T5-BYG-406

Per ...... *ness*

157 F834
Personal ......
00640

Personality
and Personal Illness

G. A. FOULDS

in collaboration with
T. M. CAINE

and with the assistance of
ANNE ADAMS
and ### ANNA OWEN

TAVISTOCK PUBLICATIONS

First published in 1965
by Tavistock Publications Limited
11 New Fetter Lane, London EC4
SBN 422 71420 8
First published as a Social Science Paperback in 1972
SBN 422 75360 2
Printed in Great Britain
in Monotype Plantin
by T. & A. Constable Ltd
Edinburgh
© *G. A. Foulds, 1965*

Distributed in the U.S.A. by
Barnes & Noble Inc.

157
F824p

Contents

Contents

Contents

Contents

Preface

Clinical psychologists are fortunate in entering an area in which the subjects of their inquiries have been so thoroughly observed by their psychiatric colleagues. In no other branch of psychology are psychologists at such an advantage. It seems unduly optimistic to assume that general psychology has so much to offer that psychologists can, with scant regard for existing psychiatric knowledge, abruptly set up their experiments and produce meaningful results. Psychiatrists, on the other hand, are apt to dismiss research findings which confirm what they already know clinically. It would be surprising and, indeed, disquieting if the foundations of an experimental science of abnormal behaviour looked utterly different from what psychiatrists had always thought them to be. This is not to say that the roof may not eventually look different; meantime psychiatrists should bear the confirmation of their observations with benign resignation.

In endeavouring to hold a line of argument consistently in the focus of attention one is apt to sound more dogmatic and tendentious than one intends to be. Frequent qualifications and modest disclaimers are time-consuming and sometimes as irritating as their absence. I hope this brief intropunitive response will serve to bring my 'Direction of Punitiveness' score not too exasperatingly far from the normal mean.

I would like to thank Dr Cecily de Monchaux and Professor Hilde Himmelweit for reading the MS and for their helpful criticisms.

Many of the investigations carried out at Runwell Hospital were made possible by grants from the Medical Research Council.

Finally, the title is intended to reflect the influence of Professor John Macmurray's *Persons in Relation*. Indeed, this book could have been called 'Persons out of Relation'.

G. A. FOULDS

Medical Research Council
Unit for Research on the Epidemiology of Psychiatric Illness
Department of Psychiatry
Edinburgh

Acknowledgements

The authors wish to thank the individuals and publishers concerned for permission to quote material from the following books and journals:

Basic Books Inc., New York, in respect of *The Open and Closed Mind* by Milton Rokeach; Chatto and Windus Ltd, London, in respect of *Thought and Action* by Stuart Hampshire and *Experience into Words* by D. W. Harding; Faber and Faber Ltd, London, in respect of *Persons in Relation* by J. Macmurray; Oxford University Press, New York, in respect of *Psychiatric Dictionary* by L. E. Hinsie and R. J. Campbell; Tavistock Publications, London, in respect of *Community as Doctor* by Robert N. Rapoport; John Wiley and Sons, New York and London, in respect of *Psychological Differentiation* by H. A. Witkin, R. B. Dyk, H. F. Faterson, D. R. Goodenough, and S. A. Karp; the Editor of the *British Journal of Medical Psychology* in respect of 'The obsessional: on the psychological classification of obsessional character traits and symptoms' by J. Sandler and A. Hazari; the Editor of the *Journal of Consulting Psychology* in respect of 'Questionnaire measure of the hysteroid: obsessoid component of personality' by T. M. Caine and L. G. Hawkins; and the Editor of the *Journal of Mental Science* in respect of 'Melancholia: a clinical survey of depressive states' by A. J. Lewis.

Deux excès: exclure la raison; n'admettre que la raison.
Pascal: PENSÉES

PART I

The Distinction between Personality Attributes and Psychiatric Illness

CHAPTER ONE

Introduction

The main arguments of this book are:

1. That it is important to distinguish between personality traits and attitudes on the one hand, and the symptoms and signs of mental (or personal) illness on the other. These symptoms signal a disruption of the normal continuity of the personality. Such a distinction is a necessary prelude to any further understanding of the interaction between personality and illness which might lead to advances in the diagnosis, treatment, aetiology, and prophylaxis of the mentally ill.

2. That it is the logical inadequacy of existing systems of psychiatric classification rather than the inappropriateness of classification as such that has led to current dissatisfactions. An attempt is accordingly made to work out a more cohesive system.

3. That the neuroses and the functional psychoses can be regarded as illnesses of the person and not merely of the organism. Since the person is only a person in relation to others, such illnesses can usefully be viewed, *inter alia*, as indicative of increasing degrees of failure to maintain or to establish mutual personal relationships.

4. That, contrary to the view of the behaviour therapists, symptoms and signs alone are not regarded as constitutive of the illness. They are not regarded as constitutive of the illness because they are sometimes present in persons who are functioning not only adequately, but unusually effectively. A neurotic or a psychotic illness must carry some implication of a failure in functioning which is so distressful to the individual or to his nearest associates as to lead to recognition of the need for outside intervention.

Although the distinction between personality types and psychiatric syndromes has been made by many authors over many years, surprisingly little attempt has been made to utilize this distinction in practice. This failure probably stems in part from the lack of adequate quantitative measures of the relevant variables.

3

Personality Attributes and Psychiatric Illness

In his early days in clinical psychology the writer found himself diagnosing hysteria more frequently than his psychiatric colleagues. They would send cases diagnosed provisionally as anxiety states or as neurotic depressives, which would be duly returned as hysterics. Not infrequently, after about a fortnight, the psychiatrist would change his diagnosis to hysteria. This apparently flattering confirmation became more bewildering than satisfying with increasing experience. The possibility presented itself that the attention of the psychiatrist might be fixed on symptoms and that of the psychologist on personality traits. If such a confusion existed in practice, there were grounds for thinking that it should not do so, since widely read psychiatric texts had stated the position unequivocally: 'True obsessive-compulsive states may develop in personalities with little or no evidence of obsessional characteristics in their previous make-up' (Curran & Guttmann, 1949). 'The hysterical personality . . . is not found in all patients who show hysterical symptoms, but nearly all people of hysterical personality show hysterical symptoms' (Lewis & Mapother, 1941).

Obsessoid personalities are described as: 'Extremely cleanly, orderly and conscientious, sticklers for precision; they have inconclusive ways of thinking and acting; they are given to needless repetition. Those who have shown such traits since childhood are often morose, obstinate, irritable people; others are vacillating, uncertain of themselves, and submissive' (Lewis & Mapother, 1941).

Hysteroid personalities are described as: '. . . over-active, unsatisfied with their own capacities and, therefore, pose and pretend; they show lability of affect and exuberance of fancy, egotism, untruthfulness, longing for prestige, sympathy and love; they use illness to satisfy these needs; they show heightened suggestibility, hypomnesia is common; it occurs more frequently in women who may be both coquettish and frigid' (Lewis & Mapother, 1941).

These are, of course, the obsessoid and hysteroid personalities as observed in neurotics. It seems likely that there are innumerable hysteroid personalities who do not use illness to satisfy their needs, but use rather the stage or writing for women's magazines. Similarly, there may be innumerable obsessoid personalities working happily in banks, and some averting a neurosis by spending their time trying to tease out these distinctions. This aside, however, a distinction is clearly being attempted between symptom-sign clusters (syndromes) on the one hand, and personality trait and attitude clusters (or types) on the other.

4

Introduction

A number of studies, which preceded those to be reported fully in Part III, were carried out to try to determine whether or not this distinction had any practical or heuristic value. It was thought desirable initially to limit the number of groups. Accordingly two neurotic groups were selected – hysteria and dysthymia – and two personality types – the hysteroid and the obsessoid. The subjects of the studies were, therefore, divided into four groups: hysterics of hysteroid personality; hysterics of obsessoid personality; dysthymics of hysteroid personality; and dysthymics of obsessoid personality. The dysthymic group comprised anxiety states, neurotic depressives, and obsessionals. The justification for the inclusion of obsessionals may be questionable. For practical purposes this was of little account since they formed only about 5 per cent of the sample.

Diagnostic classification was carried out in the usual way by psychiatrists. Personality classification resulted from ratings by psychiatrists on a hysteroid : obsessoid scale, based on the descriptions of these personality types mentioned above. Given this double classification, it became possible to determine whether various psychological test measurements and other clinical data were related to symptom clusters or to personality trait clusters.

In the first study (Foulds & Caine, 1958), where the subjects were neurotic women admitted to hospital, three of the test measures differentiated between hysterics and dysthymics regardless of personality type, and five differentiated between hysteroid and obsessoid personalities regardless of diagnostic class. Since the majority of measures reported in later investigations were of the questionnaire type, it is perhaps worth remarking that only two of the eight referred to here were of this type.

A similar study was carried out with neurotic men (Foulds & Caine, 1959). Once again some test measures differentiated between personality types regardless of diagnosis; whereas others – or rather, with men, one measure only – differentiated between diagnostic groups regardless of personality type. The measures were not, however, the same for men and for women. Psychiatrists experienced greater difficulty in diagnosing men – as evidenced by more frequent changes of diagnosis and the use of more unusual terms to describe the conditions. This greater apparent difficulty was reflected in the test results.

The third study (Foulds, 1959) was a successful replication of the first, in that 77 per cent of cases were classified similarly by the tests and by the psychiatrists, as against 78 per cent in the original study.

In the fourth study, reported in the same paper, it was predicted that: (i) diagnostic measures would change more than personality measures, even after one month; (ii) in view of the widely accepted better prognosis in dysthymia, the diagnostic measures of dysthymics would change more than those of hysterics in such a way that (*a*) hysterics and dysthymics would cease to be distinguishable on re-test; whereas (*b*) hysteroid and obsessoid personalities would be distinguishable both on test and on re-test. All these predictions were confirmed. The difference between the change in diagnostic scores and the change in personality scores was statistically significant. The difference between hysterics and dysthymics on first testing was significant; whereas on re-test the difference was nowhere near significant. Hysteroid differed significantly from obsessoid personalities on first testing and on re-testing. There was a tendency for the difference to diminish; but it was not obscured.

A retrospective study of the case histories showed that some of the data were related to diagnosis and some to personality type. Thus within the depressive group – virtually the only one to be given ECT – this treatment was confined almost exclusively to those rated as having an obsessoid personality rather than a hysteroid personality. This applied to both men and women.

As predicted, some improvement had been recorded in the case notes within the first week with significantly greater frequency among hysteroid than among obsessoid personalities, regardless of diagnosis, although dysthymics were more often judged to have recovered or improved greatly on discharge.

It would appear that psychiatrists, in arriving at a diagnosis, sometimes changed their universe of discourse from symptom clusters to personality trait clusters, and conversely. A female patient initially diagnosed as having an anxiety state, but a hysteroid personality, was often found to settle down within a week or so of entering hospital. This may be because entering hospital is part of her perhaps pre-conscious campaign for bringing her husband to heel; whereas entering hospital may be viewed by the obsessoid person as an admission of failure. In the first case the psychiatrist may become more aware as time passes of the histrionicity, and the lability and shallowness of affect, than of the now quiescent palpitations, tremors, and free-floating anxiety. He may then shift his attention from symptoms to personality traits and, in the light of the present argument, mistakenly change his diagnosis to hysteria.

The results of these preliminary studies led to the hope that utilization of a double classificatory system, in terms of syndrome and of personality type, might reduce this tendency and thus increase the reliability of the classification of neurotic patients. It then seemed desirable to attempt to produce quantitative scales which could serve as criterion measures for personality and diagnosis, and to extend the studies to the functional psychoses.

Some theoretical criteria for making this distinction and some definitions of the relevant terms are discussed in Chapter 2. In Chapter 3, the history of the obsessoid and hysteroid concepts is reviewed, followed by a description of the criterion personality measure – Caine's Hysteroid : Obsessoid Questionnaire – which is central to the studies to be reported in Part III.

Part II deals with theoretical views on the nature of psychiatric classification, and with empirical results obtained with the criterion diagnostic measures derived from the Symptom-Sign Inventory.

The position is adopted that, in so far as we enter into mutual personal relationships, we lose that detachment which is the prerequisite of scientific study. As scientists, we can know people only impersonally and thus partially. This does not mean that we have to go to the extreme of studying behaviour only to the exclusion of experience.

Selective attention is as characteristic of the observed as of the observer, and is at least initially very often governed by intention, though later much of it may be governed by that residual agglomeration of former intentions which have become largely habitual. The road to integration is paved with past intentions. Although the person is not merely a bundle of habits, his present intentions are not functionally autonomous, but are in dynamic relationship with his past. In the strictest sense, he does not act out of character, although he may act in such a way as to enrich or degrade his character.

While Allport (1937) is probably right in holding that a man's stated intention is one of the most important keys to the way he will act, our predictions will be the better the more, within limits, we know of his past, the more we know whether, as a matter of fact, he has usually been truthful, and whether he has been in the habit of carrying out his intentions. Intentions are but flexible guides, changing to meet changing circumstances, for the range of our freedom of choice is always to some extent determined. We cannot make the mountain come to Mahomet. We cannot make someone love us. Inner, as well as outer, resistances may defeat our purpose, such as persistent unconscious motivation. The more this is so the more will the individual tend to be regarded as mentally, or personally, ill. In the extreme form, the crazy paving of the schizophrenic's road to integration may well result from his loss of awareness of himself as agent of his own actions. In relatively large measure all the personally ill lose the ability to intend their own actions, and become merely motivated to behave.

As Harding (1953) has suggested: 'One of the most important of the criteria that guide our verdict of normality' is 'that we believe we can comprehend some motivation for the normal person's actions. We may, in fact, be wrong, but at least a possible motivation presents itself. We cannot in this way put ourselves in the abnormal person's place and feel that we know why he acted as he did.' There is implied a breakdown in communication between the normal and the abnormal and, as Macmurray (1961) has argued, 'to be a person is to be in communication with the Other. The knowledge of the Other is the absolute presupposition of all knowledge, and as such is indemonstrable.'

The tragedy and perhaps the essence of personal illness lie in the alienation from the rest of humanity. Sartre's *L'enfer, c'est les autres* is a statement not of the general human condition, but of the dilemma of one group of the personally ill. Another group would say, *L'enfer, c'est moi.*

Parallels have often been drawn between madness and genius. Like madness, genius too often alienates, as Alfred de Vigny realized:

> *Josué s'avançait pensif et pâlissant*
> *Car il était déjà l'Elu du Tout-Puissant.*

The withdrawal of the genius is, however, for the sake of return, even if the return may be somewhat impersonal in the form of his creative output. The insane withdraw for the sake of withdrawal, and such compensations as there may be remain purely private. To paraphrase Donne, no *person* is an island. In seeking, or being forced, so to become, the personally ill diminish themselves or are diminished, and, just as inevitably, diminish us, for, in so far as we fail in true communication, both cognitive and affective, with other persons, to that extent are we ourselves diminished as persons.

'I can't concentrate' is one of the symptoms having the highest commonality in personal illness. At the opposite end of this continuum lies Schachtel's (1954) 'focal attention'. Paradoxically, focal attention involves self-abandonment or, in the strict sense, unselfconsciousness. In the lives of most people such unselfconsciousness is achieved but rarely and, again paradoxically, those returning from these relatively rare experiences reflect that in their self-abandonment they were somehow most truly themselves, most truly alive. This self-abandonment may be achieved in mystical experience, in artistic creation, and, less esoterically, in sexual intercourse with a loved person or, indeed, in any form of deep communion with another person. In such situations experience, awareness, and communication are at one. Rogers (1961) uses the term 'congruence' to indicate such an accurate matching of experience, awareness, and communication. He goes on to say: 'I cannot choose whether my awareness will be congruent with my experience. This is answered by my need for defense, and of this I am not aware. But there is a continual existential choice as to whether my communication will be congruent with the awareness I *do* have of what I am experiencing.'

Hilgard (1954) has argued very cogently that the defence dynamisms are defences against guilt rather than anxiety. This may, however, depend to some extent on the degree of individuation achieved by the time the situation arises which evokes the defence dynamisms.

Lynd (1958), in her stimulating analysis of shame, uses the term 'shame' where Hilgard uses 'guilt', and conversely. It is shame which exposes the quick of the self. The distinction cannot be more succinctly expressed than by Lynd's example of Dmitri Karamazov. Far greater than his guilt at having murdered his father was his shame at having to take off his socks in front of the prison warder, because he had always felt that his feet were a peculiar shape and this was somehow of the essence of him, Dmitri Karamazov.

Following Lynd's usage and Hilgard's argument at least most of the way, the defence dynamisms are very frequently defences against shame. Anxiety and perhaps guilt we share with animals; but shame is probably a specifically human attribute, and self-deception, as Lawrence & Festinger (1962) have observed, almost certainly is.

Deep mutual personal relationships are possible only to the extent that we can allow ourselves to become aware of and to communicate feelings of shame, and to overcome what Suttie (1935) called the taboo on tenderness. 'In mutual trust and love there can be no incongruous or inappropriate words or behaviour. Dropping the protection of role-playing, letting oneself go freely in risking incongruity and inappropriateness is one of the delights of trusted love. Exposure can be exposure of the diversity of the good, the hopeful, the tender, as well as what may in other circumstances be accounted shameful' (Lynd, 1958).

9

It is this fusion in a deep love relationship of tenderness with what in other circumstances might be accounted shameful that Lawrence was only partially successful in describing in *Lady Chatterley's Lover*, and that Freud failed utterly to comprehend when he described fellatio as 'this excessively repulsive and perverted fantasy' (Freud, 1925); but it is through just such a fusion that one can strengthen the sense of one's own identity. 'The I can be discovered most saliently through the awareness of the you in a dynamic encounter. The I takes the risk of a transient loss of identity in every step that transcends its previous boundaries, but the endurance of the anxieties mobilized by the risk opens the potentialities of creative transfiguration' (Weigert, 1960).

One may say, then, that the integrative individual, knowing who he is, can risk allowing himself to become vulnerable and thus to become capable of entering into a mutual relationship. The partially integrated individual, fearing the possibility of modification, of rejection, of further disintegration, cannot allow himself to become vulnerable and thus cannot enter into mutual personal relationships. By protecting himself, by his inability to reveal himself, he precludes the possibility of knowing himself and, more particularly, of knowing others.

A mutual personal relationship exists when both individuals are capable predominantly of intending their own actions (which implies that any unconscious motivation will not be such as seriously to disrupt such intentions); when both individuals predominantly succeed in communicating both cognitively and affectively to a sufficient, but not necessarily conscious, degree to make possible a sharing of experience; when each individual acts predominantly for the sake of the other. It is not merely that the members of the orchestra comprehend the gestures of the conductor and that the conductor hears and appreciates the tonal values and the tempo of their mutual production. Out of the music written down by the composer, out of the imagined interpretation of the conductor, out of his and the orchestra's execution emerges a unique performance of the work. The musical notation represents those dominant traits and attitudes that are awakened by personal interaction, the issue of which may transcend the previous expectations of each. Once having thus been elicited these emergent qualities are added to the reservoir of potentialities for the future.

It will be necessary at many points to refer to mutual personal relationships. What will be described will be something of the substrate. This is essentially serious or, more accurately perhaps, *sérieux*. Such a description, in isolation from the qualities which these relationships can release, may sound rather solemn and pretentious. It is important, therefore, to emphasize that deep, unguarded relationships tend not only to be unashamed of shame and tenderness, but also be to unselfconsciously gay and even absurdly childish. As someone once wrote, love is not (and one would add 'only') the distant moan of a violin, but the triumphant twang of a bed-spring. It contains every notch along the continuum from Dante to Rabelais. Perhaps it has never been more felicitously sought after in one single work of art than by the early Puritan, Andrew Marvell, in that most nearly perfect minor masterpiece, 'To his coy mistress'.

Such mutual personal relationships can usefully be distinguished from certain other types of relationship. Transatlantic Togetherness, for example, is a Mutual Reassurance Society for the Preservation of Personae. Each individual may predominantly intend his own actions; but, if he does so, he intends *not* to reveal himself and he acts mainly for himself rather than for the other, since he is primarily motivated by the desire to be liked and accepted for what he is not. It is therefore, in essence, defensive behaviour.

Within this framework one can understand why a personal relationship between two schizophrenics suffering from the passivity phenomenon is virtually impossible. They cannot intend their own actions; they cannot reveal themselves so that their experience can be shared; and, since they feel their actions are not their own, they cannot act for the sake of the other. In essence their behaviour is impulsive, which is to say that it is a sudden, transient, undeliberated action prompted by feeling or by, or in relation to, an external stimulus. This is to be distinguished from spontaneous action, which is a sudden, undeliberated action arising from deeply ingrained attitudes or traits elicited by and in relation to some external stimulus.

The psychotherapeutic relationship is an unusual one. The patient may be largely unable to intend his own actions, owing to the disruptive influence of unconscious motivation. He may act predominantly for his own sake rather than for the sake of the other – initially at least; but he may unwittingly reveal much more of himself because of the special circumstance that the other, the therapist, is an expert. The therapist may be able predominantly to intend his own actions; but he does not for the most part reveal himself. That he does act for the sake of the other is his ethical justification for utilizing techniques for acquiring more information about the patient than the patient is aware of supplying. In essence, the behaviour of the therapist is similar to that in any protective relationship, such as that of parent and child or teacher and pupil, in that one person intends to act for the sake of the other without necessarily revealing himself.

When the therapeutic relationship has reached the stage at which the patient has been largely able to abandon his defensive and impulsive behaviour in favour of spontaneous action, which is of the essence of mutual personal relationships, it is time to terminate treatment.

The increasing appreciation in psychotherapy of the significance of the transference situation and of 'working through' rather than of insight is a shift in emphasis to the dynamic importance of personal relationships. Increased insight alone has proved of little therapeutic value. That it should ever have been expected to have been otherwise results from hypostatizing the self. There is a deep-seated belief that the reward for profound, unabashed, inner contemplation will be the discovery of what 'I' really am; but 'I' am the negative after-image that fades the longer it is fixated, the spots before the eyes that drift uncontrollably from view. It is only when 'I' have acted spontaneously, particularly in relation to other persons, and have later reflected on the action and the relationship, that I discover who and what I really am. The spontaneous – but not the impulsive – action is accompanied by a feeling of rightness, of appropriateness, because it arises out of all that I truly am and have been over many years; all that, as a result of the complex interaction between my physical make-up and my osmotic experiencing, I have valued and longed for; all that I have sought out and tried to understand in order that I might feel more at home in the world and, in particular, more at ease with my fellow beings.

It is argued that the loss of ability to maintain or to establish mutual personal relationships increases from neurosis, to integrated psychosis (in the main, melancholics, paranoiacs, and probably most manics), to non-integrated psychosis (in the main, the schizophrenics). In consequence there is some ground for regarding the major classes of personal illness as lying along a continuum.

A number of psychologists apparently accept the claim that because the results obtained by normals, neurotics, and psychotics on certain objective tests require two dimensions for their explanation, it has been demonstrated once and for all that two dimensions are necessary to explain the differences between normals, neurotics, and psychotics, and that these groups cannot, therefore, be on a continuum.

Introduction

One can determine by statistical means whether or not a claim be true that normal, neurotic, and psychotic subjects lie along a continuum in respect to particular operations. One cannot determine by statistical means whether normality, neurosis, and psychosis require one or two dimensions for their description independently of particular operations. And the number of operations is infinite. As Hampshire (1959) puts it: 'Everything resembles everything in some respect . . . we pick out resemblances in certain respects as the basis of our classifications and neglect other resemblances which, in pursuance of some new need or interest, may be marked later. . . . Reality by itself sets no limit. The limit is set by changing practical needs and by the development of new powers and new forms of social life.'

Sometime in the future it may be demonstrated that, for *most* purposes, a two-dimensional model is more useful than a one-dimensional system; but it will never be demonstrated once and for all that there are *no* purposes for which a one-dimensional is better than a two-dimensional system.

In considering the usefulness of a system it is important to take account of the fact that some attributes may be central and others peripheral to the concepts involved. In a trivial sense, any tests that serve to discriminate between groups are relevant to some differences between those groups. Dancing forwards or backwards, using or not using the expression 'never ever', may differentiate efficiently between men and women without telling us anything very fundamental about masculinity and femininity. One is obliged to ask, in order to uncover the essential grounds of the classification, 'If one encountered a set of things exactly similar in other features to things of the kind in question, but different in this one, apparently essential respect, would one apply or withhold the concept?' (Hampshire, 1959). About subsequently ascertained differences between groups, we will wish to ask: 'What is the nature of the difference?'; 'Is it essential or superficial?'; 'What work will it do for us?'

Rao (1952) points out that there is a logical gap between the study of measurements and the study of characteristics. He says, of ethnological data, that any similarities or differences between groups which are derived from measurements alone must be interpreted in the light of historical and geographical considerations. Interpretations of psychological measurements must presumably be in the light of psychological considerations. To deny this is recklessly to anticipate the day when it may safely be assumed that the psychologist need know nothing about human nature.

13

The argument may be stated in the form: 'X, Y, and Z can be described in terms which are not -A. Therefore, there are no terms in which X, Y, and Z can be described as A.' When stated in this form, the argument is clearly false; tends to lead to dogmatic and sterile dissension; and implies a hypostatization, in this instance, of psychiatric classes, a belief that they are somehow individuated 'out there', independently of our forms of reference to them.

The position to be taken up is then that, at the *genus* or class level, there is a continuum of increasing degrees of failure to maintain mutual personal relationships from normality through personality disorders, personal illness, psychosis, to non-integrated psychosis. It is further claimed that all non-integrated psychotics share those characteristics which are common to all groups of psychotics, to all groups of the personally ill, and to all groups of the personality disorders. All groups of psychotics share those characteristics which are common to all groups of the personally ill and to all groups of the personality disorders. All groups of the personally ill share those characteristics which are common to all groups of the personality disorders. Those who are psychotics, but not non-integrated psychotics, will be called integrated psychotics; those who are personally ill, but not psychotics, will be called neurotics; those who are personality disorders, but not personally ill, will be called psychopaths.

Within each genus or class one has to search for differentiae for the groups. At the group level, the concept of 'contained within' does not apply. Thus, within the classes, non-integrated psychotics will have those symptoms which are common to all psychotic groups plus some specific to their own class. On the other hand, within the integrated psychotic class, paranoiacs will have symptoms in common with melancholics and with manics which make them integrated psychotics; but they will have symptoms which differentiate them from melancholics and from manics, which make them paranoiacs. Similarly, melancholics will have symptoms in common with manics and with paranoiacs which make them integrated psychotics; but they will have symptoms which differentiate them from manics and paranoiacs, which make them melancholics.

Having established the Symptom-Sign Inventory and the Hysteroid : Obsessoid Questionnaire as reasonably valid quantitative criterion measures for diagnosis and personality respectively, Part III will deal with a number of studies in which these measures are related to certain

Introduction

other measures. The criterion diagnostic measure and any other measures correlated with it are expected to change with treatment; whereas the criteron personality measure and any measures not related to diagnosis are expected not to change. There is, however, one exception to this latter prediction, which is reported by Caine in Chapter 13. It concerns neurotic patients in a hospital specializing in community therapy: here, with lengthy treatment in this type of setting, it was thought that changes might be effected in attitude, though not in trait, measures.

Of all the methods of treatment employed in psychiatry, community therapy comes closest in practice to the therapeutic use of real inter-personal relationships. Accordingly, it stands closest to the practical application of the theoretical position developed in the earlier sections.

With the possible exception within the functional psychoses of the extremely withdrawn, the profoundly depressed, or the overexcited, it is impossible to conceive of twenty or thirty people living together for a period of months without the emergence of positive and negative feelings towards each other. Both have a part to play in increasing self-knowledge and knowledge of others. The often highly hostile reception by the patient community of certain attitudes and behaviour displayed by some patients is in marked contrast to the impersonal analytic interpreter or the 'sympathetic echo' of the Rogerian.

There is suggestive evidence that interpersonal relationships have a bearing on attitude change when subjected to analysis and understanding in the community setting. Further studies will, of course, be required to determine just what factors are operative in the therapeutic process. One may guess that ability to empathize, egocentricity, rigidity, and motivation to change will be rewarding areas for study. In the meantime, there is nothing to gainsay the belief of many of those most closely engaged in this field that it is the development and understanding of personal relationships between and by patients, with the staff acting largely as catalysts, which is the stuff of community therapy. If the aim of the psychiatric treatment of the functional psychoses and of the neuroses is to enable those who could not do so more fully to intend their own actions and to re-establish satisfying personal relationships, any treatment that stops short of supplying such help in these areas is a partial treatment. Partial treatment may on occasions be unavoidable and, on occasions, even desirable; but it should be clearly recognized as such, and its efficacy justified in comparative studies with the more complete form of treatment. Caine has attempted to supply one baseline for

15

such comparative studies. Community therapy seems a particularly suitable baseline, since it should not be necessary to justify treating patients as persons.

There is no intention of implying that all patients at all stages of their illness will benefit from community therapy or that there is anything less than a very important part to be played by the physical treatments and by various forms of individual psychotherapy. The physical treatments are seen principally as means of bringing excessively preoccupied patients back to the possibility of more or less adequate communication. These problems, particularly in relation to the treatment of psychotic depressives and to the nature of schizophrenic withdrawal, are considered in more detail in Part IV.

REFERENCES

ALLPORT, G. W. (1937). *Personality*. New York: Henry Holt.

CURRAN, D. & GUTTMANN, E. (1949). *Psychological medicine*. Edinburgh: Livingstone.

FOULDS, G. A. (1959). The relative stability of personality measures compared with diagnostic measures. *J. ment. Sci.*, **105**, 783.

FOULDS, G. A. & CAINE, T. M. (1958). Psychoneurotic symptom clusters, trait clusters and psychological tests. *J. ment. Sci.*, **104**, 722.

FOULDS, G. A. & CAINE, T. M. (1959). Symptom clusters and personality types among psychoneurotic men compared with women. *J. ment. Sci.*, **105**, 469.

FREUD, S. (1925). *Collected papers*, IV. London: Hogarth.

HAMPSHIRE, S. (1959). *Thought and action*. London: Chatto & Windus.

HARDING, D. W. (1953). *Social psychology and individual values*. London: Hutchinson.

HILGARD, E. R. (1954). Human motives and the concept of self. In H. Brand (Ed.), *The study of personality*. New York: Wiley; London: Chapman & Hall.

LAWRENCE, D. H. & FESTINGER, L. (1962). *Deterrents and reinforcement*. Stanford: Stanford University Press; London: Tavistock Publications.

LEWIS, A. J. & MAPOTHER, E. (1941). In *Price's Textbook of the practice of medicine*. London: Oxford University Press.

LYND, H. M. (1958). *On shame and the search for identity*. London: Routledge & Kegan Paul.

MACMURRAY, J. (1961). *Persons in relation*. London: Faber.

RAO, C. R. (1952). *Advanced statistical methods in biometric research*. New York: Wiley.

Introduction

ROGERS, C. R. (1961). *On becoming a person*. London: Constable.
SCHACHTEL, E. (1954). The development of focal attention and the emergence of reality. *Psychiat.*, **17**, 313.
SUTTIE, I. D. (1935). *The origins of love and hate*. London: Kegan Paul.
WEIGERT, E. (1960). The subjective experience of identity and its psychopathology. *Comprehen. Psychiat.*, **1**, 18.

CHAPTER TWO

Personal Continuity and Psychopathological Disruption

INTRODUCTION

For the purposes of an investigation limits must be set as to the order of the observations to be made. This, as Rogers (1961) has pointed out, is a subjective, personal choice. For the psychologist this is true regardless of the level of personality functioning with which the investigation is concerned. Studies are pursued of memory, set, attitude, perception, and the like. Textbooks of psychology have chapters on learning, intelligence, aptitudes, personality, and motivation. The biographer attempts to see the total person in all his relationships; but the scientist must divide him up into the pieces and segments which are to be the constant subject of reference for the investigation at hand. Even the therapist deals with a certain segment only of his patient. His province is essentially that of symptoms and unconscious conflicts. It can be argued that the therapist is concerned predominantly with that aspect of the patient's behaviour which is inappropriate to the situation in which the patient finds himself, and it is often inappropriate because, unlike much normal behaviour, it is determined.

The feeling that one is free to choose from a number of possible lines of action is much reduced in those who are mentally ill, and this has been well described by Rogers. Freedom of choice of behaviour, which for the healthy person will have interpersonal connotations, places serious limitations on prediction for the social scientist.

The claim that the science of psychology can study the person as a whole is illusory. 'I can know another person *as a person* only by entering into personal relation with him. Without this I can know him only by observation and inference; only objectively. The knowledge which I can obtain in this way is valid knowledge; my conclusions from observations can be true or false, they can be verified or falsified by further observation or by experiment. But it is abstract knowledge, since it constructs its object by limitation of attention to what can be known about another person without entering into personal relations with them' (Macmurray, 1961). Rogers, in his discussion of the conflict within him of the 'experientialist' and the 'scientist', arrives at a similar conclusion.

The social sciences suffer from the handicap that the object of study, the organism, answers back. When the organism insists on becoming a person, we leave the realm of science. Psychologists have long since recognized this; but, in so doing, they have often tended to believe that we also leave behind the possibility of valid knowledge. This is probably a more heinous error than would be the extreme opposite view that we should use science only when we cannot do any better.

It is perhaps somewhat easier to study the mentally ill more completely than the normal individual, because mental illness is illness of the person, not merely illness of the organism, and this implies that the individual becomes less of a person and more of an organism falling within the purlieu of determinism. The personally ill are less able than the normal to intend their own actions. We are increasingly forced, as Peters (1958) points out, to ask not '*Why* did X do Y?'; but 'What *made* X do Y?'

PERSONALITY ATTRIBUTES AND PSYCHIATRIC SYNDROMES

Whereas those abstractions which we designate personality traits and schemata emphasize the continuities in behaviour, symptoms and signs of neurotic or of psychotic illness emphasize the discontinuities.

As Claude Bernard (1878) pointed out, the inner environment has to be more constant than the outer. In a sense in which Wordsworth probably did not intend it, the world *is* too much with us – or, more strictly, too much of the world is with us – and so we have to partial some of it out. Experience tends to get organized, consciously or unconsciously, into something which is simpler than the original, in ways which Bartlett (1932) has demonstrated. Characteristically in man, much of this organization is predigested for him by the culture in which he lives. That this selectivity serves needs deeper than man's sloth is evidenced by the fact that in the past hypermanic patients, at the mercy of almost all stimuli, have been known to die of exhaustion.

Terms like 'trait' and 'attitude' were introduced into psychology to describe certain aspects of this economy of organization which imply or lead to personal continuity. Traits and attitudes on the one hand can be distinguished from symptoms and signs of personal illness by means of three criteria:

1. Traits and attitudes are universal; symptoms and signs are not.
2. Traits and attitudes are relatively ego-syntonic; symptoms and signs are distressful, either to the patient or to his closest associates.
3. Traits and attitudes, particularly the former, are relatively enduring.

In order to pursue this argument further a number of definitions must first be set out.

A *personality variable* may be viewed as a convenient abstraction of behavioural qualities which fall along a continuum differentiable from other such continua. It thus provides a distinguishing feature in personality in general. Examples of such continua might be affective expressivity or affective dependency.

Personality variables, as assessed by people with a common frame of reference, are always universal in the sense of applying to the total population under observation. They are not, of course, universal in the sense that all cultures will utilize the particular concepts. Thus, with the variable of affective expressivity, certain behaviour is categorized as indicative of affective expressivity and all other behaviour as not indicative of affective expressivity. If the extremes of this variable are 'flamboyant display of emotions' and 'extreme control of emotions', everyone must fall at or between these extremes. The dimension can never be irrelevant to anyone. Such variables are variables shared in more or less degree by all of us. We are all more or less labile in affect; more or less longing for prestige, sympathy, and love; more or less conscientious; more or less obstinate. The extent of the more or less is the *personality trait*, or the *personality attitude*. The personality trait, or attitude, denotes a rather consistent position in respect to a personality variable. If all individuals manifested all forms of behaviour from completely uninhibited display to completely inhibited control of emotions in an apparently random way, the variable of affective expressivity might still be identifiable, but the trait would not. Widespread inconsistency and specificity do not, however, seem to be the rule, and the trait and attitude concepts serve to classify the relative generality, consistency, and continuity of responses to somewhat similar situations.

Newcomb (1950) considers that 'a complete account of personality would have to show how characteristic patterns of expression are related to characteristic patterns of direction', where temperamental factors determine the manner of expression and attitudes determine the direction of the behaviour expressed.

Allport (1937) believes that 'Both *attitude* and *trait* are indispensable concepts. Between them they cover virtually every type of disposition with which the psychology of personality concerns itself. Ordinarily *attitude* should be employed when the disposition is bound to an object of value, that is to say, when it is aroused by [or presumably seeks out] a well-defined class of stimuli, and when the individual feels toward these stimuli a definite attraction or repulsion.'

A trait, or attitude, may be *common*, if the position on the particular variable is one that is shared by many other people; or it may be *uncommon*, if it is rarely found in the same degree in others – for example, extreme conscientiousness. Reference is to inter-individual variation. It should be noted that a change from even extreme conscientiousness to over-conscientiousness is not a linear extension, but a step-function. Over-conscientiousness implies that the individual finds his preoccupation with rectitude distressful. The step is from an attitude to a symptom.

A personality trait, or attitude, may be *prominent* if other traits are rarely found in the same degree in the same person. Reference is to intra-individual differences. An individual may, for example, be extremely conscientious, but only moderately quick, only moderately intense in affect. The uniqueness of the person could probably be accounted for on the basis of his position on a single variable had we measures sufficiently sensitive; but there would certainly be little difficulty in doing so with the multiplicity of possible variables which might be chosen. The uniqueness of any person is a resultant in part of different strengths of traits and attitudes, *inter alia*, relative to other people and within himself. The different strengths of traits and attitudes, both between and within individuals, will have arisen as a result of the interaction between different constitutions and situations which the individuals did little or nothing to seek out, and between different constitutions and situations which already differing traits and attitudes have predisposed the individuals to seek out in order to exercise them.

The term 'trait', then, is being used as a constellation of expressive behavioural characteristics, which are in part constitutional and in part a result of early learning. It does not drive. Reference to any inferred tendency underlying a constellation of expressive behavioural characteristics would require some such term as *trait-construct*, which 'might be conceived of as lowered thresholds for certain types of response' (Earl, 1954).

A *personality type* is a constellation of traits and attitudes which can be distinguished from other such constellations. An example would be the hysteroid personality as described by Lewis & Mapother (1941).

Personality traits, attitudes, and types emphasize the continuities in behaviour; whereas symptom and sign clusters signal a disruption of continuity, arising from the failure of defence dynamisms adequately to reorganize conflicting forces, to maintain a sufficient integration of the self-concept to enable the individual to continue to be in satisfying relationships with other persons.

A *symptom* may therefore be viewed as a change in bodily or mental functioning which the subject reports because it is distressful to him. For example, 'I am afraid to go out alone' or 'I have lost interest in almost everything'.

Signs can be of two kinds – subjective or objective:

A *subjective sign* is a change in bodily or mental functioning which the subject reports, of the significance of which he is not aware, but which to the skilled observer is indicative of such maladaptation as is likely to cause or to have caused danger or distress to others or to himself. For example, 'I know of people who are trying to poison me or make me ill in some way' or 'Sometimes I think of doing away with myself and those I love because the world is such a wicked place'.

An *objective sign* is a change in bodily or mental functioning which the subject does not report, but which to a skilled observer is indicative of such maladaptation as is likely to cause or to have caused danger or distress to others or to himself. For example, clang association or thought blocking.

A *syndrome* is a constellation or cluster of symptoms and subjective and objective signs, which tends to occur rather commonly and which is distinguishable from other such clusters of signs and symptoms. Symptoms or signs may occur in more than one syndrome; but the syndromes *per se* must be mutually exclusive.

We are all more or less dependent, more or less quick, more or less retiring, and we are so, with possibly some modifications in the more or less, throughout our lives. We do not, however, all have functional paralyses, fugues, anaesthesias, fits, or anorexia nervosa; nor do those who have them have them all their lives. The distinction is not always simple. We do all wash our hands. The obsessional neurotic may wash his hands more often. This is a quantitative distinction only. The normal person, even if he is of obsessoid personality, feels free to decide whether or not he will wash his hands; the obsessional neurotic feels no such freedom and would be distressed by this compulsion itself or by interference with it. This is a qualitative distinction, which implies either a symptom or a subjective sign.

A factor analytic study carried out by Sandler & Hazari (1960) isolated two relatively independent factors of obsessional neurosis and obsessional character traits. The distinction they make is very similar to the above.

Personality traits refer, as McClelland (1951) has pointed out, to the 'how' of behaviour. How did X do Y? He did it quickly, gracefully, without fuss, independently. We do not seek for recondite motives for his conduct. He did Y_4 because he had previously done Y_1, Y_2, and Y_3, and, well, he is the sort of person who does that sort of thing. Predictions can be made, as Peters (1958) has argued, without knowing the cause of behaviour. Symptoms, on the other hand, are an indication that the normal consistencies and continuities of behaviour have been interrupted. We seek for an explanation of behaviour that seems strange to us. If we ask someone why he acted in a particular way or why he holds a particular belief and he is unable to tell us, or he offers an explanation which seems altogether unconvincing, we suspect that an unconscious wish may be operating which conflicts with reality.

Most people would probably agree that the following reasoning of a patient was unconvincing and invited explanation in terms of unconscious wishes. This patient argued that he was unfit to live, but that he was too cowardly to kill himself. He would, therefore, have to get someone else to do it. The only way to do this would be to kill someone else and then he would be hanged. He was, however, a very sensitive man and did not want to kill anyone with dependent relatives who would be left to grieve for his victim. The only person he could think of who had no dependent relative, other than himself, was his mother. If he killed his mother, he would be hanged and, therefore, there would be no dependent relative left to grieve.

Picture 6 GF of the Thematic Apperception Test shows a man leaning towards a seated woman who is half-turning towards him. Women of predominantly obsessoid personality typically give stories of a husband and wife discussing where to go for their holidays, whether to go to the cinema or not, or some such undramatic situation. Women of predominantly hysteroid personality give stories of a husband coming home early and finding his wife writing to her lover, or stories of the boss putting an unbusiness-like proposition to his secretary. In the absence of strong evidence to the contrary, a sufficient explanation can be found within Peters's rule-following behaviour model. These particular stories are probably consonant with the normal interests, daydreams, or actual experiences of the obsessoid and hysteroid personalities. When, however, a patient says that both the people in the picture are looking very anxious and that maybe the house is on fire, such explanations do not seem sufficient. When the same patient is shown the same picture some time later, she says again that they both seem very anxious. Perhaps there is a flood and they are waiting anxiously for it to subside. Inquiry reveals that she has never been in fire or flood. Her sole complaints were of depersonalization and emotional flattening. She could never get excited about anything. What made X do Y? What made her give this extremely unusual story? Her husband was so afraid of their having another child that he had for some time been sleeping in the kitchen, and their only sexual relations consisted of mutual masturbation. Not infrequently the wife had been left unsatisfied, in a state of considerable excitement. Now she complained of being unable to get excited about anything; but the husband and wife in the stories were waiting anxiously for the flood to subside or for the fire to go out. Thus the breakdown in normal rule-following behaviour could be traced to the intervention of an unconscious wish, or to the defence against that wish. The form her story took was determined more by her symptomatology than by her personality traits.

The distinction between symptoms and signs has gone out of fashion; but it can still prove useful to both psychiatrists and psychologists. In the schizophrenias (the non-integrated psychoses) reliance must often be placed most heavily on the objective signs in arriving at a diagnosis. In some catatonics, who are mute, withdrawn, and manneristic, this is entirely so. In some simple schizophrenics, with virtually no complaints and minimal thought disorder, reliance may be mainly on the observation of emotional flattening. In such cases, the psychologist may think in terms of techniques for measuring thought disorder, flattening of affect, or expressive movement.

In the integrated psychoses, such as melancholics and paranoiacs, subjective signs may assume a greater importance. Delusional beliefs can often be elicited without much difficulty by a questionnaire. Studies of perceptual vigilance and defence may be particularly suitable for such groups. The guilt of the one and the hostility of the other are so all-pervading that they do not need to be evoked artificially.

In the neurotically ill, symptoms will play a more significant part, so that questionnaires will again have their uses. Though we may be able to see the tremor, the hand-washing ritual, or the paralysed arm, we cannot see the tight band round the head, the constantly recurring blasphemous thoughts, or the low back pain. For much of the diagnostic evidence one has to rely on report or on inference from report.

It is not intended to imply in the foregoing discussion that the individual who is personally ill will be abnormal in all respects. On the contrary, many of the enduring personality characteristics seem to remain identifiable, except perhaps in the most chronic disintegrated psychotic conditions. It is believed that there is practical value in identifying them and in distinguishing them from the symptoms and signs of psychosis or of neurosis, and that failure to do so has led to much confusion.

EXTRAVERSION : INTROVERSION = HYSTERIA : DYSTHYMIA

The use of hysterics and dysthymics as criterion groups for extraversion and introversion by Sigal, Star & Franks (1958) and by Eysenck (1958) has already been criticized (Foulds, 1961) and has led to further discussion (Eysenck, 1962; Foulds, 1962; Ingham, 1962) and experiment (Crookes & Hutt, 1963). These arguments will not be reiterated here. Germane to this discussion, however, is a more recent study.

Ingham & Robinson (1964) conducted a particularly useful investigation through following the illogical practice of classifying in terms of symptomatology or personality at whim, as though they were in the same universe of discourse. There is no logical reason why a person of hysterical personality should not suffer a neurotic depression or a phobic anxiety state, and, in fact, he not infrequently does. The crux of the difficulty lies here. When faced with the presence in the patient of both anxiety symptoms and a conspicuously hysteroid personality, some psychiatrists choose between them in making their diagnosis, instead of using a double classification in terms of symptoms and of type of personality. In the choice situation, one psychiatrist may be more impressed by the symptomatology and another by the personality traits and attitudes. It is not that they disagree about what they see. They are just looking different ways. Presumably the hysterical personalities of Ingham & Robinson were, in the main, cases which were rather free from symptomatology, particularly from dysthymic symptomatology.

What Ingham & Robinson did was to divide the hysterics into conversion hysterics (including dissociative states, pseudo-dementias, etc.) and hysterical personalities, and to examine the MPI E scores of these two groups along with dysthymics and normals. Hysterical personalities were more extraverted than the normal sample, and both dysthymics and conversion hysterics were just slightly more introverted than the normal sample. This finding with regard to conversion hysterics is, therefore more nearly in line with the clinical opinions of Fenichel (1960), Glover (1949), and, indeed, of Jung (1921), whose view has been incorrectly stated, than with the opinion of Eysenck.

Jung (1921) distinguished both traits and symptoms from his concepts of introversion and extraversion, which describe the direction of mental energy or libido. The extravert gives his fundamental interest to the outer or objective world, attributing an all-important and essential value to it, becoming emotionally involved with it in a highly 'differentiated' way. He knows and understands it through his emotions. In contrast, the introvert is more concerned with his own thoughts, and withdraws emotionally from the world the better to think about it. The introvert uses his thought as the function of adaptation, thinking beforehand about how he will act; whereas the extravert feels his way into the object by acting. In extreme cases, one limits himself to thinking and observing, and the other to feeling and acting. In Macmurray's (1961) terminology, the introvert might be said to have a high ratio of withdrawal to return; whereas the extravert has a low ratio.

In this theory hysteria was opposed to dementia praecox and psychasthenia, the contrast resting 'on the almost exclusive supremacy of extraversion or introversion' respectively. Hysteria is characterized by a centrifugal tendency of the libido, whereas in the other two conditions the tendency is centripetal. 'The reverse occurs, however, when the illness has fully established its compensatory effects.' In a fully developed illness the hysteric becomes introverted, the precocious dement and the psychasthenic become extraverted. Jung's theory of the neuroses – for the details of which there is virtually no empirical support – implies an imbalance of extraversion and introversion and a corresponding maladjustment to environmental demands.

Although acknowledging Jung, Eysenck does not follow him in distinguishing between hysterical illness and premorbid personality; nor does he subscribe apparently to Jung's view that in the fully developed illness the hysteric becomes introverted. He admits (Eysenck & Claridge, 1962) that Jung's original theory of extraversion : introversion as direction of libidinal flow has been diluted and, indeed, altered in the interests of theory and the hypothetico-deductive method; but he believes nevertheless that his hypothesis 'does not postulate a one-to-one correspondence . . . it preserves the distinction between personality, on the one hand, and symptomatology on the other' (Eysenck, 1962). It preserves the distinction between personality and such symptomatology as is common to all neurotics (that is, between extraversion and neuroticism); it confuses the distinction between personality and such symptomatology as is specific to each of the neurotic groups (that is, between extraversion and hysteria). It is in this respect that the fundamental difference lies between his approach and the one suggested here.

Those adopting the present standpoint would wish to re-examine much of the voluminous data in this area. To take but one example, Vernon Hamilton (1957) found – on a number of measures of intolerance of ambiguity – that conversion hysterics and obsessional neurotics were highly intolerant of ambiguity, whereas anxiety states were not. One might suppose that his conversion hysterics, following Ingham & Robinson, were somewhat introverted or obsessoid in personality. The majority of obsessional neurotics are probably of introverted or obsessoid personality (Foulds, 1955); anxiety states probably divide rather evenly between hysteroid and obsessoid types (Foulds & Caine, 1958). If intolerance of ambiguity were, in fact, related more to the personality dimension than to diagnostic groups, one would still predict Hamilton's results with these particular diagnostic groups. One might, incidentally, argue that the fact that anxiety states did not make decisions about ambiguous stimuli, where obsessionals and hysterics did, does not point unambiguously to their greater tolerance of ambiguity. They may have been exceedingly anxious about and intolerant of their inability to make up their minds.

SUMMARY

It has been suggested that traits and attitudes are universal, relatively ego-syntonic, and of very long duration. The trait concept is concerned with processes and the attitude concept with content. Signs and symptoms, on the other hand, are relatively rare, are distressing, and provide

Personality Attributes and Psychiatric Illness

evidence of a break in the normal continuity of behaviour. In the main, symptoms and subjective signs, like attitudes, are concerned with content and may, indeed, be abnormal attitudes; whereas objective signs will tend to be process disorders and thus more like traits in this respect.

It has been argued that the use of hysterics and dysthymics as criterion groups for extraversion and introversion is fundamentally at odds with the distinction proposed here between symptoms, attitudes, and traits, and that it involves a shift of universes of discourse resulting from unsound deductions from Jung's untested and, indeed, incorrectly stated hypothesis.

REFERENCES

ALLPORT, G. W. (1937). *Personality*. New York: Henry Holt.

BARTLETT, F. C. (1932). *Remembering*. Cambridge: Cambridge University Press.

BERNARD, C. (1878). *Leçons sur les phénomènes de la vie communs aux animaux et aux végétaux*. Paris: Baillière.

CROOKES, T. G. & HUTT, S. J. (1963). Scores of psychotic patients on the Maudsley Personality Inventory. *J. consult. Psychol.*, **27**, 243.

EARL, C. J. C. (1954). Some methods of assessing temperament and personality. In H. Brand (Ed.), *The study of personality*. New York: Wiley; London: Chapman & Hall.

EYSENCK, H. J. (1958). Hysterics and dysthymics as criterion groups in the study of introversion : extraversion: A reply. *J. abnorm. soc. Psychol.*, **57**, 250.

EYSENCK, H. J. (1962). Correspondence in *Brit. J. Psychol.*, **53**, 455.

EYSENCK, H. J. & CLARIDGE, G. S. (1962). The position of hysterics and dysthymics in a two-dimensional framework of personality description. *J. abnorm. soc. psychol.*, **64**, 46.

FENICHEL, O. (1960). *The psychoanalytic theory of neurosis*. New York: Norton.

FOULDS, G. A. (1955). Psychiatric syndromes and personality types. *Psychol. Forschuung*, **25**, 65.

FOULDS, G. A. (1961). The logical impossibility of using hysterics and dysthymics as criterion groups in the study of introversion and extraversion. *Brit. J. Psychol.*, **52**, 385.

FOULDS, G. A. (1962). Correspondence in *Brit. J. Psychol.*, **53**, 456.

FOULDS, G. A. & CAINE, T. M. (1958). Psychoneurotic symptom clusters, trait clusters and psychological tests. *J. ment. Sci.*, **104**, 722.

GLOVER, E. (1949). *Psychoanalysis*. New York: Staples.

HAMILTON, V. (1957). Perceptual and personality dynamics in reactions to ambiguity. *Brit. J. Psychol.*, **48**, 200.

28

INGHAM, J. (1962). Correspondence in *Brit. J. Psychol.*, **53**, 458.

INGHAM, J. & ROBINSON, J. O. (1964). Personality in the diagnosis of hysteria. *Brit. J. Psychol.*, **55**, 276.

JUNG, C. G. (1921). *Psychologische Typen*. Zürich: Rascher. Trans. *Psychological types*. London: Kegan Paul; New York: Harcourt Brace, 1923.

LEWIS, A. J. & MAPOTHER, E. (1941). In *Price's Textbook of the practice of medicine*. London: Oxford University Press.

MACMURRAY, J. (1961). *Persons in relation*. London: Faber.

MCCLELLAND, D. C. (1951). *Personality*. New York: Sloane.

NEWCOMB, T. M. (1950). *Social psychology*. New York: Dryden.

PETERS, R. S. (1958). *The concept of motivation*. London: Routledge & Kegan Paul.

ROGERS, C. R. (1961). *On becoming a person*. London: Constable.

SANDLER, J. & HAZARI, A. (1960). The obsessional: on the psychological classification of obsessional character traits and symptoms. *Brit. J. med. Psychol.*, **33**, 113.

SIGAL, J. J., STAR, K. H. & FRANKS, C. M. (1958). Hysterics and dysthymics as criterion groups in the study of introversion : extraversion. *J. abnorm. soc. Psychol.*, **57**, 143.

CHAPTER THREE

Obsessoid and Hysteroid Components of Personality

HISTORICAL SURVEY

The view that the symptoms of hysteria and of obsessive-compulsive states can and should be considered separately from hysteroid and obsessoid personality traits has been advanced by many leading clinical psychiatrists, clinical psychologists, and psycho-analysts. Although these distinctions have a long history, reaching back to the turn of the century, at least for the obsessional symptoms and obsessoid personality, differentiation has, until recently, been purely in terms of clinical description. Of later years, however, attempts have been made to measure these different attributes of personality functioning and to provide a logical framework for the general problem of symptoms and traits, their categorization and interrelationship. The present chapter outlines something of the history of these concepts, as far as the neuroses are concerned, and describes the development, construction, and validation of a new measure of the hysteroid : obsessoid component of personality.

Mackinnon (1944), in tracing the history of personality typologies, ascribed to Janet the first attempt to dichotomize symptoms and personality types in neurotics. The former were classified by Janet into hysteria and psychasthenia, the latter into hysteroid and obsessoid, to use Mackinnon's precise terminology. This terminology with regard to the personality types has been followed in the present discussion as being more clearly distinguishable from symptoms than are the terms hysterical and obsessional or obsessive, and because the '-oid' ending implies a lesser commitment with regard to the association between symptoms and traits.

Mackinnon has criticized personality typologists on the ground that the basis of their work is clinical observation rather than experimental. One must agree with him that in most investigations the details of procedure have not been made clear, the basis of the selection of subjects has not been specified, and statistical treatment of the results is usually lacking. To these criticisms must be added the dangers involved in generalizing from highly selected clinical groups to the population in general. The analyst describes what he may consider to be 'neurotic personality traits' as they appear in his patients. He has no opportunity to observe the incidence of these same traits in the general population under the same conditions.

Nevertheless, clinical observation may, and indeed should, precede scientific refinement, and one cannot agree with Mackinnon that clinically the concepts of the hysteroid and the obsessoid personalities have not withstood the test of time. On the contrary, despite differences in terminology, most clinicians make a distinction between symptoms and traits, and standard psychiatric texts contain sections devoted to the description of the hysteroid and/or the obsessoid personality traits and their relation to symptoms and other personality variables. Among such authors are to be found Kretschmer (1926); Bowlby (1940); Fenichel (1945); Lewis & Mapother (1941); Curran & Guttmann (1949); and Mayer-Gross, Slater & Roth (1954). The present researchers have aimed at quantifying this hysteroid : obsessoid dimension originally described by Janet.

Obsessional Neurosis
One of the most recent articles on the classification of obsessoid character traits and obsessional symptoms is that of Sandler & Hazari (1960). These authors point to the confusion that exists in the use of the term 'obsessional'. They list four popular usages of the word, namely: as denoting a type of character in both normal and disturbed subjects; as denoting either a symptom complex or a single symptom; and, finally, as a term of abuse.

In considering the many definitions of obsession and compulsion that appear in the literature, Sandler & Hazari find sufficient agreement among these various authorities, at the symptomatic level at least, to formulate the following definitions:

'*An Obsession* is an unwanted but repetitive thought which forces itself insistently into consciousness and recurs against the conscious desires of the person concerned. Such thoughts may include intrusive doubts, wishes, fears, impulses, prohibitions, warnings and commands. Neither reason nor logic can influence these pointless, repugnant, insistent and absurd thoughts, and they persist so tenaciously that they cannot be dispelled by conscious effort. On the whole they are recognized by

31

their owners as largely irrelevant and irrational. *A Compulsion,* in addition to having many qualities in common with obsessions, is generally thought of as expressed in action. It can be regarded as a morbid, intrusive, insistent and repetitive urge to perform some stereotyped act – apparently trifling and meaningless – which is contrary to the patient's ordinary conscious wishes or standards. Failure to perform the compulsive act usually results in anxiety, while once it has been carried out, there usually occurs some temporary lessening of tension.'

Freud (1907) and many subsequent authors maintain that an obsessional act is an expression of an obsessional thought. Henderson & Gillespie (1950), although agreeing that both obsessive-ruminative and obsessive-compulsive states can be included in the general classification of obsessive psychoneurosis, point to a clinical differentiation between patients who perform compulsive acts and those in whom ruminations do not necessarily lead to such activity. The common practice of classifying both conditions as obsessional neurosis suggests that for most diagnosticians the distinction is a superficial one; but, doubtless partly because of the rarity of the conditions, systematic studies are lacking.

Obsessoid Personality
Many authors distinguish between obsessions and compulsions as symptoms on the one hand, and the obsessoid (anal, obsessional) character on the other. Freud (1908) first described the traits of orderliness, parsimony, and obstinacy as constituting the cardinal triad of the anal character. This descriptive difference between symptoms and trait complexes he later elaborated (Freud, 1913, 1949) in his discussions of the aetiology of the two phenomena. Character formation in Freudian theory involves three distinct processes, namely: (i) incorporation within the child of moral dictates, attitudes, and judgements of the parents; (ii) identification with the parents and other authority figures in superego formation; and (iii) repression and repudiation of undesirable impulses arising from the id by means of reaction-formations and sublimations. These undesirable impulses are bound up with Freud's theory of the four phases of libidinal development of the growing infant: namely oral, anal, phallic, and genital. Libidinal fixation may occur at any one of these phases as a result of experience at the hands of parents or significant 'objects' in the environment. What is important for character formation is how much each of the earlier phases is carried over to the next, obtaining permanent representation in the economy of the libido and thus in the character of

the individual. In normal development the repression of the primitive impulses from the id, including pregenital drives, results in sublimations and reaction-formations along socially approved lines. From his analysis of persons of obsessoid character Freud concluded that their characteristic orderliness, parsimoniousness, and obstinacy proceed from the dissipation of their primitive anal eroticism and its employment in other ways. In similar manner he expected other traits of character to be derived from pregenital libidinal formations.

With the neuroses, on the other hand, frustrating environmental experience may prohibit successful sublimations and reaction-formations at some point in libidinal development. As a result, the individual experiences a regression of libidinal organization to an earlier stage of development where adjustment was more successful. Freud maintained that certain regressions are characteristic of certain forms of illness. The hysteric, for example, regresses to the phallic level, the obsessional to the anal.

Support for Freud's triad of traits – orderliness, obstinacy, and stinginess – has come from Sears (1936, 1943) and from Beloff (1957). In a study of ratings obtained from university students Sears found correlations of the following order: stinginess and orderliness 0·39; stinginess and obstinacy 0·37; obstinacy and orderliness 0·36. He points out that, although the correlations are not very high, they are all positive and in the expected direction. This is particularly interesting when it is considered that orderliness is regarded as a desirable trait; whereas stinginess and obstinacy are regarded as undesirable. Beloff confirmed the findings with regard to the intercorrelation of the traits; but she found no significant relationship with mode of upbringing. In their review of work in this area O'Connor & Franks (1960) found no conclusive evidence to support the regression theory as such.

The inadequacy of any personality theory which fails to take cultural determinants into account has been stressed by cultural anthropologists. Bateson (1944) argues that childhood experiences at these significant periods of development will have different meanings for the participants and will take different forms in various cultures: '. . . in the ordinary course of everyday life, apart from the extremes of deprivation, we must expect every one of the simple physiological behaviours, such as eating, defecation, copulation, and even sleep, to have special meaning for the individual, and this meaning will be culturally determined and will vary from culture to culture.'

33

Personality Attributes and Psychiatric Illness

It is as fallacious to assume that bowel training will in every case be entirely culturally determined as it is to equate prototypical situational evocations of particular modes of behaviour with the cause of that behaviour. Nevertheless, as we have shown, there is some evidence that the obsessoid (if not anal) traits of parsimony, orderliness, and obstinacy do tend to cluster together. In later years the obsessoid traits have been extended to include cleanliness, conscientiousness, inconclusiveness in thinking and acting, repetitiveness, deep feeling with inhibition of emotional display, constancy of mood, and self-effacement. Experimental evidence for this extension is, as yet, meagre.

Within our Western culture at least, descriptive distinctions between obsessional neurosis and obsessoid personality traits have been persistently maintained by authors representing a number of disciplines: Jones (1918) and Abraham (1921) from the psycho-analytic discipline; Curran & Guttmann (1949), Mayer-Gross *et al.* (1954), and Lewis & Mapother (1941) from the general psychiatric; Foulds & Caine (1958, 1959) and Sandler & Hazari (1960) from the psychological.

Hysteria

Although the first psychiatric observations on obsessional neurosis seem to date only from 1860 (Rado, 1959), physicians have been concerned with the phenomenon of hysteria since the dawn of medicine with the early Greeks. Chodoff & Lyons (1958) have described five senses in which the term hysteria is currently used: '(i) A pattern of behaviour habitually exhibited by certain individuals who are said to be hysterical personalities or hysterical characters; (ii) A particular kind of psychosomatic symptomatology called conversion hysteria or conversion reaction; (iii) A psychoneurotic disorder characterized by phobias and/or certain anxiety manifestations called anxiety hysteria; (iv) A particular psychopathological pattern; (v) A term of opprobrium.'

Chodoff & Lyons, in common with a number of writers, confine their attention to the first two senses. The term anxiety hysteria was introduced by Freud to describe a type of psychoneurotic disorder in which repression, the principal defence, is supported by the dynamism of displacement. They argue that, while there may be considerable justification for this view, it has not been demonstrated that every clinical case of a phobia has these dynamisms as its basis, or that in every instance repression and displacement will cause the appearance of phobic anxiety. Since, however, necessary and sufficient conditions have not been un-

34

equivocally demonstrated for any other clinical category, this objection is rather a frivolous one. Freud was forced by his definition of anxiety hysteria (now rarely accepted) to seek another term for what most people would now regard as anxiety states (perhaps in a hysteroid personality). To have lighted on a combination of two already existing class names was no more justifiable logically than the current use of the term schizo-affective.

With regard to item (iv), Chodoff & Lyons contend that, in the present state of our knowledge, psychopathological patterns (presumably Freud's regression theory) are not sufficiently reliable and invariable to be used as the only criteria for diagnoses, a view shared by O'Connor & Franks (1960). On the whole, they conclude that symptom complexes, however imperfect and overlapping, should be used as the basis for diagnosis. With this conclusion one would agree; but one certainly cannot agree with Chodoff & Lyons's equation of conversion hysteria and 'psychosomatic symptomatology'. The distinction between the psychosomatic and the personal illness, made in Chapter 5, is in no way an unconventional one.

Charcot & Marie (1892) and Janet (1901) have given the classical description of the hysterical illness, and there is considerable agreement among later authors in their descriptions of what may constitute hysterical symptoms, although the differentiation from the psychosomatic and purely organic still presents a diagnostic problem. The contentions of Mayer-Gross *et al.* (1954) are fairly representative. Hysteria can mimic almost any disease. There is a tendency to dissociation seen in hysterical paralysis, anaesthesias, twilight states, and fugues, which is often accompanied by *la belle indifférence* described by Janet. Some clinicians stress the manipulative aspect of the symptoms and seek to establish the gain derived by the patient from them.

Hysteroid Personality
The concept of the hysteroid (or hysterical) personality is of more recent origin. Chodoff & Lyons found no articles specifically on the hysteroid personality until that of Wittels (1930), who described the traits of suggestibility, emotionality, impulsiveness, and histrionicity. They consider that Charcot was concerned with symptoms rather than with traits. Freud, as far as they were able to discover, never described the hysteroid personality or used the term. The contributions of Janet were apparently overlooked in their review. In *The Mental State of Hystericals* (Janet,

1901), he devotes a chapter to the description and explanation of the 'hysterical character'. Although his view that the traits were the product of the illness (a weakening of the will, intelligence, and personal synthesis) would not be subscribed to now by most people, his descriptions of the personalities of his patients are still pertinent. Janet listed affective shallowness and lability, exaggerated and disproportionate emotional display, egocentricity, jealousy, and sexual frigidity. He felt that many persons might share these traits with hystericals, particularly criminals, imbeciles, and small children. Two traits only he felt were peculiar to the hysteric, namely the lability and contradictory nature of the affects and traits. The hysteric passes from hope to despair, from liveliness to apathy, from suggestibility to stubbornness, from affection to indifference.

This uncomplimentary view of Janet's undoubtedly sprang from his conviction, shared with Charcot, that hysteria was a degenerative disease. Although castigating the witch hunters, he raised a substitute bogey of his own which has pursued the unfortunate hysteroid personality to the present day under the cloak of 'medical' or 'scientific' observation. The list of hysteroid personality traits gleaned from the literature by Chodoff & Lyons indicates the moral repugnance with which hysteroid personalities are still viewed by medical writers:

1. Egotism, vanity, egocentric, self-centred, self-indulgent.
2. Exhibitionism, dramatization, lying, exaggeration, play acting, histrionic behaviour, mendacity, pseudologia phantistica, dramatic self-display, centre of attention, simulation.
3. Unbridled display of affects, labile, affectivity, irrational emotional outbursts, emotional capriciousness, deficient in emotional control, profusion of affects, emotions volatile and labile, excitability, inconsistency of reactions.
4. Emotional shallowness, affects fraudulent and shallow, go through the motions of feeling.
5. Lasciviousness, sexualization of all non-sexual relations, obvious sexual behaviour, coquetry, provocative.
6. Sexual frigidity, intense fear of sexuality, failure of sex impulse to develop towards natural goal, sexually immature, sexual apprehensiveness.
7. Demanding, dependent.

Number 8 should obviously be a Thurber drawing of a predatory female bearing down on a timorous male psychiatrist.

Obsessoid and Hysteroid Components of Personality
The Relationship between Symptoms and Personality
Although there seems to be considerable agreement about the feasibility of making the distinction between symptoms and personality traits and attitudes, there are at least three main schools of thought about the nature of the relationship.

The first school is represented by Janet who considered that the underlying weakness of personal synthesis produces both symptoms and traits. Presumably the distinction he would make between the two would be that the symptoms are peculiar to the fully developed hysterical illness; whereas the traits are shared with other 'degenerates', such as criminals and imbeciles. In the aetiology of hysteria 'pathological heredity plays a preponderant part'. Physical illness, and emotional shocks and crises can precipitate a breakdown. Successive breakdowns weaken the predisposed constitution with a resultant mental disintegration, which may be permanent and complete. Little convincing evidence is offered for these views.

Fenichel (1945) agrees with Janet that the respective character traits may develop simultaneously with the symptoms, but thinks that the development of the character structure *may* ward off definite symptoms.

The second school maintains that the symptoms are dependent on the traits. Masserman (1946) and Noyes (1954) hold that an obsessive-compulsive neurosis appears when the defensive thoughts and acts of the person of obsessoid character become too widely pervasive and deviant. Reich (1949) believes that there are merely fluid transitions from compulsive symptoms to the corresponding character attitudes. Michaels & Porter (1949) consider that an obsessional neurosis is a pathological exaggeration of the normal character. A certain degree of compulsiveness may be regarded as an asset, being represented by a normal concern with cleanliness, orderliness, responsibility, and law-abidance, which, according to these American authors, are the stuff of civilized society. In Chapter 2 it was argued that the difference between an obsessoid trait of cleanliness, for example, and a compulsive washing symptom is a qualitative, and not merely a quantitative, difference. Rapaport (1948) thinks that the breakdown of the obsessional character is inevitably followed by the development of obsessional neurosis. This view is, however, patently at odds with the findings of the Slaters, to be discussed under the third school.

As regards the relationship between symptoms and traits, Jung belongs with the second school. He considers (1920) that the traits precede the illness and are more enduring: 'Psychiatrists know very well that before either illness [hysteria and dementia praecox] is fully developed patients already present the characteristic type, traces of which are to be found from the earliest years of life. As Binet pointed out so well, the neurotic only accentuates and shows in relief the characteristic traits of his personality.'

In general, the second point of view is, then, that traits precede symptoms and are more enduring; but that, when symptoms do develop, they are an exacerbation of the pre-existing traits and this is a sufficient explanation of the form the symptoms take.

This standpoint is challenged by the third school, which maintains that there is no absolutely necessary connection between symptoms and personality traits. Mayer-Gross *et al.* (1954), Curran & Guttmann (1949), Lewis & Mapother (1941), and Chodoff & Lyons (1958) support the view in stating that not all persons exhibiting obsessional or hysterical symptoms have the supposed corresponding constellations of personality traits. Anxiety states, and neurotic and psychotic depressives are more commonly associated with obsessoid personalities than are obsessive or compulsive symptoms. The present series of studies supports this view.

The most thoroughgoing evidence has come from the work of the Slaters (1944, 1950). They hold that the relation between personality and symptoms is a close one and that personality is exhibited in the symptoms shown in neurotic illness: 'Not only is the type of symptom partly determined by the make-up of the personality but every personality seems to have its own threshold to different types of strain, below which a successful adaptation is still made, above which breakdown is likely.' In an investigation into the personalities and symptoms of neurotic soldiers during the second world war, Slater & Slater (1944) found that the relation between personality and neurotic symptoms was not equally close for all types of symptoms. Obsessional and compulsive symptoms were found to correlate with the obsessoid personality at the order of 0·8. Hysterical and paranoid symptoms were connected with the corresponding character traits by correlations around 0·5, and those of anxiety and depression with the corresponding personality types by a correlation of about 0·4. Hypochondriacal symptoms were relatively loosely connected with hypochondriacal personality traits with a correlation of 0·2.

In his summary of research findings, particularly in the field of genetics, Slater (1950) concluded that personality has a physical basis, but that neurosis is essentially a reaction between the personality and the environment. Environmental factors play an important part in precipitating the illness and, to a lesser extent, in determining its nature and symptomatology. 'The specific quality of the neurotic reaction is, however, principally derived from the personality.'

The standpoint taken throughout our studies comes closest to that of the Slaters. We would argue that personality is to be regarded biosocially, as Murphy (1947) has suggested, and that the environment is partly thrust upon the individual and is partly of his own choosing. With the possible exception of some traumatic neuroses, the pertinent environment for the neurotic is usually another person or persons in relation to whom the situation is one potentially capable of producing such feelings of shame as would seriously disrupt the individual's self-concept. The symptoms which are thrown up to avert this disaster may in part be determined by personality dispositions and in part by their unconsciously assessed teleological serviceableness in the particular circumstances.

In summary, the great majority of authors distinguish between traits and symptom complexes. This distinction is largely in terms of the more enduring nature of personality traits, which are regarded as pre-dating any illness and as having a constitutional basis. This is particularly interesting in view of the almost universal condemnation of the hysteroid traits, which are purported to be associated with immaturity. In spite of the emphasis on the possible constitutional aspects of trait development by many authors, including social psychologists such as Newcomb (1950) and Katz & Schanck (1938), it is difficult to believe that social pressures do not have a profound effect on the expression or inhibition of certain reaction patterns and that these pressures will not vary from culture to culture and from class to class.

There is an increasing tendency to regard the hysteroid and obsessoid traits as falling within the normal range of behaviour and as having some ego-syntonic value. Neurotic symptoms are usually seen as a later development more closely associated with environmental stress.

The problem of the relationship between symptoms and traits remains largely unsolved, with efforts towards its solution resting more on the theoretical bias of the authors than upon experimental evidence. Mackinnon's criticisms remain largely pertinent some eighteen years after his formulation.

THE HYSTEROID : OBSESSOID QUESTIONNAIRE
Construction

One of the great difficulties in arriving at a fuller understanding of the nature of personality trait and symptom complexes is the lack of valid measuring instruments. Cronbach (1949) considers that the disappointing results so often encountered in personality testing by questionnaire have arisen from inadequate preparation of the testing instruments and from inadequate theories of personality. In only a few instances, according to Maller (1944), have personality tests been validated against an outside criterion. There is no doubt that many so-called personality inventories are a mixture of symptoms and traits. It is reasonable to argue, therefore, that the logical separation of these two concepts, involving the distinction of the more general from the more specific, the more permanent from the more transient, and the inhibitors from the promoters of adjustment, should be a first step in the development of an adequate theory and an adequate measuring instrument. The rest of this chapter is concerned with the description of the development of a questionnaire based on the principles of classification propounded above.

It had been found in previous work that *self*-ratings on the hysteroid : obsessoid rating scale (Foulds & Caine, 1958, 1959) by observer-rated hysteroid and obsessoid persons failed to distinguish between the two groups sufficiently accurately to be of much practical value. Untrained subjects found rating-scale principles hard to grasp, some of the items had moral implications as worded, and the nine-point scale was too short for high reliability. To escape these difficulties the Hysteroid : Obsessoid Questionnaire (HOQ) was constructed.[1]

The hysteroid : obsessoid rating scale consisted of the following traits placed on a five-point scale:

Hysteroid	*Obsessoid*
1. Excessive display of emotion	Scarcely any display of emotion
2. Vivid day dreams	Inability to indulge in fanciful thinking
3. Frequent mood changes	Constant mood
4. Under-conscientious	Over-conscientious
5. Given to precipitate action	Slow and undecided owing to weighing of pros and cons
6. Over-dependent	Obstinately independent
7. Careless and inaccurate	Stickler for precision
8. Shallow emotionally	Feels things deeply
9. Desire to impress and gain attention	Self-effacing

[1] The HOQ is reproduced in Appendix A (pp. 50-52 below).

In constructing the HOQ several statements were framed which were thought to be pertinent to each of these nine items. As far as possible statements having a moral implication and statements having to do with symptoms were avoided. Rating-scale item 9, for example, formed the basis of the following true/false statements:

'I like to wear eye-catching clothes'
'I keep quiet at parties or meetings'
'It pleases me to be the centre of a lively group'
'I like discussing myself with other people'

In this way 48 statements were compiled, each of which could be scored in a hysteroid or in an obsessoid direction.

Establishment of the Outside Criterion (Behaviour Ratings)
The therapeutic community approach to psychotherapy employed at Claybury Hospital has been described by Martin (1962). It can be claimed that such a milieu is a particularly favourable one for obtaining ratings of behaviour. The medical, nursing, and occupational therapy staff work closely together and share the opportunity to observe the patients in a very wide range of activities at work, recreation, meals, visiting days, and in different types of group.

In the case of the community wards for neurotics, from which the bulk of the validation sample came (76 cases), ratings were called for two weeks after admission, when staff members felt confident of making a reasonably accurate assessment. Patients from the acute admission wards had been observed for somewhat longer. All members of the ward staff had access to the case papers, and there would be some discussion of patients among the staff during the period. The rating forms and the approach to be adopted were discussed with each rater. Staff were urged to base their ratings on observed behaviour, with as little interpretation as possible, even though this might be regarded as superficial. Detailed instructions concerning the use of the rating forms were available on the wards, with explanatory notes as to the meaning of the items. Periodically, on the neurotic wards, rating results were communicated to each of the raters, so that assessments could be compared with those of their colleagues. Individual difficulties were discussed with the psychologist when they arose.

Ratings on all patients were obtained from medical, nursing, and occupational therapy staff, using a form of the rating scale described in the previous study (Foulds & Caine, 1958). The number of raters per patient varied from three to eleven with a mean of 7·5.

An analysis of the internal consistency of the rating-scale items showed that only six of the eleven original traits were being successfully differentiated for the groups by the raters, namely: attention-seeking, emotional display, speed of decision, lability of affect, conscientiousness, and shallowness of affect. These six items formed the subsequent basis of the hysteroid-obsessoid rating allocation.

An analysis of the mean rating was computed, and from this confidence limits were calculated. Despite the safeguards taken in the rating scheme these calculations showed that the dependability of the ratings was in question. Although this is a common and recognized weakness of ratings, a factorial experiment was carried out in an effort to improve the validation criterion. Five of the raters each rated ten male and ten female patients twice, with a ten-day interval between ratings, making a total of 200 ratings. An analysis of variance was carried out with raters, replications of ratings, and patients as the sources of variance. The between-raters, between-patients, and rater/patient interaction variances were significant, but the between-replications was not. The between-raters variance was too small to be of practical significance and, since the rater/patient interaction could not, in practice, be allowed for, it was included in the residual variance.

The experiment was collapsed into a 5 (raters) × 20 (patients) factorial design. Estimates of the variance of the factors were made on the assumption of model (II) of the analysis of variance (Snedecor, 1956). The variance of the raters was only ·35, while that of the patients was 4·37. The error variance was 2·69. One may conclude from the factorial experiment that raters tended to show something of a bias in one direction or another but that this bias was too small to be worth correction, and that the raters differed frequently from each other in their individual classifications. The reliability of the mean rating of each patient (averaged over the 5 raters and measured by an intraclass correlation coefficient) was ·92.

The distribution of the patients' ratings was not significantly different from a normal distribution having the same mean and standard deviation. Degree of hysteroidness or obsessoidness as observed by trained observers was thus not related to hospital admission.

To establish the hysteroid or obsessoid rating classification the ratings for each patient were pooled, taking the total hysteroid score less the

Obsessoid and Hysteroid Components of Personality

total obsessoid score as the allocation. This allocation yielded 65 obsessoids, 27 hysteroids, and one indeterminate.

Subjects

The Hysteroid : Obsessoid Questionnaire was administered to all neurotic patients entering Forest and Orchard House community wards of Claybury Hospital during the period December 1959 to February 1961. In addition, all patients referred to the psychologist from the acute admission wards as hysteroid or obsessoid personalities were included in the validation sample. A minimum of Grade IV on the Mill Hill Vocabulary scale, that is above the 10th centile, using the Synonym scale only, was set.

Altogether 93 patients were tested on the HOQ and rated. Of those rated as hysteroid, 21 were women and 6 were men; of those rated as obsessoid, 31 were women and 34 were men. The association with sex was significant (chi-square being 7·024, for $n=1$, and p being $<·01$). The ages of the two groups were very similar: for hysteroids, the ages ranged from 20 to 53 with a mean age of 33·72 (s.d. 8·78); for obsessoids, the range was from 19 to 54 with a mean of 33·95 (s.d. 9·50).

The scores of 34 normal subjects (18 women and 16 men) were available for the HOQ and for the Maudsley Personality Inventory (MPI). These were all members of local associations. In addition, 54 student nurses completed the HOQ. The ages ranged, for the total group of 88 subjects, from 19 to 56 with an average of 33·95.

Administration of the HOQ

The HOQ, together with certain other tests of questionnaire type, was completed by each patient several days after admission and again after six weeks. A number of the referred cases had been in hospital for some months and these were tested only once.

The instructions for completing the questionnaire were that the questions had to do with the patient as he 'really was', as he was 'usually', rather than as he might be on an 'off' day or as he might be in some transitory mood. The patients were pressed to answer each question as true or false, but some qualification by writing the word 'mostly' after a response was allowed. In a case of extreme indecision an item could be left blank, but this procedure was discouraged. In fact, only a very few patients availed themselves of it, and the largest number of blanks was five in one extreme case.

43

Personality Attributes and Psychiatric Illness

The score recorded was the number of items marked in the hysteroid direction, since each item had to score either hysteroid or obsessoid with the very few exceptions mentioned.

Other Tests and Clinical Data

The diagnosis accepted was that of the senior psychiatrist in charge of the case, usually of consultant status.

A number of other test results were available for 77 of the patients. These included the standard Minnesota Multiphasic Personality Inventory (MMPI) scales of K, Hs, D, and Pt. In addition, certain other specially devised scales were employed, namely the $(D-Hs)$ score distinguishing between hysterics and dysthymics among female neurotics (Foulds & Caine, 1958); the $(D+Pt)$ score distinguishing between hysterics and dysthymics among male neurotics (Foulds & Caine, 1959); the Extrapunitive : Intropunitive scales of the MMPI (Foulds, Caine & Creasy, 1960); and combinations of these last two.

The breakdown of the Extrapunitive scale into Acting-out Hostility, Criticism of Others, and Delusional Hostility, and of the Intropunitive scale into Self-criticism and Delusional Guilt, is described in detail in Chapter 5; the total of all five scales is referred to as General Punitiveness, the total extrapunitive – the total intropunitive score as Direction of Punitiveness.

Fifty-three neurotics completed the Maudsley Personality Inventory (MPI) (Eysenck, 1959). Eysenck (1962) claims that the MPI measures neuroticism and extraversion in normal samples. Although recent research has failed to substantiate the validation claims that it is a test of extraversion in neurotic samples (Eysenck, 1962; Sigal, Star & Franks, 1958; McGuire, 1962), the test was included here to establish its relationship with the HOQ.

An analysis of the HOQ was conducted to determine the association of items within the questionnaire. In this analysis each item was placed with that item with which it had highest agreement; agreements lower than the ·05 level of significance were ignored.

Results

As with the ratings, the scores on the HOQ were found to be normally distributed. No sex difference was found, and the mean score for those rated as hysteroid in personality was 27·08 (s.d. 6·64); that of those rated

44

as obsessoid in personality was 19·08 (s.d. 4·20). This difference between the means was significant at beyond the ·001 level, with a 78 per cent agreement between the rating scale and the questionnaire when each was dichotomized. The correlations of the other clinical and test data are shown in *Table 1*.

TABLE 1   *Clinical and test correlations with the HOQ*

	N	Correlation	$p <$
Re-test (after 6 weeks' therapy)	62	·77	·001
Rating classification	92	·68	·001
Diagnosis (hysteria or dysthymia)	86	·28	·01
Age	93	·23	·05
MMPI scales			
K	77	·08	
Hs	77	− ·14	
D	77	− ·15	
Pt	77	− ·11	
$(D-Hs)$	41	·00	
$(D+Pt)$	36	·32	
General Punitiveness $(E+I)$	77	− ·07	
Direction of Punitiveness $(E-I)$	77	·31	·01
Maudsley Personality Inventory			
Neurotics			
Extraversion	53	·84	·001
Neuroticism	53	− ·40	·01
Normals			
Extraversion	35	·81	·001
Neuroticism	35	·11	

The 2nd and 3rd correlations are bi-serial. Correlations between MPI E and MPI N are, for neurotics, − ·46; for normals, ·06.

Mean score comparisons between the HOQ scores of the normal sample and those of the neurotic groups are shown in *Table 2*.

TABLE 2   *Mean HOQ score comparisons between normals and neurotics split on clinical diagnosis and personality rating*

	N	Mean	s.d.	t	p<
NORMALS	88	24·07	5·51		
NEUROTICS	92	21·42	7·03	2·96	·01
Hysterics					
hysteroid	7	27·71	3·95		
obsessoid	6	21·83	5·40	2·21	·05
Dysthymics					
hysteroid	15	28·26	6·59		
obsessoid	58	16·96	5·20	6·01	·001
All neurotic hysteroids	27	27·08	6·64	2·11	·05
All neurotic obsessoids	65	19·08	4·20	6·50	·001

Six cases were not placed in either the hysteric or the dysthymic class; but these cases have been included in other break-ups.

Items showing the highest agreement within the HOQ could be identified under the following traits, using the hysteroid direction of response: (i) imaginative thinking; (ii) unconcern with details and standards; (iii) social poise; (iv) self-display, fashionable clothes; (v) quickness of decision; (vi) lack of conscientiousness; (vii) many acquaintances rather than a few friends; (viii) dependence on others; (ix) display of emotions; (x) lability of affect.

All items tended to agree with each other, with the exception of No. 33 – 'My party manners are pretty good'. About nine out of ten said 'yes' to this and it was misplaced in the agreement analysis.

Discussion

Despite the fallibility of the ratings, these analyses show that there is a considerable measure of agreement between them and the HOQ. It can be claimed that for a personality test the HOQ has a reasonably high validity in terms of an outside criterion, and a high re-test reliability in spite of intervening psychotherapy. Sex differences on the HOQ are minimal; but, in this Claybury sample, there is a slight correlation with age. The older patients have a slightly higher hysteroid score, a finding at variance with the view that hysteroid traits are associated with the immaturity of the young. One cannot, of course, generalize from a selected population such as the present one. The fact that both the rating classifications and the HOQ scores are distributed normally has been remarked; but neurotics have significantly lower scores than the normal sample, as do those scoring high on the MPI Neuroticism scale. Either obsessoids tend to be at greater risk of a neurotic breakdown, or neuroticism results in subjects distorting their self-description in an obsessoid direction.

There is a significant correlation between the HOQ and diagnosis, with the diagnosed dysthymics in the Claybury sample tending to have obsessoid personalities. It should, however, be noted that the difference between the means of subjects rated as hysteroid and obsessoid is considerably greater than that between the means of hysterics and dysthymics. This certainly underlines the need to distinguish between symptoms and traits.

There is no correlation between the HOQ and any of the standard MMPI scales used in the study.

Whereas the HOQ is quite unrelated to General Punitiveness, it is significantly related to Direction of Punitiveness, which is in line with previous studies (Foulds & Caine, 1958, 1959), and with more recent studies (Martin & Caine, 1963) at Claybury and at Runwell Hospital, as reported elsewhere in various chapters. The evidence for the association between the hysteroid type of personality and extrapunitiveness is, therefore, very strong.

The HOQ and the MPI are obviously very closely related and have the same order of agreement with the Neuroticism scale of the MPI in both neurotic and normal groups. This is not surprising in view of Eysenck's (1953) clinical identification of hysteroid attitudes and traits with hysterical diagnosis and extraversion. As Eysenck & Claridge (1962) point out, the E scale is heavily dependent on sociability items, which are probably related to the attention-seeking items of the HOQ.

It might be argued that as long as a test is predictive it does not matter what it measures. This view is justified only for certain types of problem. Mechanical information and spatial ability tests may be highly correlated and equally useful in predicting mechanical ability in adults; for this purpose they might be interchangeable. If one were investigating the development of spatial ability in children, however, one would be

47

ill-advised to employ tests of mechanical information rather than spatial tests in the investigation. It can equally well be argued that tests of extraversion: introversion should be tests of direction of psychical 'libidinal flow' rather than tests of associated personality traits, if indeed they are associated traits.

In their original senses the concepts of extraversion: introversion and of hysteroid: obsessoid represent different levels of personality functioning. The former indicates the direction, the latter the 'how' of behaviour. Too ready an identification of the two aspects may obscure important differences. An extraverted thinking type might well occur in an obsessoid personality. This would certainly seem to hold good for a considerable number of scientists and engineers. Darwin has been described as an extraverted thinker (Fordham, 1959); but his behaviour in pursuing his researches was that of an obsessoid. In this sense it is the obsessoid who is typically extraverted. He requires and seeks more and more information from the environment before he can make a decision. He distrusts his own intuitive judgement and must check with the facts. He has difficulty in making up stories on the Thematic Apperception Test, as clinical psychologists well know, 'because there is not enough to go on', and, as a result, he becomes preoccupied with the details of the pictures. The hysteroid, on the other hand, has little difficulty in this respect, being prepared to give free rein to his fantasy, sparked off by minimal cues. It is the obsessoid who studies his environment and depends upon it in making decisions. It is the hysteroid who lacks interest in details, in precision, and who is prepared to make extreme judgements on minimal evidence, in which an element of wishful thinking is discernible.

No doubt it is this failure to distinguish between different aspects of personality functioning that has given rise to the conflicting views as to the nature of extraversion: introversion. The close association of the HOQ and the MPI *E* scale suggests that the latter is related to personality traits rather than symptom complexes, and thus the differences postulated by Eysenck would not follow of necessity. In the studies reported in Chapter 1, half the dysthymics had hysteroid personalities. In the Claybury sample, although more dysthymics had obsessoid personalities, approximately half the hysterics had obsessoid personalities. Again, it was reported in Chapter 2 that Ingham & Robinson (1964) found that conversion hysterics tended to be introverted, and it was hysterical personalities who were extraverted.

Obsessoid and Hysteroid Components of Personality

If one is prepared to differentiate between symptom complexes, attitudes, traits, and direction of psychical 'libidinal flow', a number of interesting possibilities arise in considering psychiatric classifications, personality types, and extraverted thinking. Do extraverted-thinking obsessoids develop the same symptom patterns as introverted-thinking obsessoids? Since their attention is directed outwards, do they develop hysteria rather than dysthymia? Extraverted thinking may help to explain the inward or outward direction of hostility. One would expect the extraverted thinker to look for the cause of frustrating situations in the environment; whereas the introverted person would look, intropunitively, into himself.

The elucidation of such problems and relationships will depend very largely upon the development of appropriate measuring instruments. The HOQ was designed to measure the hysteroid : obsessoid component of personality and the experimental evidence suggests that it does so. Of the validation material the most significant agreement of the HOQ is with the personality rating, and the items of the scale group themselves in accordance with the hysteroid : obsessoid trait constellations. Hysteroid and obsessoid personalities are well-established clinical entities about which there is considerable agreement. On the other hand, there is a great deal of controversy as to the nature of extraversion : introversion both conceptually aud experimentally. The data constituting the present research can be adequately explained in terms of two entities, i.e. symptom and personality trait constellations.

The Hysteroid : Obsessoid Questionnaire

SURNAME.....................CHRISTIAN NAMES................................

AGE.........SEX.........OCCUPATION............................DATE.........

Instructions

Read over each question and decide whether it is a true description of
how you *usually* act or feel, then put a circle round the T (true) if the
statement describes you or round the F (false) if it does not. Do not spend
too much time over any question. Take your first reaction bearing in
mind your usual way of acting or feeling. Do not miss any questions.
There are no right or wrong answers.

1. I find it hard to think up stories	T F
2. I like to wear eye-catching clothes	T F
3. I keep my feelings to myself	T F
4. I am slow in making up my mind about things because I weigh up all the pros and cons	T F
5. I am a moody sort of person, with lasting moods	T F
6. I have rigid standards I feel I should stick to	T F
7. When I am working I like a job which calls for speed rather than close attention to details	T F
8. I like to ask for other people's opinions and advice about myself	T F
9. I don't feel awkward when meeting people because I know how to behave	T F
10. I prefer to be popular with everyone than to have a few deep lasting friendships	T F
11. I cannot shake off my troubles easily even if I get the opportunity	T F
12. I have a good imagination	T F

13. I keep quiet at parties or meetings   T   F

14. I feel better after I've had a good row and got it off my chest   T   F

15. I am quick in sizing up people and situations   T   F

16. My mood is easily changed by what happens around me   T   F

17. My conscience seldom bothers me   T   F

18. I keep a place for everything and everything in its place   T   F

19. I'm rather lacking in the social graces   T   F

20. I have the same friends now as I had years ago   T   F

21. It pleases me to be the centre of a lively group   T   F

22. I like to show people exactly how I feel about things   T   F

23. The first impressions or reactions are usually the right ones in the end   T   F

24. I do not mind if things turn out badly as long as I know I've done the right thing   T   F

25. I can lead more than one life in my imagination   T   F

26. I like discussing myself with other people   T   F

27. I do not show my emotions in front of people   T   F

28. When someone asks me a question I give a quick answer and and look for the reasons later   T   F

29. If I am not in the right mood for something it takes a lot to make me feel differently   T   F

30. I usually get by without having to worry about whether I've done the right thing morally or not   T   F

31. One can understand most things without having to go into all the details   T   F

32. It is important to be fashionable in your opinions, clothes, etc.   T   F

33. My party manners are pretty good   T   F

34. The only friends I make I keep   T   F

35. If I happen to be upset about something it seems to carry over into all I do for a long time   T   F

36. I cannot completely lose myself in a book or story   T   F

37. I like to sit in the background or in an inconspicuous place at socials, meetings, etc. T F
38. I act out my feelings T F
39. I wait until I am sure of all my facts before I make a decision T F
40. I spend a good deal of time worrying about the rights and wrongs of conduct T F
41. When going into a room or meeting someone for the first time I get a strong general impression first and only gradually take in the details T F
42. When meeting people I haven't met before I usually feel I make a rather poor impression T F

43. It upsets me to leave friends and make new ones even if I have to T F
44. When watching a play I identify with the characters T F
45. My feelings about things and towards other people seldom change T F
46. I do not like taking a leading part in group activities T F
47. Mistakes are usually made when people make snap decisions T F
48. If two people find they disagree about things they shouldn't try to carry on being close friends T F

REFERENCES

ABRAHAM, K. (1921). Contributions to the theory of the anal character. In *Selected papers on psychoanalysis*. London: Hogarth Press.

BATESON, G. (1944). Cultural determinants of personality. In J. McV. Hunt (Ed.), *Personality and the behavior disorders*, Vol. 2. New York: The Ronald Press.

BELOFF, H. (1957). The structure and origin of the anal character. *Genet. Psychol. Monogr.*, Vol. 55, 141.

BOWLBY, J. (1940). *Personality and mental illness*. London: Kegan Paul, Trench, Trubner.

CHARCOT, K. M. & MARIE, P. (1892). Hysteria. In H. D. Tuke (Ed.), *A dictionary of psychological medicine*, Vol. 1. Philadelphia: Blakiston.

CHODOFF, P. & LYONS, H. (1958). Hysteria, the hysterical personality and hysterical conversion. *Amer. J. Psychiat.*, 114, 734.

CRONBACH, L. J. (1949). *Essentials of psychological testing*. (2nd edn., 1960.) New York: Harper.

CURRAN, D. & GUTTMANN, E. (1949). *Psychological medicine*. Edinburgh: Livingstone.

EYSENCK, H. J. (1953). *The structure of human personality*. (2nd edn., 1960.) London: Methuen.

EYSENCK, H. J. (1959). *Manual of the Maudsley Personality Inventory*. London: University of London Press.

EYSENCK, H. J. (1962). Response set, authoritarianism and personality questionnaires. *Brit. J. soc. clin. Psychol.*, 1, 20.

EYSENCK, H. J. & CLARIDGE, G. S. (1962). The position of hysterics and dysthymics in a two-dimensional framework of personality description. *J. abnorm. soc. Psychol.*, 64, 46.

FENICHEL, O. (1945). *The psychoanalytic theory of neurosis*. New York: Norton.

FORDHAM, F. (1959). *An introduction to Jung's psychology*. Harmondsworth, Middlesex: Penguin Books.

FOULDS, G. A. & CAINE, T. M. (1958). Psychoneurotic symptom clusters, trait clusters and psychological tests. *J. ment. Sci.*, 104, 722.

FOULDS, G. A. & CAINE, T. M. (1959). Symptom clusters and personality types among psychoneurotic men compared with women. *J. ment. Sci.*, 105, 469.

FOULDS, G. A., CAINE, T. M. & CREASY, M.A. (1960). Aspects of extra- and intro-punitive expression in mental illness. *J. ment. Sci.*, 106, 599.

FREUD, S. (1907). Obsessive acts and religious practices. In *Collected papers*, II. London: Hogarth Press, 1948.

FREUD, S. (1908). Character and anal erotism. In *Collected papers*, II. London: Hogarth Press, 1948.

E

FREUD, S. (1913). The predisposition to obsessional neurosis. In *Collected papers*, II. London: Hogarth Press, 1948.

FREUD, S. (1949). *New introductory lectures on psychoanalysis*. London: Hogarth Press.

HENDERSON, D. K. & GILLESPIE, R. D. (1950). *Textbook of psychiatry*. (7th edn.) London: Oxford University Press.

JANET, P. (1901). *The mental state of hystericals*. New York & London: Putman.

JONES, E. (1918). Anal erotic character traits. In *Papers on psychoanalysis*. London: Baillière, Tindall & Cox, 1938.

JUNG, C. G. (1920). *Collected papers on analytic psychology*. London: Baillière, Tindall & Cox.

KATZ, D. & SCHANCK, R. L. (1938). *Social psychology*. New York: Wiley.

KRETSCHMER, E. (1926). Hysteria. *Nerv. & Ment. Dis. Monogr.*, 44. New York.

LEWIS, A. J. & MAPOTHER, E. (1941). In *Price's Textbook of the practice of medicine*. London: Oxford University Press.

MCGUIRE, R. J. (1962). A study of the MPI used with psychiatric in-patients. *Bulletin of the Brit. Psychol. Soc.*, **47**, 56.

MACKINNON, D. W. (1944). The structure of personality. In J. McV. Hunt (Ed.), *Personality and the behavior disorders*, Vol. I. New York: The Ronald Press.

MALLER, J. B. (1944). Personality tests. In J. McV. Hunt (Ed.), *Personality and the behaviour disorders*, Vol. I. New York: The Ronald Press.

MARTIN, D. V. (1962). *Adventure in psychiatry*. Oxford: Cassirer.

MARTIN, D. V. & CAINE, T. M. (1963). Personality change in chronic neurotics in a therapeutic community. *Brit. J. Psychiat*, **109**, 267.

MASSERMAN, J. H. (1946). *Principles of dynamic psychiatry*. London & Philadelphia: Saunders.

MAYER-GROSS, W., SLATER, E. & ROTH, M. (1954). *Clinical psychiatry*. (2nd edn., 1960.) London: Cassell. Baltimore: Williams & Wilkins, 1955.

MICHAELS, J. J. & PORTER, R. T. (1949). Psychiatric and social implications of contrasts between psychopathic personality and obsessive-compulsive neurosis. *J. nerv. ment. Dis.*, **109**, 122.

MURPHY, G. (1947). *Personality: a biosocial approach to origins and structure*. New York: Harper.

NEWCOMB, T. M. (1950). *Social psychology*. New York: Dryden.

NOYES, A. P. (1954). *Modern clinical psychiatry*. London & Philadelphia: Saunders.

O'CONNOR, N. & FRANKS, C. M. (1960). Childhood upbringing and other environmental factors. In H. J. Eysenck (Ed.), *Handbook of abnormal psychology*. London: Pitman Medical Publishing Co.

RADO, S. (1959). Obsessive behaviour. In S. Arieti (Ed.), *American handbook of psychiatry*. New York: Basic Books.

Obsessoid and Hysteroid Components of Personality

RAPAPORT, D. (1948). *Diagnostic psychological testing*, Vol. 2. Chicago Year Book.

REICH, W. (1949). *Character analysis*. New York: Orgone Institute Press.

SANDLER, J. & HAZARI, A. (1960). The obsessional: on the psychological classification of obsessional character traits and symptoms. *Brit. J. med. Psychol.*, **33**, 113.

SEARS, R. R. (1936). Experimental studies of projection: I. Attribution of traits. *J. soc. Psychol.*, **7**, 151.

SEARS, R. R. (1943). Survey of objective studies of psychoanalytic concepts. Bulletin No. 51, *Soc. Sci. Res. Com. Bull.* New York.

SIGAL, J. J., STAR, K. & FRANKS, C. M. (1958). Hysterics and dysthymics as criterion groups in the study of introversion : extraversion. *J. abnorm. soc. Psychol.*, **57**, 143.

SLATER, E. (1950). The genetical aspects of personality and neurosis. *Congrès Internat. de Psychiatrie, Paris*. VI, *Psychiatrie Sociale, Génétique et Eugénique.*

SLATER, E. & SLATER, P. (1944). A heuristic theory of neurosis. *J neurol. Psychiat.*, **7**, 49.

SNEDECOR, G. W., (1956). *Statistical methods*. (5th edn.) Iowa: Ames.

WITTELS, F. (1930). *Med. Rev. of Rev.* **36**, 186.

PART II

A Quantitative Classification of the Functional Psychoses and the Neuroses

CHAPTER FOUR

Diagnostic Classification

THE PROBLEM OF CLASSIFYING

Psychiatric diagnosis has suffered a steady decline in prestige among both psychiatrists and psychologists. This is due principally to a misunderstanding about the nature of classification and secondarily to a confusion between inadequacy and unsuitability in respect of existing methods of classifying.

One must distinguish between 'What is X?' and 'What like is X?' classification. 'What is X?' 'X is a human being.' Clearly he will always remain in this category as long as he exists. 'What like is X?' 'X is active.' Clearly, for a variety of reasons, he may cease to be active. Psychiatric diagnoses should be concerned with 'What like is X?' questions.

In medicine the 'What is X?' view was represented by the disease entity model, and at one time psychiatric diagnosis was associated almost exclusively with that model. There are, indeed, still some epiphenomenologists left in psychiatry who, while paying lip-service to a multidisciplinary approach, clearly believe that a single physical cause will eventually be found for at least the psychoses. Many suggestions have been put forward as to what this cause is, particularly in the case of schizophrenia. In the main these speculators rely on the disease entity model. This model has been illustrated by Eysenck (1960), utilizing the example of tuberculosis. 'We have a "cause", namely the tubercle bacillus, acting on an organism predisposed by constitutional and environmental factors to react to the bacillus. The illness, when it develops, is characterized by various symptoms. . . .' 'When it develops' indicates that the tubercle bacillus is *not* the cause of tuberculosis, that it is a necessary but not a sufficient condition of the disease. Inability to tolerate the uncertainty inevitable in the face of an immensely complex set of relationships leads to the premature acceptance of a simplified and prejudiced solution. A striking factor is selected out of a set of factors that are jointly sufficient and independently necessary to the production of the effect. As Stebbing (1930) has put it, 'Common sense fails to

recognize that what we have to take into account is a system the parts of which are in mutual dependence. This dependence is causal dependence.' The cause of tuberculosis is not, therefore, the tubercle bacillus, but the 'tubercle bacillus, acting on an organism predisposed by constitutional and environmental factors to react to the bacillus'. Organicists in psychiatry should lower their sights. They may find necessary conditions for schizophrenia; they will not find a single cause.

Those who began to appreciate the unsuitability of the disease entity model tended to overlook the possible alternatives or to despair at the inadequacy of their reliability and, in consequence, felt constrained to abandon diagnosis altogether. Although many went through this process in their minds, few had the courage of their lack of conviction, so that in practice they clung with a defensive and self-conscious scorn to their rejected concepts. In their despair they wished to relegate inter-individual comparison to the servants' quarters and to entertain intra-individual comparison alone. Knowledge cannot, however, be pursued at all without classification. As Hampshire (1959) points out:

'a language must provide a means of differentiating, of dividing reality into the pieces and segments which are to be constant subjects of reference. Reality and experience cannot be thought about unless we have rules that correlate experience, in such a way that any familiar use of a particular group of signs will be taken as a reference to some particular element in experience.'

Later he states that:

'the two most general types of rules attaching words and thoughts to reality are first, the rule that singles out a so-and-so as the same so-and-so, the rule of identity; secondly, the rule that prescribes that anything resembling a particular thing, already singled out, in certain respects is also to be classified as a so-and-so, the rule of resemblance. All so-and-sos must resemble each other in some respect, the resemblance in that particular respect being the ground of the classification. It is also necessarily true that everything resembles everything in some respect. . . . We pick out resemblances in certain respects as the basis of our classifications and neglect other resemblances which, in pursuance of some new need or interest, may be marked later. . . . Reality by itself sets no limit. The limit is set by changing practical needs and by the development of new powers and new forms of social life.'

Diagnostic Classification

Adam was no doubt able to identify Eve as the same so-and-so any day of the week. A shrewd observer, had there been one available at the time, would have been able to note certain resemblances between Adam and Eve which differentiated them from all other things in the Garden. To arrive at his classification he would have been prepared to overlook certain differences between them. With the advent of Cain and Abel, his interests might have shifted and he would perhaps have noted that Cain and Abel bore a greater resemblance to Adam than to Eve in certain respects. Had he wished to select the two tallest to pick apples, the classification would become Adam and Eve and not Cain and Abel. Had he wished to select the two darkest, the classification might have changed again, say, to Adam and Cain on the one hand and Eve and Abel on the other. Had the observer been a psychiatrist he might have thought to himself: 'This Eve seems to be dissatisfied with her own capacities and to be always trying to manipulate poor Adam, who seems pretty normal to me, and so does Abel. Cain takes after his mother, I should say; but he has got a frightful temper, never stops to think. Nasty piece of work. I'll call him an aggressive psychopath. Of course, I can see that Cain and Abel have some things in common; but, for what I'm interested in at the moment, it's these differences that are most important. Yes, Adam and Abel seem all right; but I believe those other two could do with some treatment.' With increasing experience he finds that there are many other people needing treatment who remind him of Eve and of Cain. As a result of this accumulated knowledge he must teach himself, in the words of Abercrombie, what to look for, but not what to see (Abercrombie, 1960).

Such is the confusion over the nature and purpose of classification that some clinicians, bent on belittling the diagnostic function, unwittingly destroy the arguments in favour of the clinical experience which at other times they would extol. Thus Henderson & Gillespie (1950) state: 'Fortunately it is not diagnosis that matters, but the understanding of the disorder, and of the patient who suffers from it – under what circumstances it arose, how it is related to the patient's normal condition, what the disorder means, what light is shed on his problems, and what can be done to help towards a favourable outcome.' Noyes (1953) argues that 'the principal value of classification is not in the categorizing of a disease entity but in quickly eliminating those considerations which will be least useful in understanding the patient and in directing attention to those which are likely to be relevant'. Having thus adequately justified

classification, he goes on to say immediately, 'except in organic disorders a classificatory diagnosis is less important than a psychodynamic study of the personality. The psychiatrist should be interested in processes, not in labels . . . we should endeavour not so much to fit the symptoms into a classificatory scheme as to understand the sick person in terms of his life experience.'

The term 'label' has, in this connexion, come to have an almost exclusively pejorative connotation; but labels, as we have tried to indicate, can be extremely informative. We learn a great deal about a modern Adam who wears a blue rosette on Election Day, and we learn it very succinctly. The same Adam may wear a red rosette on Cup Final Day, and again we learn something. The fear of the anti-classifiers that the classifiers are stripping the individual of his uniqueness is quite unwarranted. Adam's total collection of rosettes may be altogether unique. Those who refuse to classify at all are apparently prepared to educe relations of difference, but not of similarity, between the mentally ill. Theoretically they approach each new case as psychiatric virgins; in practice nobody does so.

'It is not diagnosis that matters' is certainly not true for the research worker and ought not to be for the clinician. The clinician is, nevertheless, quite right to insist that one of his major concerns is with the individual patient, as far as possible, as a whole. He is interested in historical facts and attitudes in the life of a particular person and in their antecedents and consequents. Criteria can be worked out, as Dalbiez has shown (1941), for evaluating what are good and what are bad reasons for accepting inferences from such data, just as criteria can be established for the valuation of good and bad reasons for accepting ethical judgements (Toulmin, 1960). When the psychiatrist has made psychodynamic studies of several personalities, he must, if he is to formulate a cohesive, teachable body of knowledge, compare one with another. With comparison comes classification; without it, comes a tendency to feel things in one's bones, and such rheumatoid sensitivity is notoriously difficult to convey to the tiro.

The two functions of the psychiatrist which are insufficiently differentiated are the diagnostic and the aetiological. Each has its own particular purpose and its own particular techniques. It may be that the clinical interview is a somewhat unsuccessful method of arriving at a diagnosis because an attempt is made to combine the two rather incompatible functions at the same time.

Diagnostic Classification

The diagnostic function consists principally in ascertaining *what* the subject does, *what* he believes, *how* he does what he does, the style of his behaviour, and *why* he thinks he did what he did.

A man was picked up by the police in a confused and exhausted state and was admitted to hospital. During the first interview it was ascertained that what he had done, among other things, was to cycle from Edinburgh to London. He had then ridden three times round Buckingham Palace and set off for Scotland again. What he believed, among other things, was that the Queen was in danger and that he could avert the danger by riding three times round Buckingham Palace. He also believed that he could control the weather. The explanation of why he thought he had done it was to avert the danger to the Queen. This, together with certain other information, was sufficient for the psychiatrist to arrive at a diagnosis of paranoid schizophrenia. This type of interview is in essence an extensive or horizontal process.

It has been objected that the clinician does not need to ask more than a limited number of questions to obtain a clinical diagnosis and that, in any event, he has not the time to do otherwise. A distinction should perhaps be made between attaining a diagnosis for clinical purposes and attaining one for research purposes. Clearly a systematic and wide coverage of all relevant questions must precede any clinical selectivity, since it is only upon the systematic assessment of the salient characteristics of each group that selectivity can be based. Even had these salient characteristics been satisfactorily established, many difficulties would remain. We will wish to argue that there is a hierarchy, not only of symptoms within a syndrome, but of illnesses within the total group of those who are mentally ill. Thus, many – and perhaps all – who may be legitimately diagnosed as psychotics have neurotic symptoms; but those who can legitimately be diagnosed as neurotics do not have psychotic symptoms. If, therefore, the presence of psychotic symptoms is established early in the interview, it may, for purely diagnostic purposes, be unnecessary to inquire about neurotic symptoms. If, for example, hallucinations and delusions are manifestly present, the elicitation of a feeling of tension in the back of the neck or of a fear of going out alone is not likely to be of much diagnostic consequence. The converse, however, does not hold. Early detection of the feeling of tension or of the fear of going out alone does not provide a stopping point, since further inquiry may unearth the delusions and hallucinations, which would result in a change of diagnosis.

A Quantitative Classification

In order to build up the best possible picture of the characteristics of these diagnostic groups it is essential that the interview should be systematically structured. The same questions must be asked of all subjects, so that one knows that the absence of any record of a symptom means that the patient has not got that symptom and not that the psychiatrist might not have asked the question. This danger was illustrated by a woman who gave, in addition to a number of anxiety symptoms, several obsessional symptoms on the inventory to be described later. The case was diagnosed clinically as an anxiety state and there was no mention at all of obsessional features. When asked if she had mentioned these obsessional symptoms to the doctor, she said that she had not because he had not asked her. She did not like to volunteer information and, indeed, asked the psychologist if she would tell the doctor.

This single fact of not knowing whether a blank means 'no' or 'not ascertained' sets a severe limitation on the use of routine case notes for certain research purposes. To overcome this limitation it is necessary to trail the largest practicable standard net in order to catch as many traits, symptoms, and signs as possible. The catch will probably be a mixed one; but it will most probably contain a sufficient degree of similarity with certain other catches and a sufficient degree of difference from yet other catches to be classified with the former rather than the latter.

The aetiological function with mental patients, at least on the psychological side, consists principally in ascertaining *what made him* do what he did, *what made him* believe what he believes.

There might be circumstances, such as a race, in which it might be reasonable to cycle from Edinburgh to London, and even to cycle three times round Buckingham Palace; but the patient's explanation of his behaviour left little doubt that he was suffering from a delusion. The purpose of an aetiological interview would be to ascertain how he came to have such beliefs. What did the Queen signify for him? What was the significance of cycling three times round? How did this tie up with his belief that he could control the weather? What did he fear he could *not* control? This is an intensive or vertical approach. In this type of interview the approach may be much more selective and rather unsystematic. The clinician may have a characteristic way of opening such an interview; but, when clues are presented, he will follow them to the exclusion of questions which might have been asked had different clues been presented. Thus, if a response to some question indicated the presence of a paranoid delusion, the patient's reason for believing whatever it may

64

be would be inquired into, and he would probably not be asked if he tended to wake early. In other words, having elicited some information, the clinician sets up a hypothesis which he confirms or disconfirms by further restricted inquiry. If the hypothesis is disconfirmed, he tries another. In this type of interview the clinician is fishing with rod and line. He casts, and, if he does not get a bite, he casts again. It is difficult to fish at one and the same time with a large standard net and rod and line. It is not of the essence of The Compleat Angler that he should do so.

The upshot of the foregoing argument is that the choice is between diagnosing well and diagnosing badly rather than between diagnosing and not diagnosing. Better diagnoses might be made if the diagnostic and aetiological types of interview were kept more consciously and deliberately distinct than is perhaps customary.

SOME METHODS OF CLASSIFYING

Some psychiatrists and psychologists, who recognize the need for some form of classification, emphasize specificity. Diagnosis is by symptoms rather than by syndromes. This comes out clearly in certain therapeutic approaches.

Behaviour therapists, in a series of ingenious experiments, have endeavoured to concentrate on the most important symptom, and claim that the removal of such a symptom often results in the disappearance of the remainder. It has not been claimed that learning theory provides the means for selecting the dominant symptom or for eliciting the stimulus-hierarchy; nor, since it cannot as yet be claimed definitively that it is the conditioning procedure which removes the dominant symptom, can the disappearance of the remaining symptoms be attributed to the removal of the dominant symptom. The cooperation of patient and therapist in a combined attack on the patient's problem in the setting of a personal relationship conducive to the operation of suggestion may be a potent factor in such apparent successes as are achieved.

The treatment of isolated symptoms by conditioning seems likely to be more successful when they have become functionally autonomous; but this type of treatment has found at least equal favour with the pharmaceutical companies, who have not been slow to appreciate the possibilities of the atomistic doctrine. They have sometimes advocated the combined use of two drugs, one to treat the anxiety component and

one to treat the depressive component. It would seem that the possibilities have not as yet been fully explored and exploited. It may be, however, that this approach involves the type of assumption that a pure top C is equally pleasing whether it occurs in the right or the wrong place in an aria. The expert skittles player takes into account the interrelationships of the skittles and aims to knock down the essential skittle, that is that skittle which will have the greatest determining influence on the remaining skittles. In other words, he will seek to knock down that skittle which will knock down another skittle, which will knock down another skittle, and so on. Theoretically, those who reckon to treat symptoms take one bowl per skittle; practically, they act in ignorance of the interaction side-effects of the drugs.

In those disorders in which no necessary conditions of a physical nature have been discovered, the commonest practice is to diagnose in terms of syndromes. A syndrome is not just an aggregate of symptoms, but a hierarchical arrangement of symptoms, some at least of which are probably mutually dependent. There is thought, for example, to be a tendency for certain clusters of symptoms to occur more frequently than others. Suicidal ideas, psychomotor retardation, feelings of unworthiness, and delusions of poverty would be expected to occur together more commonly than functional paralysis, psychomotor retardation, *folie de doute*, and visual hallucinations. The syndrome concept is, therefore, as Eysenck (1960) has pointed out, a statistical concept. Its hierarchical nature can be taken care of to some extent by means of appropriate statistical weighting derived from a discriminant function analysis. Thus, although a functionally paralysed leg would be of much less frequent occurrence than low back pain, even in a group of hysterics, it would probably have greater differentiating power, so that it might receive a weighting of, say, 4, against only 2 for low back pain. The hierarchy would be a hierarchy of increasing power of differentiation.

The hierarchical nature of the syndrome is shown by the fact that an anxiety state, in a patient who neither felt anxiety nor manifested any of the autonomic signs associated with this emotion, would be inconceivable. The mood of anxiety is, therefore, a necessary condition for the diagnosis of an anxiety state. The mood of anxiety is not, however, a sufficient condition for the diagnosis of an anxiety state, since it can occur in, among others, a schizophrenic syndrome. Here it is implied that, even if this particular patient were not anxious, the remaining symptoms would seem to cluster in such a way as to make the diagnosis

appropriate. The mood of anxiety would not in this case be a necessary condition for the syndrome. The same type of symptom may, therefore, be a necessary condition for one syndrome, and present in, but not a necessary condition for, another.

With the schizophrenic syndrome we may be in a somewhat different case. The necessary condition for the diagnosis of schizophrenia might be accepted as a certain degree of flattening of affect or of incongruity or of thought disorder or of the passivity phenomenon. Unlike the case of anxiety, the presence of a certain degree of flattening of affect (assuming its adequate definition and measurement) or of thought disorder or of the passivity phenomenon may each be a sufficient condition for the diagnosis of schizophrenia, at least in the absence of known toxicity. We do not have much difficulty in understanding what is meant by an involutional melancholia with obsessional features; but an involutional melancholia with schizophrenic features is incomprehensible, except perhaps to those who believe in a schizo-affective syndrome. 'Where the greater malady is fixed, the lesser is scarce felt' has implications for classification to which it will be necessary to turn later. It was a view that was certainly supported by Bleuler (1950) when he said: 'The symptomatological differentiation of schizophrenia from manic-depressive psychosis can only be based on the presence of the specific schizophrenic symptoms. All the phenomena of manic-depressive psychosis may also appear in our disease; the only decisive factor is the presence or absence of schizophrenic symptoms.'

In the meantime there are certain confusions in the use of the syndrome concept which are particularly discouraging to the student, who, on picking up a textbook of psychiatry, is apt to get the impression that everything occurs in everything. This is due to the confusion between syndromes and symptoms. Thus, Skottowe (1953) argues:

'It is conventional to sub-classify psychoneuroses into four groups: *anxiety neuroses, obsessional neuroses, hysteria* and *neurasthenia*. These are syndromes, rather than sharply defined categories, and they are not mutually exclusive. Obsessional symptoms appear in many anxiety neuroses; few obsessional patients do not show some, sometimes intense, anxiety; patients with anxious or obsessional states may develop hysterical or fatigue syndromes, and so on.'

In trying to illustrate the supposed fact that the syndromes are not sharply defined categories, Skottowe has confused syndromes and symp-

toms. The anxiety syndrome may be characterized by symptoms *A*, *b*, *c*, *d*, and *e* – where *A* is a necessary condition for this syndrome. The obsessional syndrome may be characterized by symptoms *H*, *c*, *d*, *f*, and *g* – where *H* is a necessary condition for this syndrome. Thus, the anxiety state might have the following symptoms: *A*, free-floating anxiety (anxiety state would not be diagnosed in the absence of both this and phobias); *b*, feeling of having a tight band round the head; *c*, fear of insanity; *d*, palpitations and breathlessness; *e*, tremor. The obsessional neurotic might have: *H*, a compulsive symptom, say, handwashing (without this or some ruminative symptom the diagnosis would not be made); *c*, fear of insanity; *d*, palpitations and breathlessness; *f*, fear of doing something wrong against one's will; and *g*, being troubled by silly, pointless thoughts. If, in fact, fear of insanity and palpitations and breathlessness occur more frequently in anxiety states than in any other group, it is quite unobjectionable to describe the second case as an obsessional neurotic (syndrome) with anxiety features (symptoms); but Skottowe's conclusion – that, because the symptoms overlap, the syndromes are not distinct – is false.

The syndromes *qua* syndromes, when considered at the same level of classification, must be distinct, or they are not true classes. If principles of division have been arrived at which enable one to speak of a schizophrenic syndrome and of an affective syndrome, it is not logically permissible to speak of a schizo-affective syndrome, since this term denies the original principles of division. It would, however, be possible for a particular individual to fall into both classes and, therefore, to be described as a schizophrenic with psychotic depressive features.

In our present state of ignorance patients perhaps fall into more than one class oftener than they should do so, because of our inability to distinguish between a symptom which is a necessary condition for allocation to one particular class and a symptom which is secondary and of more frequent occurrence in some other class. Again, we may accept evidence for the existence of a symptom from, say, a psychopath, which he does not in fact have. With increased skill in assessing evidence and in handling data, the frequency of so-called borderline or mixed cases may well decrease.

The clustering of symptoms is not a random affair. Given symptom *A*, the probabilities of the simultaneous presence of symptoms *B*, *C*, or *D* will vary, just as the occurrence of the word 'the' in conversation is more likely to be followed by a noun or an adjective than by other parts of

speech.[1] Symptom clusterings can perhaps best be coped with by principal component analysis. At present, however, statistical skills are running ahead of conceptual and clinical skills, so that we have to be on our guard against trying to make silk purses out of sows' ears.

Another method of classifying is Eysenck's two-dimensional model for psychoneurosis (Eysenck, 1947) – the normal-neurotic and the extravert-introvert continua; the concepts of extravert and introvert being operationally defined in terms of their closeness of fit with hysteria and dysthymia respectively. Eysenck believes that psychiatrists are wrong to diagnose in terms of categories, because neuroticism and normality are not qualitatively, but only quantitatively, different. Albino (1953) has pointed out that 'Eysenck's continuum may mean that the processes underlying neurosis and normality are continuous as well as that the symptoms are continuous. But this is not necessarily so.'

A woman of 39 complained of a fear of walking down the street because she felt as though she were naked and people were looking at her. Independently of this phobia, she complained that her husband often made her parade about in the nude for half an hour at a time. She seemed unconscious of any relationship between the two complaints. Let us suppose that she was physically afraid of her husband, that she was quite untrained in any means of earning her own living, and that she had small children for whose sake she was prepared to endure these activities which were morally repugnant to her. Let us suppose further that she became very anxious about the situation – anxious because she feared her husband and loathed the activity, and yet always felt that there must surely be some way out (had she not felt this, she might have reacted with depression). She would be fully aware of the conflicting tendencies and of the relationship between them. She would be suffering anxiety, perhaps intense anxiety; but she would not be suffering from an anxiety neurosis. It is difficult to conceive that there would be any motivation for the phobia of walking down the street. Let us suppose, on the other hand, that we add to this account a lurking pleasure that she, at 39, should still be considered by at least one man to be worth looking at in the nude for half an hour. It might have been much more traumatic had he seen her in the nude and promptly reached for his hat. She might covertly wish to extend her entertainment value to a larger audience; but these naughty ideas might be inconsistent with her concept of herself as

---

[1] Certain aspects of schizophrenic thought disorder might be measurable by analysis of probabilities of word sequence.

A Quantitative Classification

a respectable woman. Naughty ideas are no respecters of persons. When she picks up her shopping basket, dons her coat and her respectability, and walks down the street, she *knows* she is not naked; but she *feels* naked and that people are staring at her. She is suffering from an anxiety neurosis.

Most people have some notion of the implications of being seen by a psychologist in a psychiatric unit. Such preconceptions may be sufficient to evoke the patient's problems and the concomitant affect during the performance of a task to which, in other circumstances, little anxiety might attach. On the type of psychological tests that psychologists are apt to administer the woman suffering anxiety and the woman suffering from an anxiety neurosis might well be indistinguishable. It might, therefore, be more discreet for psychologists to state that neuroticism and normality are quantitatively and not qualitatively different on the measures which they usually tend to employ. If we use a ruler for our measuring, we cannot expect the answer to come out in pints.

The most famous classificatory system in psychiatry, that of Kraepelin, was formulated at a time when the layman thought of matter as being made up of discrete particles, of mind as being made up of discrete faculties, and of mental illness as an entity dissociable from the person suffering from it. The classification and description of symptom clusters by the modern method of factor analysis may bear a close resemblance to the Kraepelinian system without entailing acceptance of all Kraepelin's opinions on the nature of symptoms. The view that the factors of the mind may be ordering concepts derived, by a necessary limitation of attention, from operations carried out for the convenience of the investigator, rather than complete explanations or descriptions of what is 'out there' to be observed, can well be applied to the classification of those who are mentally ill.

THE RELIABILITY AND VALIDITY OF PSYCHIATRIC DIAGNOSES

Many psychologists, as well as psychiatrists, have attacked the present systems of psychiatric classification. Roe (1949) suggests that:

'much of this research [the use of various psychological devices for making psychiatric diagnoses] is not only a waste of time, and a perpetuation of errors, but is actually preventing advance in the field.

There are many reasons why this is true, but one of the most potent is that it involves clinging to a classification which has long since been outlived. I submit that using techniques which are not too precisely validated at all, to place patients in psychiatric categories, the inadequacy of which is admitted by all concerned, is a treadmill procedure guaranteed to keep us moving in circles.'

Many psychologists, as well as psychiatrists, would agree with this estimate and yet the curious fact is that there is little or no evidence for this wholesale condemnation, as a review of the few, and mainly inadequately conducted, studies will seek to show.

Roe states that one of the most potent reasons for not using tests for diagnostic purposes is that psychiatric classification has long since been outlived. Yet ten years later the *American Handbook of Psychiatry* (Arieti, 1959) and the *Handbook of Abnormal Psychology* (Eysenck, 1960), protestations to the contrary notwithstanding, lean heavily on just such classification.

It is true, as Roe says, that the inadequacy of psychiatric classification is admitted by all concerned; but inadequacy is no reason for abandonment, unless something more adequate can be substituted. This, critics have notably failed to supply. There is still the possibility of making the inadequate more adequate. An adequate reason for abandoning existing categories would be their demonstrable unsuitability. If our supply of burgundy were inadequate, we would endeavour to make it more adequate by ordering more and better vintages; if our supply were unsuitable – for example, all the bottles were corked – we would abandon it and try to obtain something more suitable.

The position would appear to be that the inadequacy of psychiatric classification is indeed recognized by all concerned, but that its unsuitability is not so recognized. Many citations could be made to justify this view; but two will perhaps suffice. Zubin (1953) writes:

'While the reaction-pattern type of model to explain the etiology of neurosis is an attractive one, it does not lend itself as readily to experimental manipulation as the disease-entity model with the potential physiological, biochemical and genetic factors that enter into the postulation of disease models. If one regards the problem, not as a search for basic etiology, but as a search for serviceable models leading to further knowledge about etiology . . . the disease model is to be preferred.'

71

A Quantitative Classification

Wittenborn's (1951) argument comes closer to the present one, namely that:

'If a well-formulated logically coherent theory for the psychoses were available, the intervening variables of this theory could provide the basis for economical description. Since no such theory is available, any phenomenal clustering tendency provides a plausible conceptualization and allows us to use some of the advantages of theory, i.e. measurement based on intervening variables. . . . The manifestation of symptom clusters, regardless of the exact conditions responsible for their appearance, takes us a step nearer to our goal.'

Is the psychodiagnostic procedure guaranteed to keep us moving in circles? It may do so; but it is not guaranteed to do so. If it should turn out that the test categories agree in the main with reasonably reliable psychiatric categories, then the way is opened up for the description and measurement by means of these tests of hitherto undiscovered attributes of these categories and of their interrelationships. This is a not unimportant task for the psychologist. Wittenborn has, indeed, shown, in a number of factorial studies using a specially designed rating scale, that the factors he has been able to extract are rather congruent with the well-known psychiatric categories (Wittenborn, 1951) and that this holds even when psychiatrists from different institutions participate (Wittenborn et al., 1952). A study of these factors may well help to isolate underlying processes which can be brought under experimental control. There seems no reason then for agreeing with Noyes that psychiatrists, and psychologists, should be more interested at this stage in processes than in labels.

Psychiatric diagnoses have been used as the criterion for classifying groups of subjects in innumerable psychiatric and psychological researches, and yet the reliability of these diagnoses has received surprisingly little attention. The following studies, which will be treated in chronological order, have dealt with this subject:

Doering & Raymond (1934) carried out a comprehensive investigation, using case records. This meant that semantic difficulties had not been cleared up and that no attempt had been made to secure the use of mutually exclusive categories. Apart from these limitations, as Kreitman (1961) remarks, 'the results of this study are too loosely organized to permit any firm conclusions'.

Masserman & Carmichael (1938) found that about 40 per cent of cases

seen at follow-up one year after discharge required reclassifying, though not always to a major extent. Kreitman believed that this finding had more relevance to the problem of the validity of diagnosis than to its reliability; but he might equally well have repeated his comment that the study was too loosely organized, at least in relation to this particular aspect, to permit any firm conclusions.

Ash (1949) reports agreement of 58 to 67 per cent on major diagnostic categories between pairs of psychiatrists, and of $31\frac{1}{2}$ per cent on specific categories. This is regarded as discouraging. There are, however, a number of unusual features in this study which make the results a dubious guide for most psychiatric practice. Only 35 of the 139 cases were said to have indicated a clear-cut psychopathology, interviewing was carried out jointly, and categories were used which were not mutually exclusive. Within the specific category of psychopathy are found, for example, schizoid, constitutional inferiority, drug addiction, epileptoid, etc. Clearly there is no reason why a schizoid psychopath should not exhibit constitutional inferiority and be a drug addict and epileptoid. When account is taken of these facts, it is not surprising that the figures are low.

Mehlman (1952) found that the incidence of different diagnostic categories differed substantially among a number of psychiatrists; but Kreitman calculated from the rather scant details that the discrepancies were of the order of 20 per cent, and adds that the APA classification used in the study had changed during the course of the study. Once again, therefore, we have no firm evidence for or against the reliability of diagnosis.

Hunt, Wittson & Hunt (1953) report on a series of service personnel. They estimated the agreement between psychiatrists at the pre-commission station and at the hospital to which the cases were subsequently sent. The diagnoses were virtually uncontaminated. Agreement on unsuitability for further service was about 94 per cent. The average agreement on the major categories – psychosis, psychoneurosis, and personality disorder – was 54 per cent, and on specific categories 33 per cent. This again is treated as discouraging; but once more categories were used which were not mutually exclusive. Among psychoneurotics are to be found the following: mixed, anxiety, unclassified, hysteria, situational, neurasthenia, psychasthenia, traumatic, hypochondria, inadequate, reactive depression. Logically, this is like asking: 'Is this an elephant? (if so, what sort?) *or* is it from Africa? *or* from not very good stock? *or* a bit of both? *or*, if you don't know, say so.' There are at least three distinct

A Quantitative Classification

principles of division, one denial of these principles, and one expression of inability to apply these principles.

The authors went on to examine the changes in diagnosis between the two centres and these were found to be rather consistent. As they put it: 'The changes were nearly all neighbourly changes which did not involve much clinical displacement and raise the question as to whether the "practical" reliability of the diagnosis (in terms of the care, treatment and disposition of the cases) is not larger than "pure" statistics would indicate.' This raises another question, which does not appear to have been dealt with at all, whether the use in all of these studies of a simple dichotomy of agreement-disagreement is inadequate, if not unsuitable. If one psychiatrist made a diagnosis of paranoid schizophrenia, another of paraphrenia, and a third of hysteria, there would almost certainly be general agreement that the views of the first two psychiatrists were much closer together than that of either with the third. A scale which takes account of partial agreements was constructed and used in a study which dealt only incidentally with the reliability of psychiatric diagnosis (Foulds, 1955).

Schmidt & Fonda (1956) assessed the agreement between trainees and their teachers, with an interval of three weeks between diagnoses, on a modified APA classification. Agreements on the general category for the 426 patients were as follows: organic disorders, 92 per cent; psychoses, 80 per cent; and neurotic and personality disorders, 71 per cent. Agreements on specific diagnoses within the general categories were: organic disorders, 74 per cent; psychoses, 47 per cent; and neurotic and personality disorders, 24 per cent. In view of the fact that one of the pair in each case was a trainee these figures are likely to be lower than if both psychiatrists had been experienced.

Pasamanick, Dinitz & Lefton (1959) looked at incidence figures in three wards of the same hospital for female patients who had been allocated at random. The greatest discrepancies occurred in the psycho-neurotic and personality disorder groups; but overall the differences were not statistically significant (Kreitman, 1961).

Norris (1959) compared diagnoses made at an observation unit with the diagnoses subsequently made at the mental hospitals to which the patients were later admitted, the time interval usually being between two and four weeks. Agreements on general category were: functional psychoses, 89 per cent; neuroses, 46 per cent; character disorder, 44 per cent. Agreements on specific diagnoses within the general category were:

74

functional psychoses, 66 per cent; organic psychoses, 53 per cent; neuroses and character disorders, not given.

Kreitman (1961), using experienced clinicians only, found the following agreements. For general categories: organic disorders, 85 per cent; functional psychoses, 71 per cent; neuroses, 52 per cent. For specific diagnoses: organic disorders, 75 per cent; functional psychoses, 61 per cent; neuroses, 28 per cent.

It is clear that the more recent studies are much less unsatisfactory than the earlier ones and that they indicate that psychiatric diagnoses are less unreliable than had previously been thought. The results of these more adequate studies are consistent in showing that psychiatrists can achieve a useful degree of agreement in diagnosing patients as organic disorders or as functional psychoses. Their level of agreement as to what type of organic disorder the patient is suffering from is also reasonably high. Their level of agreement in allocating patients to the general category of neurosis or to the particular sub-class of functional psychosis is indifferent. The outstanding difficulty is in determining the sub-class of neurosis: here the extent of agreement is so low as to be unusable.

Kreitman *et al.* (1961) have performed a useful function in examining the reliability of the various sources of information which are utilized in arriving at a diagnosis. Their results supply little comfort to those who, despairing at the inadequacy of diagnostic categories, fall back, without question, on description by symptoms rather than by syndromes.

Kreitman (1961) has pointed out that 'the problem of diagnosis is ultimately one of "validity", which implies the use of some other criterion, such as the natural history or pathology of an illness against which the procedures of clinical diagnosis can be checked. Hence the contribution which studies of reliability can make is necessarily limited.'

It is not proposed to review the vast literature on studies which might be conceded to throw some light on the question of the validity of psychiatric diagnosis, since there would probably be very general agreement that they are inadequate. This is, in part, due to the fact that the individuals working in the psychiatric field have not until relatively recently had the technical knowledge necessary for carrying out such studies and, in part, because of the inherent difficulties in this field of work. It might nevertheless be of some value to try to illustrate the types of validity outlined by Cronbach (1949) as they relate to psychiatric diagnosis.

A Quantitative Classification

Concurrent Validity

As Cronbach indicates, the principal use of this procedure is to substitute a more convenient X for a less convenient Y. When X is the clinical diagnosis, it is hard to conceive of any Y being less convenient. For example, does X (clinical diagnosis of, say, retarded psychotic depression) permit an estimate of a certain present performance Y (say, speed of tapping)? Clearly it is much easier to get the subject to tap than it is to diagnose him. As this type of statement can almost certainly be generalized, the question of the concurrent validity of psychiatric diagnosis scarcely arises.

Content Validity

Is the content of the clinical interview and whatever else is used to arrive at a diagnosis representative of what is thought to be relevant to such a procedure? Since clinical interviews are customarily unstandardized and only very partially recorded, one cannot be very optimistic about the content validity of everyday procedures. On this score, questionnaires and rating scales have perhaps much more to offer than some practising clinicians seem ready to admit.

The items of information should all relate to symptoms and signs of illness, and should not include, we would argue, personality characteristics which have been virtually life-long and relatively ego-syntonic. There are certain other facts which ought not to be taken into account in arriving at diagnosis, such as age. Given that a patient seems to present with some sort of organic picture and that he is 63 years of age, in the absence of unequivocal neurological or psychological evidence, the clinician may be wise to guess arteriosclerotic dementia rather than senile dementia. The neuropathologist may confirm this guess some years later; but the clinician has still made only a good guess, not a clinical diagnosis. In the case of a functional condition, such precise possibilities for predictive validity may well be absent and the guess will have falsified the age of onset distribution for the category of the clinician's choice. Body type is another such example.

Predictive Validity

Does X (clinical diagnosis) predict a certain important future event (say, outcome of illness)? Here the literature is too vast for review for our present purpose. There does, however, seem a wide measure of agreement that almost regardless of the particular treatment employed certain

76

diagnostic groups have a better prognosis than others. It would be difficult to believe that any experienced psychiatrist or psychologist would
put up a case for hebephrenic schizophrenia, hysteria, or simple schizophrenia against psychotic depression or anxiety state. Although much of
the evidence is vulnerable to criticism in many ways, it does suggest that
there is far too much concordance for it to be dismissed as valueless.

Construct Validity
How can the syndromes be explained? Why do some symptoms tend to
occur together more frequently than certain others? Let us take the
example of non-paranoid schizophrenia. We might predict that a certain
degree of withdrawal over a certain period of time was sufficient to
account for thought disorder, flattening of affect, the holding of bizarre,
unshared, beliefs, and so forth. An investigator might examine the
histories of all cases diagnosed by clinicians as non-paranoid schizophrenia and find that, in fact, all of them had the specified degree of
withdrawal. He might then argue that, if he could produce this degree of
withdrawal in seemingly normal people, he could turn them into schizophrenics. Assuming that he were allowed to carry out an inhumanely
prolonged sensory deprivation experiment, and that he in fact succeeded
in producing schizophrenia in the majority, he would have added to the
construct validity of his withdrawal psychosis. Apart from all the more
blatant improbabilities in our example, the experiment might break
down because *we* were withdrawing the normal subject; whereas
schizophrenics withdraw themselves.

The commonest area in which construct validity has been sought is
that of anxiety. Giving people electric shocks and telling them how badly
they have done in some psychological experiment bears little relationship
to anxiety neurosis. Rosenwald (1961) has shown his awareness of this
fact and has carried out an experiment which gives greater promise for
studies of construct validity. In the meantime, one must conclude that
the evidence is slight either for or against psychiatric diagnostic categories as they are generally identified at present.

SUMMARY

It has been argued that the decreasing attention paid to classification in
psychiatry is, in part, a result of the persistence of the 'What is *X*?' view
of classification. The inadequacy of this view has been recognized; but

77

A Quantitative Classification

the unwarrantable generalization has often been made that classification is intrinsically not only inadequate, but unsuitable, in psychiatry.

The view has been expressed that classification for research purposes and for clinical purposes may entail different procedures, but that the latter must be dependent on the former. Today's clinical assumptions are, or should be, yesterday's research. The procedures required for diagnostic and aetiological purposes will also differ, the former depending on inter-individual and the latter on intra-individual comparison.

An attempt has been made to point out the illogical nature of some methods of classification and a preference has been expressed for syndromal classification of the Kraepelinian type together with a personality classification. We should not throw out the Kraepelinian baby with the disease entity bath water, but rather we should supply him with the fresh water of current thinking about the nature of classification and of methodology. The infant is a more logical specimen than many of his successors and may still deserve well of us.

The earlier and more pessimistic studies of the reliability of psychiatric diagnosis appear to have been superseded by better-designed studies which suggest that inter-psychotic : neurotic and intra-psychotic reliabilities are satisfactorily high; whereas intra-neurotic reliabilities are low.

Some types of validity have been discussed briefly, and attention has been drawn to the difficulties in relation to psychiatric diagnosis.

Finally, a case is argued for classifying mental patients in terms of both the symptom-signs of an illness and the type of underlying personality. It is only after one has distinguished the relata as clearly and as systematically as possible that one can begin adequately to investigate all facets of their relationship and the implications that arise therefrom. The burden of this book will be to present some tentative evidence in support of this distinction.

REFERENCES

ABERCROMBIE, M. L. J. (1960). *The anatomy of judgment.* London: Hutchinson.

ALBINO, R. C. (1953). Some criticisms of the application of factor analysis to the study of personality. *Brit. J. Psychol.,* 49, 164.

ARIETI, S. (Ed.) (1959). *American handbook of psychiatry.* New York: Basic Books.

ASH, P. (1949). The reliability of psychiatric diagnosis. *J. abnorm. soc. Psychol.,* 44, 272.

BLEULER, E. (1950). *Dementia praecox.* London: Allen & Unwin.

CRONBACH, L. J. (1949). *Essentials of psychological testing.* (2nd edn., 1960.) New York: Harper.

DALBIEZ, R. (1941). *Psychoanalytic method and the doctrine of Freud,* Vol. 2. London: Longmans, Green.

DOERING, C. R. & RAYMOND, A. (1934). Reliability of observation in psychiatric and related characteristics. *Amer. J. Orthopsychiat.,* **4,** 249.

EYSENCK, H. J. (1947). *Dimensions of personality.* London: Routledge & Kegan Paul.

EYSENCK, H. J. (1960). Classification and the problem of diagnosis. In H. J. Eysenck (Ed.), *Handbook of abnormal psychology.* London: Pitman Medical Publishing Co.

FOULDS, G. A. (1955). The reliability of psychiatric and the validity of psychological diagnosis. *J. ment. Sci.,* **101,** 851.

HAMPSHIRE, S. (1959). *Thought and action.* London: Chatto & Windus.

HENDERSON, D. K. & GILLESPIE, R. D. (1950). *Textbook of psychiatry.* (7th edn.) London: Oxford University Press.

HUNT, W. A., WITTSON, C. & HUNT, E.B. (1953). A theoretical and practical analysis of the diagnostic process. In P. H. Hoch & J. Zubin (Eds.), *Current problems in psychiatric diagnosis.* New York: Proc. A.M.A.

KREITMAN, N. (1961). The reliability of psychiatric diagnosis. *J. ment. Sci.,* **107,** 876.

KREITMAN, N., SAINSBURY, P., MORRISEY, J., TOWERS, J. & SCRIVENER, J. (1961). The reliability of psychiatric assessment: an analysis. *J. ment. Sci.,* **107,** 887.

MASSERMAN, J. H. & CARMICHAEL, H. (1938). Diagnosis and prognosis in psychiatry. *J. ment. Sci.,* **84,** 59.

MEHLMAN, B. (1952). The reliability of psychiatric diagnoses. *J. abnorm. soc. Psychol.,* **47,** 577.

NORRIS, V. (1959). *Mental illness in London.* Maudsley Monogr. No. 6. London: Chapman & Hall.

NOYES, A. P. (1953). *Modern clinical psychiatry.* Philadelphia & London: Saunders.

PASAMANICK, B., DINITZ, S. & LEFTON, M. (1959). Psychiatric orientation in relation to diagnosis and treatment. *Amer. J. Psychiat.,* **116,** 127.

ROE, A. (1949). Clinical practice and personality theory: a symposium. IV, Integration of personality theory and clinical practice. *J. abnorm. soc. Psychol.,* **44,** 36.

ROSENWALD, G. C. (1961). The assessment of anxiety in psychological experimentation: a theoretical reformulation and test. *J. abnorm. soc. Psychol.,* **62,** 666.

SCHMIDT, H. O. & FONDA, C. P. (1956). The reliability of psychiatric diagnosis: a new look. *J. abnorm. soc. Psychol.,* **52,** 262.

SKOTTOWE, I. (1953). *Clinical psychiatry*. London: Eyre & Spottiswoode.
STEBBING, S. (1930). *Modern introduction to logic*. (7th edn., 1950.) London: Methuen.
TOULMIN, S. (1960). *Reason in ethics*. London: Cambridge University Press.
WITTENBORN, J. R. (1951). Symptom patterns in a group of mental hospital patients. *J. consult. Psychol.*, **15**, 290.
WITTENBORN, J. R., HERZ, M. L., KURTZ, K. H., MANDELL, W. & TATZ, S. (1952). The effect of rater differences on symptom rating scale clusters, *J. consult. Psychol.*, **16**, 107.
ZUBIN, J. (1953). In P. H. Hoch & J. Zubin (Eds.), *Current problems in psychiatric diagnosis*. New York: Proc. A.M.A.

CHAPTER FIVE

The Universe of Discourse of Ill Health and of Personality

INTRODUCTION

The remainder of Part II is taken up with an attempt to work out a more economical and logical classification of psychiatric illnesses than existing ones, and to present empirical data which accord reasonably well with the proposed system.

The attempt may fail to convince because errors of observation or of inference have been made about what are necessary and sufficient conditions for making a particular diagnosis, or because the difficulty of determining whether any particular case exemplifies the necessary and sufficient conditions is too great for it to have practical value.

It will undoubtedly be objected that the classification to be outlined is too systematic and forced. This view seems to result from confusing the necessary logical distinctness of classes and the unruliness of people. It is no denigration of human nature to say that everyone must fall either at or above the median on some scale, or else below. It is not being argued that X is a schizophrenic, a whole schizophrenic, and nothing but a schizophrenic. What is being argued is that X is a schizophrenic, a bank manager, a motorist, a husband, a father, a Chelsea supporter, a Free Mason, a Conservative, and so on. Objection may legitimately be taken to allocating X to any one of these classes, but not to allocating X.

Strictly speaking, it is not permissible to argue, as some people may be tempted to do, that there are some psychotics, for example, who do not show evidence of any delusional content in their thinking, but who do show symptoms x, y, and z. It can only be said that there are some people who do not show evidence of delusions, but who show x, y, and z, whom 'I' call psychotic. Within the framework of the classification to be outlined the obligatory answer is, 'Then argue the case for x, y, and z being necessary and sufficient conditions for something which you wish to call psychosis'. In other words, the system of classification is funda-

mentally matter of opinion and not matter of fact. It cannot, therefore, be true or false, but only useful or useless.

In summary, four principles guided the search for a system of classification:

1. There should be no shift from phenomenological to aetiological modes of classification. The use of the terms endogenous and exogenous in connection with depression, but not with any other category, is a case in point.

2. The King Lear principle that 'Where the greater malady is fixed, the lesser is scarce felt', which implies that the greater includes the lesser, but the lesser does not include the greater, can usefully be applied to personal illness.

3. It should be borne in mind that classes and groups must be logically distinct; but that nevertheless a patient may fall into more than one class on the same level of classification – either because he 'really' does or because existing techniques for discrimination are inadequate to permit of a sufficiently well-informed assessment of priority.

4. When a patient is spoken of as falling into class *X*, but with features of *Y*, particular care must be taken not to introduce personality attributes under the guise of 'features' and not to confuse symptoms with syndromes.

THE UNIVERSE OF DISCOURSE OF ILL HEALTH

Figure 1 represents Level 1 in the classification scheme. Here the universe of discourse is ill health. Those falling into P$\bar{\text{O}}$ are functionally ill, but not organically ill. The letter P is being used because it is proposed to substitute the term personal illness for mental illness throughout, in order to indicate severe disturbance in the form of the personal rather than merely in the form of the organic (Macmurray, 1957, 1961). The criteria for personal illness will be dealt with more fully below. Classifying some individuals as P$\bar{\text{O}}$ does not mean that there may not be physical consequences or concomitants of a personal illness; it does imply that any such consequences or concomitants would not in themselves warrant medical or surgical interference.

FIGURE I   *Universe of discourse of ill health*

U = Ill health

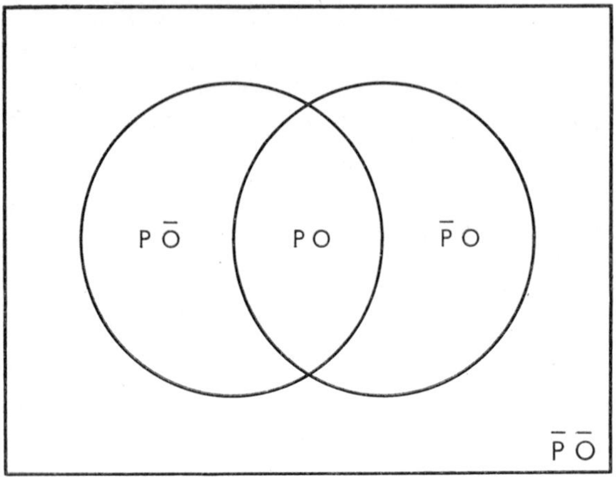

U = Universe of discourse
P = Personal illness
O = Organic illness

Those who fall into $\bar{P}O$ are organically ill, but not personally ill. Here would be found those conditions such as osteomyelitis, appendicitis, or leukaemia, which have not as yet been seriously invaded by the psycho-somatists.

Those who fall into PO may be further split into psychosomatic and somato-psychological. In the former, if one follows an aetiological form of classification, would fall, for example, ulcer, and some skin and some asthmatic conditions. In these cases it is thought that some psychological dysfunction has contributed to the production of an organic lesion – and an organic lesion which, whatever its antecedents, would justify medical or surgical interference.

In the somato-psychological group might fall GPIs, arteriosclerotics, senile dementias, epileptics, and people with neoplasms. Here some organic pathology has been followed by psychological changes. In these cases there is a primary deficiency in the organism in the sense that the organic conditions necessary for living as a person may be absent. The vascular abnormality, the spirochete, or the senile plaque may be a

sufficient condition for making the respective diagnoses. They are not, however, a sufficient explanation of the individual's inability to live as a person. They are not a sufficient explanation because some people, as Rothschild (1945) has shown, manage their affairs remarkably well with severe cerebral pathology; whereas others with relatively mild cerebral pathology do not. Rothschild cites the example of Louis Pasteur, who produced scientific papers of high calibre until shortly before his death, despite the fact that he was found on post-mortem examination to have virtually only one cerebral hemisphere left. That such instances are very much the exception rather than the rule has, however, been convincingly demonstrated by Corsellis (1962).

Eysenck (1960) has pointed out that, in terms of an aetiological classification, the division between functional and organic should logically fall between what have here been called the psychosomatic and the somato-psychological groups; but, historically, it is the somato-psychological rather than the psychosomatic who have been most often treated by psychiatrists.

When personal is substituted for functional the division does not appear as a historical accident, since it is the somato-psychological cases who are manifestly disturbed in their personal relationships. Strictly to follow this usage, it is the ulcers, asthmas, etc. which should be described as somato-psychological; and the dementia paralyticas, the senile dementias, etc. which should be described as psychosomatic. In other words, the traditional classification is an aetiological one; its reversal would be a phenomenological one and, since the greater part of the remainder of psychiatric classification is phenomenological rather than aetiological, it might be preferable to accept this modification. Doubtless, in practice, the suggestion comes too late and, since it is intended only to pursue the question of the classification of the most purely personal illness cases, this apparent oddity need be of no further concern here.

THE UNIVERSE OF DISCOURSE OF PERSONALITY

The suggested continuum from normality through personality disorder, personal illness, psychosis, to non-integrated psychosis is illustrated in *Figure 2*. The continuum is in terms of increasing degrees of failure to maintain or to establish mutual personal relationships.

FIGURE 2 *Universe of discourse of personality*

U = Personality

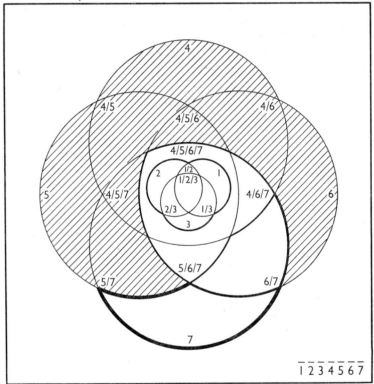

Shaded classes and 4/7 and 5/6
(not shown here) should have no class membership

The numbers 1 to 7 in the figure refer to the following symptoms or signs:

1 *Loss of awareness of the self as agent*: e.g. delusions of passivity.
2 *Thought-process disorder*: e.g. blocking, knight's move, neologisms, etc.
3 *Affective disorder (difference in kind)*: e.g. incongruity (including flattening).

G   85

4 *Perceptual disorder*: e.g. hallucinations, gross misperceptions and imperceptions.

5 *Thought-content disorder*: e.g. delusions implying a self-schema, such as grandiose, persecutory, and guilt.

6 *Affective disorder (difference in degree)*: e.g. disproportionateness.

7 *Egocentricity*: e.g. lack of empathy, treating others as objects.

These symptoms and signs are seen as barriers to the individual's achieving personhood. The likelihood of the individual's achieving or maintaining personhood decreases as one moves from 7 to 1.

Numbers 1, 2, and 3 are shown as overlapping and within 4/5/6/7. This is to indicate that, when a patient has 1 or 2 or 3, or any combination thereof, he will probably be diagnosed as schizophrenic and, for present purposes, should be classified as non-integrated psychotic. In terms of the present argument, then, he will be expected also to have 4, 5, 6, and 7. The small circles are therefore placed within the area of overlap of the four large circles. A diagnosis of non-integrated psychotic would not be made in the absence of 1 and 2 and 3.

Integrated psychotics are shown as lying within 4/5/6/7 and 4/6/7 and 5/6/7, but outside 1, 2, and 3. This indicates that, when a patient has 4 or 5 or both, he will also have 6 and 7, and will probably be diagnosed as manic, melancholic, or paranoiac.

Neurotics are shown as lying within 6/7, but outside 1 to 5. When a patient has 6, he will also have 7, and will tend to be diagnosed as a neurotic.

Psychopaths are shown as lying within 7, but outside 1 to 6.

The situation is, therefore, that:

Non-integrated psychotics have 1 and/or 2 and/or 3, and 4, 5, 6, and 7
Integrated psychotics have 4 and/or 5, and 6 and 7
Neurotics have 6 and 7
Psychopaths have 7 only.

Thus it follows that all non-integrated psychotics are psychotics, are personally ill, and are personality disorders. All psychotics are personally ill and are personality disorders. All the personally ill are personality disorders. All personality disorders are within the universe of discourse of personality. The remainder of the universe is made up of not-1, not-2, not-3, not-4, not-5, not-6, not-7.

Do patients pass from one stage to another? If they do not, it may be because their defences are adequate at one particular stage to prevent such progression in the majority of cases. With regard to those individuals who first appear to break down with a psychotic illness, it must be considered that there are very many people in the community who share some of the symptoms characteristic of those who break down with a neurotic illness who do not themselves break down. It is very hard to be sure that a patient who presents as a schizophrenic or as a melancholic was not one of those individuals. Adequate longitudinal studies are clearly lacking. A number of schizophrenics seem to present initially with neurotic symptoms, and the existence of the schizo-affective category – however illogical – suggests that they sometimes present with melancholic symptoms, since they usually turn out to be schizophrenics.

When patients remit, do they retrace their stages? It is perhaps not difficult to believe that non-integrated and integrated psychotics pass through a neurotic stage. Some evidence will be presented to show that, at least as assessed by the Symptom-Sign Inventory, melancholics pass back to a neurotic stage after treatment. The more difficult question is perhaps whether non-integrated psychotics pass back through an integrated psychotic stage. If they do not, it may be because of the age-linkage in psychosis. Different types of psychotic breakdown are associated with characteristically different types of stressful situations at different ages, encountered by people at different stages of individuation.

Much of this is matter for speculation; but it could be amenable to experimental investigation. In the meantime the continuum can be taken out of the time dimension. It can be asked: Do non-integrated psychotics have those symptoms which are common to all groups of psychotics and to all groups of the personally ill and to all groups of personality disorders? Do psychotics have those symptoms which are common to all groups of the personally ill and of personality disorders? Do the personally ill have those symptoms which are common to all groups of personality disorders? The tentative answer, excluding personality disorders, would appear to be 'yes'. If this is so, one can speak of a continuum or at least of a step-function. If one thinks, for example, that there are beliefs which are delusional, beliefs which are abnormally eccentric but not delusional, and beliefs which are definitely not delusional or eccentric, one may find a smooth continuum; if, however, one thinks one has a sufficiently stringent and clear-cut criterion for determining whether or not a belief is delusional, one may find a step-function. In

either case there is no classification out there in nature. They are human classifications which are given meaning by the forms of reference to them.

At Level 2, concern is with differentiating all personality disorders (i.e. psychopaths, neurotics, integrated and non-integrated psychotics) from normals.

Egocentricity, with its corollary of lack of empathy and its consequence of treating others merely as objects or as organisms rather than as persons, has generally been of long duration. Egocentricity is therefore in this respect more like a personality characteristic than a symptom. The difference between the egocentricity of the psychopath and that of the normal person seems to be a matter of degree and frequency. Furthermore, the psychopath more often than the personally ill individual is probably capable of intending her[1] own actions. She is, in other words, less frequently unconsciously motivated.

In those cases defined as psychopaths here, emphasis is on continuity rather than discontinuity. They do not produce symptoms because they are not appealing for help, and they are not appealing for help because they usually regard others or circumstances as to blame for their misfortunes. They do not suffer from the gross disorders of affective, perceptual, or thought processes, or of thought content.

Lack of empathy differs from flattening of affect in being a flattening only of the sympathetically induced emotions and not of the whole range of affect. The psychopath can show intense enough depression, anger, and so forth when she is herself concerned in the situation. Though not suffering from symptoms and signs of personal illness, she is frequently running into interpersonal difficulties because of her self-centredness and inability to empathize. In any interpersonal situation empathy presumably delays action. The effect of an action on the other will be weighed with (not against) the effect on oneself. If the other is treated as object, the decision-making process will be considerably simplified. Hence the 'trigger reaction' of the psychopath, who knows what she wants.

It is because these two related characteristics of lack of empathy and egocentricity are common to all who are personally ill that personality disorders have been regarded as containing personal illness, psychosis, and non-integrated psychosis. In other words, these related character-

[1] The feminine form has been generally used since the majority of the subjects investigated have been women.

istics of egocentricity, lack of empathy, and treating others as objects, in the absence of the necessary and sufficient conditions for making a diagnosis of personal illness, are themselves necessary and sufficient conditions for the identification of psychopaths, at least when they are present in such degree that they lead the individuals concerned to conflict with the law or to their being brought for treatment.

To the extent that the psychopath is basically a defensive personality – which means to the extent that she can be revealed to be such – the characteristic egocentricity and lack of empathy become distressing, at least from time to time, and the prognosis becomes correspondingly more hopeful. When such insights occur, egocentricity, lack of empathy, and treating others as objects are revealed as defences against the possibility of being modified – and thus perhaps of being destroyed – by interaction with other people. She has to manipulate other people in order to convince herself that they constitute no danger to her; while, at a deeper level, she wants them to be a danger. The moment she feels herself slipping almost imperceptibly into a mutual personal relationship she shies away and accuses the other person of making demands on her.

It is in this context of the other as an overt danger and as a covert liberator that one may understand her inconsistency in personal relations, exemplified often in an extremely complex sexual life, in which she finds it 'better to travel hopefully than to arrive'. Her promiscuity is compounded of a need to be desired superficially for the power it brings, which, in turn, is a reassurance against her fear of her own unpredictability and consequent lack of anchorage. For such a woman, going to bed with a man is like talking to him amicably enough from opposite sides of a lift door. Just as she invites entry, the doors automatically close. She hopes and dreads that some day some superman will come along who can open even automatic doors. So long as the dread is dominant she denies herself the possibility of an integrating, maturing relationship, and the face behind the mask remains always that of the pouting child, kept eternally smooth by the face-cream of dissociation and amnesia. These dynamisms serve to disrupt the normal consistencies of mood, of attitudes, of sentiments, which go to make up what we usually mean by the term 'personality', and without some degree of which personal relationships become impossible. When the other is conceived as liberator, the destroyer is dissociated and she gets onto the approach gradient; as she moves towards liberation, the destroyer emerges, the liberator is

89

dissociated, and down she goes on the avoidance gradient. Any attempt to enter into a mutual personal relationship is interpreted as a demand, a stone disturbing the calm of narcissistic reflection. If we are persons only in relation to other persons, the very methods by which the psychopath seeks to preserve her personality are those which destroy it.

If fascination is a conflict between attraction and repulsion, then most people seem to be fascinated by the psychopath. The repulsion is not difficult to understand. It *is* annoying if, when one turns the other cheek, one's pocket is picked. The attraction is perhaps little less obvious. The continuum of increasing failure in mutual personal relations is also a 'there but for the grace of God go I' continuum. Anything like complete abandonment of egocentric desires is rarely achieved by anyone, certainly not without persisting and stressful conflict. In an age of uncertainty about who we are and about the grace of God, psychopaths constitute a peculiarly magnetic threat, sufficiently powerful to ensure the box-office success of innumerable films about them. In addition to the appeal of vicarious participation, with their shallow emotional responsiveness they constitute the ultimate nagging challenge to the well-meaning lover, and it is this that gives them their Blue Angel or *Belle Dame sans Merci* destructiveness.

Some, who would here be called psychopaths, at least theoretically without any pejorative connotation, even in the absence of symptoms, seek treatment – or, perhaps more accurately, support. These cases are frequently labelled as reactive depression in psychiatric textbooks, and are generally included under the section on the neuroses. But this category is not one of neurotic illness in the sense in which the term is used here. This is not to deny that a category of neurotic depression can be described, but to claim rather that the criteria used are both inappropriate and unsuitable. In these cases there is often no displacement from the reason that is operative in bringing about their condition; they know full well what is wrong. They are disgruntled rather than depressed. They are bored with looking after too many children in their space-saving, contemporary houses, designed apparently to accommodate a limited number of Simon Stylites; bored with not getting out in the evening because their overtime-conscious husbands come home too tired to enjoy the fruits of their additional labours, because the starkly soulless new town to which they have moved has entailed late separation from the mother. As one woman announced after just such a catalogue, in terms of exasperation changing to embarrassment with the realization

of what she had let slip, 'I would be perfectly all right if only my husband would do what I say'. Such cases could usefully be differentiated from neurotic depressives.

Having set down egocentricity as the necessary and sufficient condition for the classification of personality disorders, the next consideration is the possibility of measuring it. It is obviously extremely difficult to measure directly; but many attempts have been made to assess empathy. These attempts have usually taken the form of asking subjects to predict what another person would say in response to certain questions, and then comparing this prediction with what the other person did in fact say. Though this method is certainly not without interest, it seems rather too cognitive, and for the present purpose a measure of General Punitiveness has been preferred.

The more people are able to empathize with others the more successful they are likely to be in establishing mutual relationships, and the less likely they are, even in times of stress, to resort to blaming themselves or others. As H. H. Anderson (1939) has pointed out repeatedly over the years, without being accorded the attention he deserves, such people seek an integrative solution. This he demonstrated in experiments with children. An integrative solution is more than a mere compromise in which each side gives as little as possible to gain as much as possible, the rather lowly form of behaviour on which British politicians humbly pride themselves. The integrative approach involves true mutuality. Because both parties are undefensively open to experience, the process is a creative one which permits of the emergence of new properties. Attention is centred on the solution. It is not egocentric. To resort to blame without at once going beyond it is to resort to egocentricity. The melancholic protests her utter wickedness; but she makes no move towards reparation.

The importance of the integrative approach emerges too from the therapeutic work of Rogers and his colleagues (Rogers, 1961). They, among others, have accumulated evidence that acceptance of self and acceptance of others are positively correlated, thus confirming the adjuration 'to love thy neighbour as thyself'. The reinterpretation by most churches – 'love thy neighbour, you miserable sinner' – can thus be seen in the light of modern knowledge to be psychologically inept.

So much for the rationale for regarding a measure of General Punitiveness as a possible indirect means of approaching egocentricity. Extrapunitive and Intropunitive scales were derived from the Minnesota

Multiphasic Personality Inventory (Foulds, Caine & Creasy, 1960).[1]
These terms were introduced by Rosenzweig (1934).

The *Extrapunitive scale* was broken down into three sub-scales on the basis of the following arguments. From clinical experience and experimental evidence there are three characteristically extrapunitive groups – psychopaths, paranoids, and hysteroid personalities. These three groups will be expected to express their hostility in different ways. The distinguishing feature of the psychopath, in relation to other groups, will be *acting out* his aggression, readily admitted and often more or less consciously defended. Although aggression may be ascribed to others as well, it will not be denied in himself. On the other hand, acting-out hostility will be denied by the paranoid, who will project it onto others. Thus, the paranoid will feel himself in receipt of *a direct personal attack from others to a degree such that the question of delusional thinking might well be raised.* In contradistinction to these two groups, hysteroid personalities will have neither of these predispositions to a marked degree. *Vis à vis* obsessoid personalities, hysteroids will be generally more *critical of others* in attitude, without feeling personally attacked or impelled to attack others more than verbally.

In selecting items from the MMPI for these three extrapunitive scales of Acting-out Hostility (AH), projected Delusional Hostility (DH), and Criticism of Others (CO), it was found that the AH scale presented the least difficulty. This scale consisted of relatively unambiguous items, such as G 31, 'At times I feel like smashing things', and G 32, 'At times I feel like picking a fist fight with someone'.

In selecting items for the DH scale, to differentiate it from the more critical attitude, an attempt was made to choose those items in which a direct personal receipt of hostility from others was implied, an act of open enmity about which the question of delusional thinking might be raised. Thus, $H4$, 'I believe I am being followed', or $H11$, 'I believe I am being plotted against'.

The CO scale, unfortunately, tended to be somewhat more ambiguous, since many of the MMPI items might include, in addition to criticism of others, an implication of acting out or of projection: for example, C 31, 'I have at times stood in the way of people who were trying to do something, not because it amounted to much but because of the principle of the thing'. This, although not implying violent physical assault, does

---

[1] The Punitive scales are presented in Appendix B (pp. 96-98 below).

suggest some action being taken. Most of the remaining items included in this scale were criticisms of others only, or criticisms of others with some element of projection. Thus, *C* 3, 'Some of my family have habits that bother and annoy me very much', may be criticism of others if the respondent either has not got, or does not deny, these habits in himself. It may, on the other hand, include a projective element if a majority of competent observers consider that he, rather than members of his family, has the tiresome habits. The projective element, in such an instance, though self-deceptive, would not generally be regarded as necessarily psychotic. Neither is a deliberate, active attack implied. To this extent, it should be noted, there is some unavoidable overlap in the sub-scales.

With regard to the *Intropunitive scale*, the sub-scales are simply the delusional and non-delusional self-criticism items. It was argued that melancholics, in contrast to most groups, would be high scorers on the Delusional Guilt scale (DG). This scale consists of items involving *the perpetration of actual harm to others with accompanying guilt or deserved destruction of the self by disease or by other people. The question of delusional thinking might again be raised*, as, for example, in *F* 50, 'Much of the time I feel as if I have done something wrong or evil'. On the other hand, the other known intropunitive group, the obsessoid personalities, would be distinguished from the melancholics by their absence of guilt, but also from the remaining groups by their high scores on the Self-criticism scale (SC). As distinct from the DG scale, which involves the perpetration of harm, or imagined harm, to others, the SC scale consists of items *questioning one's own ability and adequacy in particular functions*, such as *I* 41, 'I shrink from facing a crisis or difficulty'.

In an earlier study (Foulds *et al.*, 1960), all correlations between scales were found to be positive. These results could, therefore, be interpreted as indicating a 'general punitive factor' and provide the justification for using the total extrapunitive plus the total intropunitive score $(E+I)$. The correlations between the three extrapunitive scales are, however, higher on the average than their correlations with the two intropunitive scales, and the correlation between SC and DG (the two intropunitive scales) is higher than all the others. These findings support the view that the extrapunitive scores are measuring something different from the intropunitive scales and provide the justification for utilizing the $(E-I)$ score as a measure of Direction of Punitiveness, reflecting the dominance of one type of response over the other.

A Quantitative Classification

The measure which is of immediate concern is the total score on all five sub-scales. From the argument about the continuum of failure in mutual personal relationships, which would presumably involve an increasing retreat into egocentricity and, therefore, an increasing resort to punitiveness, the expected order of the groups would be: normals, psychopaths, neurotics, integrated psychotics, non-integrated psychotics. In fact, with one exception, this is the order. The one exception is that psychopaths are at the top of the list, as can be seen from *Table 3*. All groups differed from normals at the 0·001 level of significance.

TABLE 3   *Mean General Punitive scores of normals, psychopaths, neurotics, integrated and non-integrated psychotics (women only)*

E+I score	32 Normals	16 Psychopaths	60 Neurotics	36 Integrated psychotics	30 Non-integrated psychotics
Mean	12·31	26·31	17·37	19·91	26·07
s.d.	5·16	6·44	7·23	6·86	7·23

The most obvious, but perhaps not the most likely, explanation for the high position of psychopaths is that they are putting on an act of being more intropunitive than they really are, in addition to their more manifest extrapunitiveness. If this were so, it would not necessarily be at the conscious level, since being deceived by one's own persona is undoubtedly characteristic of the psychopath – certainly of the common hysteroid type.

Unfortunately the psychopaths were tested before the construction of the Symptom-Sign Inventory, so that it is not possible to say, on this basis, whether or not they were more or less symptom-free. They had all been given a primary diagnosis of psychopathy by clinicians. Nevertheless, probably the majority of psychopaths who are hospitalized are suffering from a neurotic illness and should be classified as, for example, depression or hysteria in a psychopathic personality. It may be that it is the psychopathy which accounts for the very high extrapunitive score and the neurosis which accounts for the high intropunitive score. Prison psychopaths may well score high on extrapunitiveness only, which would decrease their General Punitive score.

To this argument one might add the speculation that symptoms (but not signs), which may be viewed as abnormal attitudes, in fact drain off General Punitiveness. Symptoms are often defences against becoming fully aware of one's hostility to others or to oneself. It has been further argued that symptoms, rather than signs, predominate in neurosis and do so decreasingly in integrated psychosis, non-integrated psychosis, and, by definition, in psychopaths. A more or less equivalent General Punitiveness in all disturbed groups minus the symptom-drainage system might well account for the observed findings.

If psychopaths are regarded as outside the class of personal illness, this latter class has still to be differentiated from those who are not personally ill. For diagnostic purposes, concern is with the symptoms, and the subjective and objective signs presented by those who are personally ill which are absent in those who are not personally ill. The next chapter will therefore describe the Symptom-Sign Inventory.

SUMMARY

Certain principles underlying the present classification have been described which might help to increase the reliability of psychiatric diagnosis.

An attempt has been made to distinguish between the personally ill and the organically ill and their admixtures.

It has been claimed that it may be useful to think of a continuum from normality through personality disorder, personal illness, psychosis, to non-integrated psychosis. Necessary and sufficient conditions have been suggested for distinguishing the various classes.

Scores on a measure of General Punitiveness have been shown to distinguish between personality disorders (comprising psychopaths, neurotics, integrated and non-integrated psychotics) on the one hand and normals on the other.

APPENDIX B

The Five Punitive Scales

ACTING-OUT HOSTILITY (AH)

MMPI

D	30	In school I was sometimes sent to the principal for cutting up
E	7	I don't blame anyone for trying to grab everything he can get in this world
F	31	I easily become impatient with people
G	29	I get mad easily and then get over it soon
G	31	At times I feel like smashing things
G	32	At times I feel like picking a fist fight with someone
G	47	At times I have a strong urge to do something harmful or shocking
G	48	Sometimes I feel as if I must injure either myself or someone else
I	1	I can easily make other people afraid of me, and sometimes do for the fun of it
I	2	Sometimes I enjoy hurting persons I love
I	4	I sometimes tease animals
I	26	I am too easily downed in an argument
J	43	I get angry sometimes

> Scoring: Credit one for each statement filed as true, except in the case of I 26 where 'false' scores one.

DELUSIONAL HOSTILITY (DH)

MMPI

G	52	I have no enemies who really wish to harm me
G	53	If people had not had it in for me I would have been much more successful
G	54	Someone has it in for me
G	55	I am sure I get a raw deal from life
H	4	I believe I am being followed
H	10	I commonly wonder what hidden reason another person may have for doing something nice for me
H	11	I believe I am being plotted against
H	15	Someone has been trying to rob me
H	26	I know who is responsible for most of my troubles

> Scoring: Credit one for each statement filed as true, except in the case of G 52 where 'false' scores one.

CRITICISM OF OTHERS (CO)

MMPI

B 55   I have very few quarrels with members of my family

C 3   Some of my family have habits that bother and annoy me very much

C 31   I have at times stood in the way of people who were trying to do something, not because it amounted to much but because of the principle of the thing

D 47   Most people make friends because friends are likely to be useful to them.

D 49   I do not blame a person for taking advantage of someone who lays himself open to it

D 50   Most people are honest chiefly through fear of being caught

D 52   I think most people would lie to get ahead

D 53   I think nearly anyone would tell a lie to keep out of trouble

E 9   When someone does me a wrong I feel I should pay him back if I can, just for the principle of the thing

E 53   It is safer to trust nobody

F 30   I have often found people jealous of my good ideas just because they had not thought of them first

G 50   Some people are so bossy that I feel like doing the opposite of what they request, even though I know they are right

Scoring: Credit one for each statement filed as true, except in the case of B 55 where 'false' scores one.

DELUSIONAL GUILT (DG)

MMPI

F 50   Much of the time I feel as if I have done something wrong or evil

G 3   I believe my sins are unpardonable

G 4   I have not lived the right kind of life

G 9   I believe I am a condemned person

I 17   I wish I could get over worrying about things I have said that may have injured other people's feelings

I 36   At times I think I am no good at all

I 37   I certainly feel useless at times

Scoring: Credit one for each statement filed as true.

97

SELF-CRITICISM (SC)

MMPI

A 23   I seem to be about as capable and smart as most others around me.

C 25   I have often lost out on things because I couldn't make up my mind soon enough

C 29   I usually expect to succeed in things I do

F 33   Often I can't understand why I have been so cross and grouchy

I 13   My hardest battles are with myself

I 25   I have several times given up doing a thing because I thought too little of my ability

I 26   I am too easily downed in an argument

I 31   I have sometimes felt that difficulties were piling up so high that I could not overcome them

I 39   I am certainly lacking in self-confidence

I 40   I am entirely self-confident

I 41   I shrink from facing a crisis or difficulty

Scoring: Credit one for each statement filed as true, except for A 23, C 29, and I 40, in each of which 'false' scores one.

REFERENCES

ANDERSON, H. H. (1939). Domination and integration in the behaviour of kindergarten children and teachers. *Genet. Psychol. Monogr.* Vol. 21, No. 3.

CORSELLIS, J. A. N. (1962). *Mental illness and the ageing brain.* Maudsley Monogr. No. 9. London: Oxford University Press.

EYSENCK, H. J. (1960). Classification and the problem of diagnosis. In H. J. Eysenck (Ed.), *Handbook of abnormal psychology.* London: Pitman Medical Publishing Co.

FOULDS, G. A., CAINE, T. M. & CREASY, M. A. (1960). Aspects of extra- and intro-punitive expression in mental illness. *J. ment. Sci.,* **106,** 599.

MACMURRAY, J. (1957). *The self as agent.* London: Faber.

MACMURRAY, J. (1961). *Persons in relation.* London: Faber.

ROGERS, C. R. (1961). *On becoming a person.* London: Constable.

ROSENZWEIG, S. (1934). Types of reaction to frustration. *J. abnorm. soc. Psychol.,* **29,** 298.

ROTHSCHILD, D. (1945). Senile psychoses and psychoses with cerebral arteriosclerosis. In O. J. Kaplan (Ed.), *Mental disorders in later life.* Stanford: Stanford University Press.

99

CHAPTER SIX

Classification of Personal Illness – Classes

INTRODUCTION

In Chapter 4 it was argued that the unqualified statement that psychiatric diagnosis is unreliable is unsupported by adequate experimental evidence. There has been a tendency to review only those studies which are unfavourable and to do so uncritically. The more recent and better-designed studies of Schmidt & Fonda (1956), Norris (1959), and Kreitman (1961) suggest that earlier pessimism may not be entirely justified. At the present time it seems safest to conclude that there are some states that some psychiatrists can diagnose reasonably reliably under some conditions. Nevertheless, even if psychiatric diagnosis could be shown to be highly reliable under optimal conditions, it could serve only as the criterion by which to develop some more objective, public, and quantitative means of classification, since the optimal conditions cannot readily be met in routine clinical practice. It is desirable that any quantitative scale, such as is about to be described, should be reasonably compatible with existing psychiatric classification. As Eysenck (1960) has said: 'The degree of correspondence observed is of some interest in making possible the translation of experimental findings from one field to the other. . . . Even if there were no correspondence at all with psychiatric diagnostic classifications, this would not in any way invalidate the empirical findings.' The exactness of experimental findings is, however, no guarantee of their significance. It would be foolhardy completely to ignore generations of careful clinical observation, and alarming if experimental findings appeared to be utterly divorced from such observation. In consequence, it was thought to be prudent to base the questions in the Symptom-Sign Inventory (SSI) on psychiatric experience.

In the construction of a standard interview or of an inventory the degree of generality or specificity of questions is of critical importance. One can reasonably anticipate useful answers to the question, 'Do you feel afraid in enclosed spaces?'; but the more specific question, 'Do you feel afraid in tube trains?', would probably be unrewarding because of its relative rarity. 'Do you feel afraid in tube trains between Holborn and Tottenham Court Road, but nowhere else?' would be a complete waste of time. Such a piece of information elicited in a clinical interview might, however, be exceedingly valuable. For diagnostic purposes all one need record would be 'claustrophobia'.

The aim in compiling questions for the SSI has, therefore, been to avoid too great a specificity. An attendant difficulty is that duller subjects may be unable to make the required generalization. This problem can be coped with to some extent by having the interviewer ask for specific instances when he is in doubt about the reply. Although an element of subjective judgement may be introduced by the procedure, oral administration is probably likely to lead to more veridical results with mental patients than the more objective written administration.

The main justification for proposing yet another inventory is the attempt to include symptoms and signs of illness only and to exclude personality traits. The most widely used inventory – the Minnesota Multiphasic Personality Inventory – is, in terms of the present distinction, a hotchpotch of both. The Hysteria scale, for example, consists mainly of what would here be regarded as personality characteristics; whereas the Hypochondriasis scale contains many of the symptoms of hysteria. The Depression scale contains mostly symptoms; whereas the Schizophrenic scale contains very few symptoms.

Possible advantages of the SSI over the clinical interviews:

1. Symptoms and signs have been used and personality traits have not, at least in so far as the distinction offered earlier is acceptable.

2. All questions are put to all subjects. When several psychiatrists were asked if they questioned a patient about early waking if they had already decided he was probably a paranoid state, the answer was always 'no'.

3. Examiner influence is somewhat reduced, and suggestion, though not eliminated, is perhaps held more constant.

4. Quantitative scales are public scales, which eliminates one source of error to a large extent in replication studies and assessments of clinical change. Replication studies might fail to confirm the association between classification by means of the SSI and classification by means of clinical diagnosis, as used in a particular hospital; but SSI scores might still correlate in a similar way with other variables used in the original study. This would suggest some consistency of the measure.

5. The relationship between any symptom or cluster of symptoms and any other variables can be more precisely assessed, particularly since yet other variables can be held constant by statistical means.

6. The significance of the absence of certain symptoms can be assessed more easily than in the clinical interview. As has already been mentioned, absence of a symptom in the records of a patient is apt to be ambiguous, because one does not know whether he did not have the symptom or whether he was never asked the question.

7. No one scale can be maximally effective in distinguishing between classes A and B, C, D, etc.

Possible disadvantages of the SSI as compared with the clinical interview:

1. The SSI is perhaps more easily faked; but this has to be weighed against 3 above.

2. Symptoms are accorded equal weight. Weightings in terms of the differentiating power of various symptoms, based on frequencies, cannot take adequate account of relatively mono-symptomatic cases. These fortunately are rare; but a subject with, say, a functional paralysis and three or four minor symptoms of high frequency in most classes may be easily enough diagnosed clinically as conversion hysteria, but missed by the SSI and classified as normal.

3. Non-paranoid schizophrenics in particular often have so little insight into their condition that reliance might be expected to be more appropriately placed on objective signs in arriving at a diagnosis, although the empirical results in fact exceeded expectation. Nevertheless, a chronic manic insisted that she did not 'feel so cheerful that she wanted to wear lots of gay things, like flowers', etc., while she was actually busily decorating herself with them in classical style.

4. Phasic illnesses may be more difficult to identify without the aid of a history, although, on the Manic scale, patients are asked if they have 'ever felt', etc., as well as do they 'now feel', etc.

5. The number of symptoms does not necessarily indicate the severity of illness, although in practice it has usually been found to serve reasonably well.

6. Because of most of the points mentioned above, the SSI should ideally be supplemented by observer rating scales, such as those of Hamilton (1959, 1960) for anxiety and depression, and by objective test measures where these are available.

THE SYMPTOM-SIGN INVENTORY [1]

Content

The SSI originally consisted of 81 items. These items were derived from the MMPI, from various psychiatric textbooks, and from general clinical experience.

Ten items, thought to be associated with each of the following eight categories, were selected:

Category	
A	Anxiety state (*Ax*)
B	Neurotic depression (*Dp*)
C	Mania (*Ma*)
D	Paranoid states (*Pa*)
E	Obsessional (*Ob*)
F	Non-paranoid schizophrenia (*Sc*)
G	Hysteria (*Hy*)
H	Melancholia (*Me*)

Initially the paranoid states included all cases from paranoia through paraphrenia to paranoid schizophrenia; but later a further division is recommended.

The eighty-first item was assigned without conviction to the Melancholic (or Psychotic Depression) scale because of the widespread acceptance of an association between endogenous depression and diurnal variation. In England psychiatrists are taught that feeling worse in the morning is characteristic of endogenous depressives; in Germany the same type of variation is considered to be characteristic of exogenous depressives. Out of 50 psychotic depressives, 18 complained of this symptom; whereas of 50 neurotic depressives, 20 so complained. In so far as psychotic and endogenous on the one hand and neurotic and exogenous on the other are treated as virtually synonymous, international honours may be said to be about even. It was not possible to confirm that this was a cultural difference. Actually both groups were slightly exceeded by anxiety states, with 28 out of 50. The item was accordingly dropped.

An attempt has been made to collect data relevant to the construction of scales at each of the six levels of classification. There are, however, as yet a number of gaps. Six groups of female subjects – three from the neurotic class (anxiety, depression, and hysteria) and three from the

[1] The Symptom-Sign Inventory is presented in Appendix C (pp. 183-191 below).

psychotic class (schizophrenia, paranoia, and melancholia) – have been tested so far. In this chapter concern is with the major continuum only – from the non-integrated psychotic class through the psychotic to the personal illness class – and therefore with only three scales.

At Level 3, a Personal Illness *v.* Normal scale was constructed by selecting all those items which were given by at least 40 per cent of at least four out of the six tested groups. The frequency in all six groups was required to be significantly (at least at the 5 per cent level) in excess of normals. There were no items on which normals exceeded the abnormal groups. The following 18 items were selected:

Personal Illness v. *Normal (PI* v. *No) scale*

A 1, 2, 3, 5, 6, 8, 9, 10
B 1, 2, 4, 6, 7, 8, 9
F 6
G 5
H 5

At Level 4, a Psychotic *v.* Neurotic scale was constructed by selecting those items which were given significantly more frequently by at least two out of the three neurotic groups than by all three psychotic groups, or the converse. The 14 items were:

Psychotic v. *Neurotic (P* v. *N) scale*
Given more frequently by psychotics:

C 10
D 2, 3, 4, 7, 10
F 5, 7, 10
H 2, 4, 6

Given more frequently by neurotics:

A 7
G 5

The score was obtained by subtracting the sum of the neurotic from the sum of the psychotic items.

At Level 5, a Non-integrated Psychotic *v.* Integrated Psychotic scale was constructed by selecting those items given more frequently by the non-integrated psychotics (non-paranoid schizophrenics) than by either integrated psychotic group (paranoid states and melancholics), and those items given more frequently by at least one of the two integrated psychotic groups, where the other was at least very close in frequency.

An additional complication was introduced here. Since the relevant items for the integrated psychotics were mainly delusional items, and since paranoids, melancholics, and manics differ in having predominantly extra-, intro-, and im-punitive delusions respectively, one of each type of delusion was matched up so that one point was given for the presence of any one of the three matched items.

Non-integrated Psychotic v. *Integrated Psychotic (NIP* v. *IP) scale*
Given more frequently by non-integrated psychotics:
C 7, 8, 9
E 2, 6
F 2, 3, 4, 7, 9, 10
Given more frequently by integrated psychotics:
D1 *or* D5 *or* H 6 *and* G 6

At Level 3, data do not exist for making the differentiation between the personally ill and the personality disorders.

Administration
The inventory was administered orally and the following instructions were provided for the guidance of the interviewers:

1. Suggested opening: 'I want to ask you a number of questions. Now these are standard questions which I am asking nearly everyone, so many of them may not apply to you; but I want to ask all of them to make sure we don't miss anything and so that I can compare one person with another.'

2. In general, items need to be distressing before they are scored. Does it really bother the patient?

3. All responses should be accepted unless the interviewer feels that the item has not been properly understood, in which case he should ask for an example of what the subject means by his response.

4. The subject should be encouraged to answer the questions as they stand and not to reword them to fit his case – e.g. A 7, which reads, 'Have you a pain, or feeling of tension, in the back of your neck?' 'Well I do have a feeling as if there's a weight pressing down on top of my head.' After such a response, the actual question should be repeated.

5. In Category C (Mania), if any item is answered as true a tick is recorded. The interviewer should then ask if it applied during the

past week and, if so, he should record a second tick. It is only the latter that is used for scoring at present. The purpose of the double scoring was to try to discover the manic-depressive in the depressive phase.

6. If a known physical disability is associated with an item, the response is not scored even when positive – e.g. A 3, for heart conditions, asthma; G 5, 6, 9, 10, for epileptics.

7. If the meaning of an item is not clear to, and is questioned by, the subject, repeat the question, emphasizing the important parts. Duller subjects have a tendency to latch on to the first thought to be expressed in a question and to ignore anything that may follow. This again calls for repetition, with some such phrase as 'Yes, but what I said was . . .'

8. Complete inability to answer the question is shown as '?' and not scored, except for Category D (Paranoia) items 3, 4, 7, 10. On these items a question mark is scored as positive. It had been noted in using the MMPI that paranoids often put items relating to persecutory delusions in the 'cannot say' category, and one ought really to know whether or not one is being poisoned.

9. When the subject insists that an item does not make any sense – a very rare occurrence – even after further explanation, it is not scored. Certain items, such as D 9, seem intelligible only to those who have the symptom in question.

Many psychologists have contributed to the collection of the data. On eight occasions a second psychologist sat in and scored the inventory separately. The average number of items on which there was disagreement was about 4 and never exceeded 7 out of the 80. Entirely independent reliability studies have not been carried out.

Subjects

The SSI was given to 263 female patients and 73 normal women. The patients were drawn from three main sources:

    (i) clinical referrals, amounting to approximately 100 cases
    (ii) groups collected in the course of other research projects at Runwell Hospital, amounting to approximately 120 cases
    (iii) groups collected in the course of other research projects at Claybury Hospital, amounting to approximately 40 cases.

The possibility of contamination with the clinical diagnosis can be excluded in sources (ii) and (iii), but not with complete certainty in source (i). Some of the 100 cases were, however, referred for reasons other than diagnostic difficulty, and diagnostic reports from the psychology department were made on the basis of tests other than the SSI. Furthermore, the great majority of the referrals were placed in the first sample and were found not to differ from the second sample. It seems likely, therefore, that any possible contamination can have affected the results very little.

The normal subjects consisted of 23 members of the mental hospital staff and 50 patients convalescing on the wards of a general hospital. The normal sample was, therefore, perhaps somewhat loaded against normality.

Frequency tables were prepared for the first 25 cases in each of the following groups: hysterics, anxiety states, neurotic depressives, melancholics; for 30 paranoid states; and for 20 non-paranoid schizophrenics. Similar tables were prepared for the second sample with the same numbers in each group except the last two, in which no more cases were available at the time. Eight obsessionals and 5 manics were also tested.

The two samples were compared for each group on each item by means of chi-square tests. The average number of between-sample differences significant at the 5 per cent level over all groups was about 4, the highest being 6. It would thus appear that in each class the two samples were drawn from essentially the same type of population as regards the SSI. These samples were therefore combined to give:

50 anxiety states
50 hysterics
50 neurotic depressives
50 melancholics
30 paranoid states
20 non-paranoid schizophrenics

An additional 68 cases have been collected for a further cross-validation (see Chapter 8, Summary).

PERSONAL ILLNESS AND NORMALITY

The purely personally ill are to be distinguished from those who are not purely personally ill by means of the conjunction of three criteria. Within the personal illness class, concern is with people:

(i) who are experiencing difficulty in establishing or in maintaining mutual personal relationships;

(ii) whose difficulty is so distressing to themselves that they seek outside help in order to alleviate the symptoms which have been thrown up to defend them against facing this basic problem; or, alternatively, whose signs of illness are so distressing to their most intimate associates that the latter have sought help on their behalf for the same purpose; and

(iii) whose organic concomitants of the personal illness, if any, are not such as, in the absence of the personal illness, would warrant medical or surgical interference.

The implication of the second criterion is that it is probably unwise to categorize our friends as neurotic or our enemies as paranoid when they are functioning at least as well as we are, merely because we do not like the way they do it. The lonely lighthouse-keeper can hallucinate to his heart's content, provided he does the right thing with the lights at the right time. He can think he is God with impunity; but if he thinks that he is the Lorelei luring sailors to their doom or believes that those who bring his food supplies are trying to poison him, he may become a psychiatric problem. If we do not include this criterion, we get involved in trying to cure 'sick' societies and generally endeavouring to put the world to rights.

It is, of course, true that any competent psychiatrist would be able to recognize the fact that the lighthouse-keeper, or William Blake, had several characteristics in common with those patients whom he has learnt to call paranoid schizophrenics or paraphrenics; but the distinction between the incompetent patient and William Blake seems a not un-important one. It is not, as has recently been claimed, that neuroticism is a good predictor of academic success, but rather that many of those who are academically successful share attributes with those who enter into psychiatric treatment and who are subsequently diagnosed as neurotic. For some reason, which cannot even be sought until the prob-lem is correctly formulated, these particular students and William Blake were able to tolerate and even to utilize those attributes which debilitated others. Such a formulation would have the advantage of focusing attention on the positive as well as on the negative attributes of the individual.[1]

[1] Since this passage was written, Frank Barron (1963) has published extensive studies of creative writers and others. One of his interesting conclusions, for which he has considerable evidence, is that, compared with people in general, creative writers are 'much more troubled psychologically; but they also have far greater resources with which to deal with their troubles'.

Classification of Personal Illness – Classes

The implications of the first criterion – the failure to maintain mutual personal relationships – have been considered at some length in Chapter 1. The necessary and sufficient condition for making the diagnosis of personal illness is taken to be *disproportionateness of affect*. This is inferred when the intensity of emotion displayed seems excessive in response to the apparent stimulus, as when a melancholic protests her irredeemable guilt over some peccadillo of long ago, or, more rarely, when the response seems insufficient in relation to the apparent stimulus, as in *la belle indifférence* of the hysteric. Whereas the schizophrenic flattening of affect is generalized to all responses, *belle indifférence* is confined to the attitude to symptoms and signs of illness and does not extend throughout all the individual's interpersonal contacts.

It is this disproportionateness of affect that leads the clinician to hypothesize some covert precipitant from which the overt precipitant is presumed to be a displacement. Since this way of thinking is one of the great and well-recognized contributions of psycho-analysis to this field (A. Freud, 1937), the point requires no elaboration here.

One result of the operation of these unconscious defence dynamisms is that the neurotic and, since disproportionateness is regarded as always present in psychosis, the psychotic, too, again and again are *driven* to activity and are unable to intend their own actions. Of course the normal person sometimes acts with bias. His stated reasons for his conduct do not always seem acceptable to others as explanations. It is appropriate, therefore, at this point to emphasize that it is not strictly accurate to speak of a *person* being *a* neurotic. Some people pass through phases of maladjustment which are severe enough and distressing enough to force them to seek treatment. Such *phases* are neurotic. The vast majority of people experience phases, or areas, of maladjustment; but they can be coped with more or less successfully. These phases cannot then be construed as neurotic illness. They tend to be associated with particular stress situations or with particularly stressful situations. A lady with a phobia for the pigeons in Trafalgar Square, who consulted Culpin, was advised to walk round another way. Today we are perhaps in danger of being bowed down by, or boastful of, our quirks. There is probably very little of our food that we would eat if we always examined it first under a microscope.

RESULTS

Table 4 shows the distribution of scores on the Personal Illness *v.* Normal scale. Of the 263 personally ill subjects, 30 scored 3 or less.

There are, therefore, 11 per cent false negatives (i.e. subjects diagnosed clinically as personally ill who appear on the SSI not to be so). These are made up of the occasional exceptionally cagey paranoid, the simple schizophrenic, and a few neurotics, who might in the present framework be regarded as psychopaths. There are 16 per cent false positives, that is 12 of the 73 allegedly normal subjects who scored 4 or more.

TABLE 4 *Scores on the Personal Illness v. Normal scale of 263 personally ill and 73 normal women*

Score	Sc	Pa	Me	Ma	Hy	Ax	Dp	Ob	All	Normals
18							2		2	
17										
16			1		1	2	3		7	
15		1	5		2	4	1		13	
14	1		5		2	7	2		17	
13	2		5		3	4	10	1	25	
12	3	2	4		2	3	4		18	
11	2	1	6		8	5	7		29	
10	1	3	4			*4*	4	1	17	
9	*2*	1	3		3	5	3	1	*18*	
8		4	6		4	4	3		21	
7	2	2	5		9	2	2	*1*	23	
6		*3*	1		2	4	1		11	1
5	1	4	2	1	2	1	2	*1*	14	5
4	3	3	1	*2*	5	3	1		18	6
3	1	3	1	1	2	1	3	1	13	10
2		3			2	1	2	1	9	6
1	1		1	1	3			1	7	*16*
0	1								1	29
	20	30	50	5	50	50	50	8	263	73

In this and subsequent tables:
Sc = schizophrenia; *Pa* = paranoid states; *Me* = melancholia; *Ma* = mania; *Hy* = hysteria; *Ax* = anxiety state; *Dp* = neurotic depression; *Ob* = obsessional.
Figures in italics indicate the subjects who fell at the median score in each category.

Classification of Personal Illness – Classes

Table 5 shows the percentages of the personally ill and the normal subjects claiming to have each of the 18 symptoms.

TABLE 5 *Percentages of the personally ill and of normals claiming each symptom on the Personal Illness v. Normal scale*

Item	Normals 73	Personally ill 263
A 1	3	45
A 2	21	48
A 3	10	54
A 5	11	42
A 6	8	40
A 8	21	66
A 9	0	42
A 10	11	44
B 1	26	58
B 2	1	52
B 4	1	66
B 6	11	63
B 7	3	39
B 8	7	61
B 9	11	74
F 6	7	39
G 5	7	53
H 5	3	44

The personally ill are characterized, therefore, by the following symptoms:

A 1 Her hand often shakes when she tries to do something.
A 2 She sweats very easily, even on cool days.
A 3 She suffers from palpitations and breathlessness.
A 5 She is afraid of being in either wide-open spaces or enclosed places.
A 6 She is afraid that she might be going insane.
A 8 She has difficulty in getting off to sleep.
A 9 She is afraid of going out alone.
A 10 She has other particular fears not mentioned above.
B 1 She cries rather easily.
B 2 She has lost interest in almost everything.

111

B 4 The simplest task is too much of an effort.
B 6 She has found it difficult to concentrate recently.
B 7 The future seems pointless.
B 8 She is more absent-minded recently than she used to be.
B 9 She is slower recently than she used to be.
F 6 She often feels puzzled, as if something has gone wrong with the world or with her, without knowing what it is.
G 5 She has had black-outs, dizzy spells, or faints.
H 5 She is troubled by waking in the early hours and being unable to get off to sleep again.

These symptoms and signs seem rather consonant with the necessary and sufficient condition for the diagnosis of personal illness, namely disproportionateness of affect.

It has been argued that all psychotics are personally ill, but that not all the personally ill are psychotic. From this it follows that a Personal Illness *v*. Normal scale will be made up largely of 'neurotic' items rather than 'psychotic' items. In fact, of the 18 items, 16 came from the *a priori* neurotic scales. Had one sought to differentiate only between neurotics and normals, one item only would have been dropped from the Personal Illness scale and one different one introduced. In other words, the Personal Illness scale could equally well be regarded as a Neuroticism scale. There seems to be great difficulty in constructing a Neuroticism scale on which both normals and psychotics will score low. McGuire (1962) noted that psychotic and neurotic patients scored at much the same level on the Maudsley Personality Inventory Neuroticism scale. Trouton & Maxwell (1956) had a similar finding with the Maudsley Medical Questionnaire. These results are precisely what one would expect from the argument that all psychotics are neurotics.

Neurotic symptoms may often be less regarded when in a psychotic setting and they may be modified by the psychosis. The idea is not so unfamiliar as may at first appear – since we speak of pseudoneurotic schizophrenia, of neurotic defences against schizophrenia, such as obsessional defences, and since some psychotic depressives seem remarkably like neurotic depressives after ECT. However this may be, it is perhaps permissible to assume, with Freud, that psychotics have passed beyond the neurotic stage of failure in personal relations and that the statement that all psychotics are neurotics can be maintained without having to demonstrate the presence in all psychotics of neurotic symptoms, even though such a demonstration might well be possible.

It is just such situations as those described that have led some clinicians to feel that diagnosis is of no value; but recognition of the hierarchy and of the dominance of the greater malady over the lesser removes much of the difficulty.

It may be argued that a psychotic and a neurotic may admit to the same symptom, but that this symptom will have a very different meaning in the two cases. The neurotic may fear walking down the street because she feels naked and that people are looking at her; the psychotic may fear walking down the street because she feels, or rather knows, that 'they' are directing rays at her. The phenomenological symptom in either instance is 'fear of walking down the street'. The explanation will differ not only as between neurotic and psychotic, but within neurosis and within psychosis. The psychoticism of the ray-directing will be picked up on the persecutory items of the Paranoid scale of the inventory; but more important is the fact that we are not here concerned with aetiology. It is a matter for further and different research to determine whether there are any useful groupings of aetiological factors among all patients who admit to a fear of walking down the street.

THE UNIVERSE OF DISCOURSE OF PERSONAL ILLNESS

It is much easier for the skilled observer to point to one man and say, 'this man is psychotic', and to point to another and say, 'this man is neurotic', than it is for him to define the two concepts, as the following definitions provided by a psychiatric dictionary (Hinsie & Campbell, 1960) should make clear:

'A psychosis is usually a severer type of mental disorder in the sense that all forms of adaptation (e.g. social, intellectual, professional, religious, etc.) are disrupted. In other words, the disorganization of the personality is extensive.'

'From the psychoanalytic point of view "unconscious wish-impulses" evidently strive to assert themselves even during the day, and the fact of transference, as well as the psychoses, tells us that they endeavour to force their way through the preconscious system to consciousness and the command of "motility". Normally the wish-impulses are checked by the critical censorship, located between the unconscious and the preconscious. When the censorship is enfeebled or when unconscious excitations are pathologically reinforced, the wish-impulses gain domination over the preconscious realm, "thus directing an apparatus not designed for them by virtue of the attraction exerted by perceptions on the distribution of our psychic energy. We call this condition psychosis" (Freud, 1933).'

Neither of these definitions seems to present practicable criteria by which psychosis can readily be distinguished from neurosis. The dictionary seeks to provide such criteria thus:

'The distinctions between neurosis and psychosis are symptomatic, psychopathological and therapeutic. In the neuroses, only a part of the personality is affected (Meyer's part-reaction) [*But the same might surely be said of a Paranoid Psychosis?*] and reality is not changed qualitatively [*Is the small room not qualitatively different as between the normal person and the claustrophobic?*] although its value may be altered quantitatively (i.e. diminished). The neurotic acts as if reality had the same kind of meaning for him as for the rest of the community. [*This is again at odds with the phobic state. What about the pigeons in Trafalgar Square?*] Psychopathologically, the psychotic change in reality is partly expressed as projection, and of a type which does not occur in the neuroses. In the neuroses, language as such is never disturbed, while in the psychoses language is distorted [*But not surely in some paranoid psychoses nor in some psychotic depressives?*] and the unconscious may come to direct verbal expression. In the neuroses, the unconscious never attains more than symbolic expression, and regression to primitive levels (e.g. soiling and wetting) is not found in the presence of clear consciousness. [*Nor is it in all psychoses.*] Symptoms of neurosis include sensory, motor, or visceral disturbances, trance-states, somnambulisms, troublesome thoughts, and the like.' [*Almost all, if not indeed all, of these symptoms are found in cases usually diagnosed as psychotic (although, of course, on the view maintained here, these could be neurotic components in a psychotic illness).*]

Despite the looseness of these definitions, it has been shown in Chapter 4 that skilled observers can agree remarkably well among themselves about the differentiation of psychosis and neurosis. It can still, therefore, be maintained that psychosis represents a greater degree of failure in mutual personal relations than does neurosis, a greater degree of failure to enter into true communication with others. In this sense the greater implies the lesser and, once more, 'where the greater malady is fixed, the lesser is scarce felt'. Thus, while it is meaningful to speak of a melancholic with obsessional features, it is not meaningful

114

Classification of Personal Illness – Classes

to speak of an obsessional with melancholic features. It is meaningful to speak of a schizophrenic with anxiety features; but it is not meaningful to speak of an anxiety state with schizophrenic features. The necessary and sufficient conditions for differentiating the psychotic from the neurotic have now to be sought. The processes of perceiving, feeling, and thinking, on both the effector and the receptor sides, have to be such as to make possible content which is capable of being shared with others. It is claimed that all patients who are personally ill are more self-absorbed than is normal. It is generally considered that those whom we call psychotic are especially so, to the extent that it is frequently difficult, and sometimes seemingly impossible, to break through their preoccupation with their own inner experience. From this it would appear likely that all patients, and psychotics in particular, are deficient in their ability to understand others as compared with when they are well.

Not unnaturally, relatively little is known of the receptor as compared with the effector side. The writer did once try replying to a schizophrenic's apparent nonsense with nonsense. After about a quarter of an hour, during which time words were exchanged, the information content seemed to approximate zero; but the schizophrenic showed no evidence of perplexity. He may, of course, merely have been a very polite schizophrenic who had no higher expectation of a psychologist. On the effector side more is known, and much of what is known has been brilliantly described by clinical psychiatrists.

Loss of awareness of the self as agent, which is discussed in more detail below, is clearly not characteristic of all psychotics. It cannot, therefore, alone be both a necessary and a sufficient condition for the diagnosis of psychosis.

Affective disorders: the expression of a *kind* of emotion which seems altogether inappropriate to the apparent stimulus, though typical in schizophrenia, is not usually found in melancholics and paranoiacs. This alone cannot, therefore, be both a necessary and a sufficient condition for the diagnosis of psychosis.

It has been argued that expression of a *degree* of emotion out of keeping with the apparent stimulus is characteristic of all who are personally ill. This is not to say that this type of affective disorder may not be the outstanding feature of one or more of the psychotic groups; but, because it is not so in all psychotic groups and because it may occur in some neurotics, it cannot be the essential core of psychosis as such. It may, for example, be objected that delusions do not constitute as striking a feature in mania as the extreme mood swings. This merely means that the extreme mood swings may be a necessary and sufficient condition for the diagnosis of mania within the category of psychosis. In cases of depression it is often implied that the affective intensity is itself a sufficient sign of psychosis. There are, however, three difficulties in the way of accepting such a view.

The first difficulty is that such an implicit separation of affective expression from ideation throws one back on a purely physiological emotion, or at least on the James-Lange theory.

The second objection is that the difficulty in accepting purely physiological emotion conceptually is matched by the at least equal difficulty in measuring it.

The third objection is that, in so far as we believe we can assess it subjectively – a belief probably not without some foundation – there seems little reason to regard the intensity of the melancholic's depression as any greater than the intensity of the grief felt by countless normal people on the death of someone they greatly loved. Turgenev only epitomized and in no way exaggerated such feelings when he described, in *Fathers and Sons*, the reaction of a father to his son's death through meningitis. This conventionally devout Christian, down on his knees by the death-bed, raised his fists to heaven and cried out, 'I protest, I protest'. It is beyond credence that, along some continuum of intensity of affect, the emotion of the psychotic significantly exceeds that implied by the deep poignancy of the father's utterance, or of that of the father of the epileptic to Jesus, 'O Lord, I believe. Help thou mine unbelief.' Even in the English upper class, psychosis must surely be measured by some other yardstick. From a different cultural background Freud (1925) thought so:

'The distinguishing mental features of melancholia are a profoundly painful dejection, cessation of interest in the outside world, loss of the capacity to love, inhibition of all activity, and a lowering of the self-regarding feelings to a degree that finds utterance in self-reproaches and self-revilings, and culminates in a delusional expectation of punishment. This picture becomes a little more intelligible when we consider that, with one exception, the same traits are met with in mourning. The disturbance of self-regard is absent in mourning; but otherwise the features are the same . . . although mourning involves grave departures from the normal attitude to life, it never occurs to us to regard it as a pathological condition and to refer it to medical treatment.'

Perceptual disorders may be divided into *hallucinations* and *gross distortions* (including gross imperceptions). Having perceptual experiences in the absence of any ostensible stimuli, that is, hallucinating, is not a necessary condition for the diagnosis of psychosis, since many melancholics are never hallucinated. It cannot, therefore, constitute a necessary and sufficient condition.

Much research needs to be done before adequate criteria can be set up for determining what can best be regarded as gross distortions. In the meantime, some of the obviously gross percepts can be used illustratively. These are often noted on the Thematic Apperception Test. A paranoid patient saw a boy sitting at a table with a violin as a boy in a hole in the ground, who could not get out because of the electrical entanglement; another saw the boy as with a machine-gun rather than a violin; a third subject saw a boy kneeling on the ground by a bench, with a gun by his side, as a boy who had shot the old man in the chair. When questioned, he had seen the gun, in a condensed image presumably, as a man in a chair. The relative sizes of the old man in the chair and of the boy were rather more disproportionate than those of Gulliver and a Lilliputian. A fourth subject saw the gun as a bottle of ink spilt on the ground (though he saw it quite easily as a gun after leucotomy). Distortions of this magnitude almost certainly do not occur among neurotics, but neither do they occur among melancholics.

Disorders of thought content comprise the various delusions. Those delusions which imply a rather complete loss of awareness of the self as agent, such as delusions of passivity, are included under the loss-of-awareness-of-self category. Under delusions of thought content one is concerned with those delusions which imply the existence of a self-schema, such as delusions of influence, of reference, of persecution, of unworthiness, of grandeur, of poverty, and so forth. Such delusions, beliefs which are shared by no other member of the same culture or subculture, and which are peculiarly resistant to contrary evidence, are probably both necessary and sufficient conditions for the diagnosis of psychosis. Perhaps with still greater confidence one could say that the presence of delusions and/or of gross perceptual disorder constitutes the necessary and sufficient condition for psychosis.

When considering the differences between neurotics and psychotics many authors, as indicated in the criticisms of the dictionary definitions, have listed symptoms or signs which occur in psychosis only, but which do not occur in all psychotics. Thus, delusions have traditionally been regarded as of secondary importance to autism, thought process disorder, and flattening of affect – and so they are for schizophrenia, but not for psychosis. The differentiae must be based on conditions which, either singly or collectively, are necessary and sufficient for the class.

The view that some psychotics are not deluded is doubted for the following reasons:

Depressives who are diagnosed as psychotic simply on the basis of such symptoms and signs as insomnia, diurnal variation, and a mood of depression would not be accepted as such. Reasons for rejecting the mood of depression divorced from the thought content as evidence for psychosis have been given, and evidence will be produced to show that the first two signs are almost equally common among neurotics.

Some manics are said not to be deluded. Elation, pressure of talk, and expansive gestures unaccompanied by delusions of grandeur, or at least a delusion of wellbeing patently at odds with the situation in which the patient finds himself, seem *prima facie* improbable. Those who deny the presence of delusions would be hard put to it to evolve a theory of psychosis based merely on the manic triad.

Delusions may not always be elicited from schizophrenics because of the communication difficulty and because, for the purposes of clinical diagnosis, it may not be necessary to do so if more flagrantly psychotic symptoms or signs are unmistakably present.

Table 6 shows, at Level 4, the distribution of scores on the Psychotic *v.* Neurotic scale.

In the first sample (83 neurotics and 75 psychotics) there are 11 per cent false positives (i.e. psychiatrically diagnosed neurotics who score psychotic (2 or over) on the SSI). It can be seen that the bulk of these are cases diagnosed as hysterics; the motivation of hysterics has always been such as to upset the test results of psychologists. There are 17 per cent false negatives (psychotics who scored 0 or below). These are made up in the main of cagey paranoids, aboulic, a-everything simple schizophrenics, and a few melancholics, who may have been diagnosed as endogenous depression on the basis largely of early waking and diurnal variation, and thus had to be included among the psychotics.

Scores of 1 can be seen to be non-discriminating. They represent

TABLE 6   Scores on the Psychotic v. Neurotic scale of 105 psychotics and 158 neurotics

P-N score	Hy I	Hy II	Ax I	Ax II	Dp I	Dp II	Ob I	All	Sc I	Pa I	Me I	Me II	Ma II	All
score	25	25	25	25	25	25	8	158	20	30	25	25	5	105
9														
8													1	1
7									1	3				4
6									3	5	1			9
5		1						1	1	5	1	2		9
4				1		2		3		2	5	5		12
3	3	3		1	1	3		11	5	5	3	2	1	16
2	3	2	1	3	1	1		11	3	4	5	7	1	20
1	1	2	3	1	3	5	2	17	2	2	6	3	2	15
0	11	2	9	8	13	6	3	52	2	4	5	2		13
-1	4	14	7	8	3	3	3	42	3			3		6
-2	3	1	5	3	4	5		21						

I and II = first and second samples.

13 per cent of the sample. It seems preferable to regard these cases as uncertain and to consider them again at the next levels of differentiation. This in effect would mean that any such case would be considered on the Non-integrated Psychotic v. Integrated Psychotic scale and on the Personal Illness v. Normal scale. If the results were then, say, integrated psychotic on the one hand and personally ill on the other, the case would be carried to the next level, where it might be found that the answers were, say, melancholia and hysteria. One would then proceed to the Melancholia v. Hysteria scale for the final differentiation.

In the second sample (75 neurotics and 30 psychotics) there are 23 per cent false positives, 19 per cent false negatives, and again 13 per cent uncertain. Over the total of 158 neurotics and 105 psychotics, the figures are 16 per cent false positives, 18 per cent false negatives, and 13 per cent uncertain.

Thus, in the first sample, 73 per cent of cases are diagnosed in agreement with the psychiatric diagnosis, 13 per cent are uncertain, and 14 per cent are in disagreement. In the second sample, 66 per cent are diagnosed in agreement, 13 per cent are uncertain, and 21 per cent in disagreement. Over all cases this gives 70 per cent in agreement, 13 per cent uncertain, and 17 per cent in disagreement.

A Quantitative Classification

Table 7 shows the percentages of cases claiming each of the symptoms on the Psychotic *v.* Neurotic scale. All of these differences were significant in the first sample. The direction of the difference was always the same in the second sample, and the differences were significant at least at the 10 per cent level. Overall, the differences between the two groups were significant at least at the 5 per cent level.

TABLE 7 *Percentages of psychotics and of neurotics claiming each symptom on the Psychotic v. Neurotic scale*

Item	Psychotics 105	Neurotics 158
C 10	11	3
D 2	9	2
D 3	32	8
D 4	11	2
D 7	24	2
D 10	30	4
F 5	47	23
F 7	25	4
F 10	18	2
H 2	48	25
H 4	32	12
H 6	27	9
A 7	20	41
G 5	31	43

The psychotic is characterized, therefore, by the following symptoms or signs:

C 10 She is a more important person than most people recognize.
D 2 She has an important mission to carry out.
D 3 There are people who are trying to harm her through no fault of her own.
D 4 Someone is trying to poison her or make her ill in some way.
D 7 People are plotting against her through no fault of her own.
D 10 People can read her thoughts and make her do things against her will by a sort of hypnotism.
F 5 Other people regard her as very odd.
F 7 She sometimes hears voices without knowing where they come from.

F 10 There is something unusual about her body – like one side being different from the other and meaning something different.
H 2 She is an unworthy person in her own eyes.
H 4 She is a condemned person because of her sins.
H 6 Because of things she has done wrong, people are talking about her and criticizing her.

The neurotic is characterized by the following:

A 7 She has a pain, or feeling of tension, in the back of her neck.
G 5 She sometimes has black-outs, dizzy spells, or faints.

Only 2 out of 40 supposedly neurotic items were given significantly more often by neurotic than by psychotic patients. This is no more than might be expected by chance, and supports McGuire's results and the view that all psychotics are neurotic, but that not all neurotics are psychotic.

It can be seen that all the psychotic items, except F 5 and F 7, are delusional items. Forty items were originally chosen to differentiate particular psychotic groups from each other and from neurotics. Of these 40 items, 16 (or 40 per cent) were delusional items. Twelve items were given significantly more often by psychotics than by neurotics; of these 12, 10 (or 83 per cent) were delusional items. Thus of the 16 delusional items, 10 (or 62 per cent) turned up in the Psychotic *v.* Neurotic scale; whereas, of the remaining 24 allegedly psychotic items, only 2 (or 8 per cent) turned up in this scale.

When the six most unequivocally delusional items were scored from the Punitive scales, the results shown in *Table 8* were obtained from 40 neurotic and 40 psychotic women.

TABLE 8 *Neurotic and psychotic admissions of delusions on the Punitive scales*

Item		Neurotics 40	Psychotics 40
G	3 I believe my sins are unpardonable	2	13
G	4 I have not lived the right kind of life	4	19
G	9 I believe I am a condemned person	3	18
H	4 I believe I am being followed	1	9
H	11 I believe I am being plotted against	0	12
H	15 Someone has been trying to rob me	0	6

The score distributions for neurotics and psychotics are shown in *Table 9*. Thus 20 per cent of psychotics (the percentages for schizophrenics, paranoiacs, and melancholics all being exactly 20) gave none of these delusions; whereas 15 per cent of neurotics gave one or more.

TABLE 9 *Delusional score of neurotics and psychotics on selected items from the Punitive scales*

No. of delusions	Neurotics 40	Psychotics 40
6	0	0
5	0	0
4	0	4
3	1	10
2	2	13
1	3	5
0	34	8

Lucas, Sainsbury & Collins (1962) found that of 405 schizophrenics examined clinically, 71 per cent expressed delusional ideas, 15 per cent were either mute or so thought-disordered that evidence could not be elicited, leaving only 14 per cent of accessible cases who had never expressed delusions. This figure is very close to that obtained from the six items of the Punitive scales.

The three sources of evidence – the SSI, the Punitive scales, and the Lucas *et al.* investigations – provide considerable support for the opinion that the necessary and sufficient condition for differentiating psychosis from neurosis is the presence of delusional beliefs. These delusions can be defined operationally.

THE UNIVERSE OF DISCOURSE OF PSYCHOSIS

It is now necessary to distinguish between the non-integrated and the integrated psychotics. *Figure 2* shows the circles for the non-integrated psychotics contained within that for the integrated psychotics. This implies that all non-integrated psychotics are psychotic, but that all Psychotics are not non-integrated psychotics.

Witkin *et al.* (1962) state that integration

'refers particularly to the form of the functional relationships among system components and so speaks first of all on the patterning of the total system. When we are dealing with open systems, as in psychology, integration also refers to the form of the relationships between the system and its surroundings. . . . To say that integration is *effective* means that there is a more or less harmonious working together of system components with each other and of the total system with its environment, thereby contributing to the adaptation of the organism. In psychological systems effectiveness of integration is reflected in adequacy of adjustment. To say that integration is *complex* means that the relationships among system components and between the system and its environment are elaborate. . . . While complexity appears to be a function of level of differentiation, effectiveness of integration is not as directly related.'

By differentiation they mean individuation or awareness of personal identity, and maintenance of personality identity is mediated, as Hilgard (1954) stresses, by the continuity of memories and by the awareness of the self as an object of value which organizes many of our attitudes.

The integrated psychotics, who tend to break down in middle life, are much more complex than the non-integrated psychotics because much more differentiated, or individuated, and, as Witkin *et al.* suggest, 'among differentiated persons, impairment is apt to involve too great a separation or faulty connection of sub-systems and/or isolation from the environment. Among relatively undifferentiated persons' – such as non-integrated psychotics, who tend to break down in adolescence or soon after – 'in whom boundaries between sub-systems, as well as between inside and outside, are weak, impairment is perhaps prone to take the form of dissolution of boundaries.' In the case of the non-integrated psychotics, the stress on distortions of the body-image and on feelings of the ineffectiveness of the self (Weckowicz & Sommer, 1960), and on passivity feelings, which Langfeldt (1952) uses prominently among his criteria for distinguishing between process schizophrenia and the schizophreniform reaction, is consistent with the position presented here. These concepts can be subsumed under the phrase 'loss of awareness of the self as agent'. Strictly, loss of awareness might be called disintegration, and failure ever to achieve this awareness might be called unintegration.

It is significant that the majority of non-integrated psychotics – the simple schizophrenics perhaps most characteristically unintegrated, the hebephrenics and catatonics perhaps most characteristically disintegrated – tend to break down in adolescence or shortly after (see p. 252 below). This is widely recognized as a period in which the individual is much concerned with the problem of self-identification, of incorporating new adult roles. The paranoiac, the melancholic, and often the manic, have characteristically functioned reasonably successfully as adults for about as long as the non-integrated psychotics have lived. They know who they are, even if this knowledge is distorted by the operation of self-deceptive dynamisms, so that we do not believe them. The extreme non-integrated psychotic does not know who he is. Loss of awareness of the self as agent, which is exemplified by delusions of passivity, will only occur, but will not always occur, in non-integrated psychotics.

Some non-integrated psychotics, particularly hebephrenics and catatonics, are unusually oblivious of the presence of other people. For a person to remain a person, withdrawal, the reflective aspect of action, to follow McDougall (1908) and Macmurray (1961), is for the sake of action. Past situations are analysed, future situations are rehearsed. The non-integrated psychotic withdraws for the sake of withdrawal, because the outside world is too threatening to his integrity. His thinking becomes autistic. In our Western culture, permeated by *cogito ergo sum*, we suffer, as Macmurray stresses, from the mistaken belief that the individual thinking in isolation, rather than knowledge of the other, is the absolute presupposition of all knowledge. Schizophrenia stands witness to the falsity of this belief, with its 'I think and that's about all. Therefore I am not.' We cannot look into our own eyes without the aid of a mirror. As Macmurray has so well expressed it:

'In the human infant – and this is the heart of the matter – the impulse to communicate is his sole adaptation to the world in which he is born. Implicit and unconscious it may be, yet it is sufficient to constitute the mother-child relation as the basic form of human existence, as a personal mutuality, as "You and I" with a common life. For this reason the infant is born a person and not an animal. All his subsequent experience, all the habits he forms and the skills he acquires fall within this framework, and are fitted to it. Thus human experience is, even in its most individual elements, a common life;

and human behaviour carries always, in its inherent structure, a reference to the personal Other. All this may be summed up by saying that the unit of personal existence is not the individual, but two persons in personal relation; and that we are persons not by individual right, but in virtue of our relation to one another. The personal is constituted by personal relatedness. The unit of the personal is not the "I", but the "You and I".'

The mirror of the non-integrated psychotic is so distorted that frequently he does not even know whether he is male or female or, indeed, whether he really exists at all. His ability to communicate his emotions is so negligible that we speak of his affect being incongruous or flattened. We cannot empathize with him; nor, we believe, can he with us. There is, in that admirably descriptive phrase, a pane of glass between us. This *incongruity, including flattening, of affect* – like the passivity phenomenon – will occur only, but not always, in non-integrated psychosis.

Perhaps because he has so long withdrawn himself from personal relationships, he loses the common coinage of language. He begins very early in his illness to use words slightly incorrectly and, as Bannister (1962) has shown, to form highly idiosyncratic cognitive constructs. This process becomes increasingly bizarre until he produces neologisms and word salads and we cease to be in communication with him. This *disorder of the thought process* should, therefore, only occur, but will not always occur, in non-integrated psychosis.

The most difficult group to fit into this framework is the simple schizophrenic, whose outstanding characteristics are perhaps flattening of affect and not knowing where he is going. He may think vaguely that he would like to study Aztec history or higher mathematics (with an I.Q. of, say, 90); but he is quite unconcerned with the practical difficulty in doing so and is quite unaware of the discrepancy between his aspirations and his capacity. This may tend to suggest a fairly marked lack of an integrated self-schema; but simple schizophrenics may well turn out to be integrated schizophrenics. Where the differential diagnosis lies with schizoid psychopathy, as it so often does, the lack of integration may be less than psychotic.

The term integrated psychosis, which has been taken over from Hilgard's reference to paranoid psychoses as among the best integrated of individuals, is not strictly accurate in that, by means of their dynamisms of self-deception, they hold together a part only of their personality. They are not an undivided whole. Hilgard does, however, distinguish the *integrated* paranoid from the *integrative* normal. This distinction has been adhered to.

The non-integrated psychotic position is considered to represent a greater degree of failure in establishing or in maintaining mutual personal relationships, for which a certain integrity of the self-schema and awareness of the self as agent are prerequisite, than does the integrated psychotic position. In consequence, it makes sense to speak of a non-integrated psychosis with integrated psychotic features; but it makes no sense to speak of an integrated psychosis with non-integrated features. The next level of classification should perhaps be anticipated in order to make the illustration more familiar. It makes sense to speak of a hebephrenic schizophrenic with paranoid features or with anxiety features; but it makes no sense to speak of a paranoid psychosis with marked hebephrenic features, and still less of an anxiety state with hebephrenic features.

From the SSI a scale was derived which differentiated non-integrated psychotics from integrated psychotics – that is, in fact here, non-paranoid schizophrenics from all other psychotics. The same scale served to differentiate non-integrated psychotics from neurotics.

Table 10 shows, at Level 5, the distribution of scores on the Non-integrated Psychotic *v.* Integrated Psychotic scale. It can be seen that 75 per cent of non-integrated psychotics scored 2 or more against 25 per cent of integrated psychotics in the first sample and 30 per cent in the second sample. The figures for the two neurotic samples were 15 and 16 per cent.

If a score of 1 is taken as uncertain, then the respective percentages are: non-integrated psychotics, 10; integrated psychotics, 24 and 7; neurotics, 18 and 21.

The following percentages of each group scored 0 or below: non-integrated psychotics, 15; integrated psychotics, 51 and 63; neurotics, 67 and 63.

When all non-integrated psychotics are compared with all integrated psychotics, 59 per cent are allocated in agreement with the psychiatrists (strictly, non-paranoid schizophrenics *v.* all other psychotics), 16 per cent remain uncertain, and 25 per cent are allocated in disagreement. When non-integrated psychotics are compared with all neurotics, the corresponding percentages are 66, 19, and 15.

TABLE 10 *Scores on the Non-integrated Psychotic v. Integrated Psychotic scale of non-integrated psychotics, integrated psychotics, and neurotics*

NIP-IP score	Non-integrated psychotics 20	Integrated psychotics 85		Neurotics 158	
		I	II	I	II
9	1				
8					
7	2				
6	1	1	1		
5	2		1	2	2
4	3	1	2		
3	3	8	2		5
2	3	4	3	10	5
1	2	13	2	15	16
0	2	21	8	38	29
−1	1	7	7	13	17
−2			4	5	1
	20	55	30	83	75

Although the base-rates in this sample – and probably in any typical mental hospital population – are such as to militate against the practical usefulness of this scale, it is still of theoretical interest. Furthermore, it will be shown that the paranoid continuum can usefully be split between paranoid schizophrenia and paranoia; that the former, the largest single group of schizophrenia, belongs most properly with the non-integrated psychotic class and consequently reduces considerably the disbalance in base-rates.

Table 11 shows the percentages of cases claiming to have each of the symptoms on this scale. Again, all these differences were significant at least at the 5 per cent level in one sample and at least at the 10 per cent level in the other. The overall figures were significant at the 5 per cent level in each case.

TABLE 11 *Percentages of non-integrated psychotics and of integrated psychotics claiming each symptom on the Non-integrated Psychotic v. Integrated Psychotic scale*

Item	Non-integrated psychotics 20	Integrated psychotics 85
C 7	20	7
C 8	20	9
C 9	20	7
E 2	35	14
E 6	45	17
F 2	35	10
F 3	35	18
F 4	45	23
F 7	45	21
F 9	55	33
F 10	30	15
D 1/D 5/H 6	40	68
G 6	10	34

The non-integrated psychotic is characterized, therefore, by the following symptoms or subjective signs:

C 7   She is sometimes so cheerful that she wants to wear lots of gay things, like button-holes, flowers, bright ties, jewellery, etc. (This, and the following two items, she has felt within the past week in spite of being in hospital.)

C 8   When she gets bored she likes to stir up some excitement.

C 9   She sometimes feels so full of energy and ideas that she doesn't want to go to bed.

E 2   She is compelled to think over abstract problems again and again until she can't leave them alone.

E 6   Distressing thoughts about sex or religion come into her mind against her will.

F 2   She sometimes sees visions, or people, animals, or things around her that others don't seem to see.

F 3   She often wonders who she really is.

F 4   She sometimes has very strange and peculiar experiences.

F 7   She sometimes hears voices without knowing where they come from.

F 9   She sometimes has very strange and peculiar thoughts.

F 10   There is something unusual about her body, like one side being different from the other and meaning something different.

Items F 7, F 9, and F 10 also appear in the Psychotic *v.* Neurotic scale. It should be noted that only F 10 is a delusional item, and that implying a loss of the self-schema. The general picture is rather one of loss of identity, loss of boundaries, which again is rather consonant with the use of the term 'non-integrated'.

The integrated psychotic, as compared with the non-integrated psychotic, is characterized by the following symptoms:

D 1   People are talking about her and criticizing her through no fault of her own; *or*

D 5   She has some special power, ability, or influence which is not recognized by other people; *or*

H 6   Because of things she has done wrong, people are talking about her and criticizing her; *and*

G 6   She has been in poor physical health during most of the past few years.

Once again the scale is almost unidirectional, which supports the view that non-integrated psychotics have those symptoms that are common to integrated psychotics; but integrated psychotics do not have the symptoms that are common to non-integrated psychotics.

From *Tables 4, 6,* and *10* it can be calculated that the median scores for the 20 non-integrated psychotics, the 85 integrated psychotics, and the 158 neurotics on the Non-integrated Psychotic *v.* Integrated Psychotic scale, the Psychotic *v.* Neurotic scale, and the Personal Illness *v.* Normal scale are as shown in *Table 12*. Non-integrated psychotics thus score high on all three scales, integrated psychotics score high on two, and neurotics on one.

TABLE 12 *Median scores of non-integrated psychotics, integrated psychotics, and neurotics on the NIP v. IP, the P v. N, and the PI v. No scales*

Scales	Non-integrated psychotics 20	Integrated psychotics 85	Neurotics 158
NIP *v.* IP	3	0	0
P *v.* N	2½	2	0
PI *v.* No	9	8	10

SUMMARY

The Symptom-Sign Inventory, with its possible advantages and disadvantages, has been described and applied to a large sample of female patients and a small sample of normal women.

In this chapter the following scales have been considered: Personal Illness v. Normal (PI v. No); Psychotic v. Neurotic (P v. N); and Non-integrated Psychotic v. Integrated Psychotic (NIP v. IP).

The necessary and sufficient condition for distinguishing the *personality disorders* from normal individuals is extreme egocentricity, which is accompanied by an inability to empathize and a concomitant tendency to treat other people as objects. There are no data other than those presented in Chapter 5 relating to this comparison.

The necessary and sufficient condition for the diagnosis of *personal illness* is the presence of disproportionateness of affect, where the inference is that the overt stimulus is a displacement from some covert stimulus. A consequence of the operation of self-deceptive dynamisms is that the personally ill are less able than the normal person to intend their own actions.

The necessary and sufficient condition for the diagnosis of *psychosis* is the presence of delusions implying a self-schema, such as delusions of grandeur, of influence, of persecution, of unworthiness, of poverty, and so forth, and/or of gross preceptual disorder (including hallucinations).

Loss of awareness of the self as agent, incongruity of affect (including flattening), and thought-process disorder will each occur only in *non-integrated psychosis*, and this diagnosis will not be made in the absence of all three signs.

In each distinction it is assumed that the conditions must be sufficient to result in the individual's being brought for, or seeking, treatment.

Owing to errors of clinical diagnosis and of measurement by means of the SSI, necessary and sufficient conditions are, in practice, reduced to 'greater probabilities of occurrence'. On this basis, the results are considered to be rather congruent with the hypothetical formulations. Most of the items of the Personal Illness scale could be subsumed under the heading of 'affective disproportion'; most of the items on the Psychotic scale could be subsumed under the heading of 'delusions'; and most of the items of the Non-integrated Psychotic scale could be subsumed under the heading of 'loss of awareness of the self-schema, or of the self as agent'.

Classification of Personal Illness – Classes

It has been argued that all non-integrated psychotics are psychotics, are personally ill, and are personality disorders; that all psychotics are personally ill and are personality disorders; that all the personally ill are personality disorders. Non-integrated psychotics were, in fact, high scorers on the Non-integrated Psychotic scale, on the Psychotic scale, and on the Personal Illness scale. Integrated psychotics were high scorers on the last two scales, and neurotics on the last scale only. Psychopaths were defined as those who are personality disorders, but who are not personally ill. Neurotics are those who are personality disorders and are personally ill, but who are not psychotic. Integrated psychotics are those who are personality disorders, who are personally ill, and who are psychotic, but who are not non-integrated psychotic. Schizophrenics are those who are personality disorders, who are personally ill, who are psychotic, and who are non-integrated psychotic.

REFERENCES

BANNISTER, D. (1962). The nature and measurement of schizophrenic thought disorder. *J. ment. Sci.*, **108**, 825.
BARRON, F. (1963). *Creativity and psychological health*. New Jersey: Van Nostrand.
EYSENCK, H. J. (1960). Classification and the problem of diagnosis. In H. J. Eysenck (Ed.), *Handbook of abnormal psychology*. London: Pitman Medical Publishing Co.
FREUD, A. (1937). *The ego and the mechanisms of defence*. London: Hogarth; New York: International Universities Press, 1946.
FREUD, S. (1925). *Collected Papers*, IV. London: Hogarth.
FREUD, S. (1900). *The interpretation of dreams*. London: Allen & Unwin, 1937 and 1954; New York: Macmillan, 3rd edn., 1933.
HAMILTON, M. (1959). The assessment of anxiety states by rating. *Brit. J. med. Psychol.*, **32**, 50.
HAMILTON, M. (1960). A rating scale for depression. *J. neurol. neurosurg. Psychiat.*, **23**, 56.
HILGARD, E. R. (1954). Human motives and the concept of self. In H. Brand (Ed.), *The study of personality*. New York: Wiley; London: Chapman & Hall.
HINSIE, L. E. & CAMPBELL, R. J. (1960). *Psychiatric dictionary*. New York: Oxford University Press.
KREITMAN, N. (1961). The reliability of psychiatric diagnosis. *J. ment. Sci.*, **107**, 876.
LANGFELDT, G. (1952). Some points regarding the symptomatology and diagnosis of schizophrenia. *Acta Psychiat.*, Suppl. 80.

A Quantitative Classification

LUCAS, C. J., SAINSBURY, P. & COLLINS, J. G. (1962). A social and clinical study of delusions in schizophrenia. *J. ment. Sci.*, **108**, 747.

MCDOUGALL, W. (1908). *An introduction to social psychology.* (30th edn., 1950.) London: Methuen.

MCGUIRE, R. J. (1962). A study of the MPI used with psychiatric in-patients. *Bulletin* of the Brit. Psychol. Soc., **47**, 56.

MACMURRAY, J. (1961). *Persons in relation.* London: Faber.

NORRIS, V. (1959). *Mental illness in London.* Maudsley Monogr. No. 6. London: Chapman & Hall.

SCHMIDT, H. O. & FONDA, C. P. (1956). The reliability of psychiatric diagnosis: a new look. *J. abnorm. soc. Psychol.*, **52**, 262.

TROUTON, D. S. & MAXWELL, A. E. (1956). The relation between neurosis and psychosis. *J. ment. Sci.*, **102**, 1.

WECKOWICZ, T. E. & SOMMER, R. (1960). Body-image and self-concept in schizophrenia. *J. ment. Sci.*, **106**, 17.

WITKIN, H. A., DYK, R. B., FATERSON, H. F., GOODENOUGH. D. R. & KARP, S. A. (1962). *Psychological differentiation.* New York & London: Wiley.

CHAPTER SEVEN

Classification of Personal Illness – Groups

In Chapter 5 a continuum of increasing failure to maintain mutual personal relationships was suggested, which extends from normality through personality disorders, the personally ill, and psychotics, to nonintegrated psychotics. It is now required to consider the within-class differences, and to suggest necessary and sufficient conditions for making differentiation.

WITHIN THE SCHIZOPHRENIA CLASS

Figure 3 depicts the universe of discourse of schizophrenia. The circles for catatonic, hebephrenic, and paranoid schizophrenia are shown to overlap with each other, and to be within the circle for simple schizophrenia. This is intended to indicate that all catatonic, hebephrenic, and paranoid schizophrenics are schizophrenics; but not all schizophrenics are catatonic, hebephrenic, or paranoid. Those who do not fall into any of these groups may be called simple schizophrenics. This formulation is based on the belief that there are no symptoms which occur in simple schizophrenia which do not occur in the other forms of schizophrenia, but that there are symptoms which occur in the other forms of schizophrenia which do not occur in simple schizophrenia. This exception apart, the 'contained within' principle does not apply to within-class differentiation such as Catatonia *v.* Hebephrenia or Anxiety *v.* Hysteria. It would therefore be anticipated that the scales would not be unidirectional.

The circles for catatonic, hebephrenic, and paranoid schizophrenia are shown as overlapping. Thus, when the dominant syndrome is catatonia, the individual may constitute a rather pure case of catatonia with no other features worthy of remark; or he may have either hebephrenic or paranoid features or both. The same argument will apply when the dominant syndrome is either hebephrenic or paranoid schizophrenia.

If it is now argued that all catatonic, hebephrenic, and paranoid schizophrenics are schizophrenics, but not all schizophrenics are catatonic, hebephrenic, or paranoid schizophrenics and that those who are not will be called simple schizophrenics, a term is required for those who are not 'simple' schizophrenics. This name is presumably 'compound' schizophrenics. The term will be unnecessary if simple schizophrenics turn out to be integrated psychotics. In the meantime one must adopt this stand.

FIGURE 3   *Universe of discourse of schizophrenia*

U = Schizophrenia

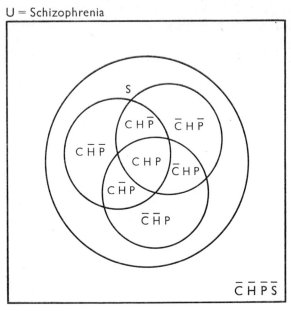

$$S = \text{Simple} \qquad C = \text{Catatonic}$$
$$H = \text{Hebephrenic} \qquad P = \text{Paranoid}$$

It is now, therefore, necessary to split off the compound schizophrenics from the total class of schizophrenics. If, for this purpose, flattening of affect is excluded from affective disorder – incongruity, and gross distortions and imperceptions are excluded from the perceptual disorders, four possible discriminants remain:

(i) Loss of awareness of self as agent
(ii) Incongruity of affect (excluding flattening)
(iii) Hallucinations
(iv) Thought-process disorder.

134

Simple schizophrenia is characterized by the absence of at least the first three types of disorder. If any of these were present, a diagnosis of simple schizophrenia would not be made.

It will be noted that none of the three types of disorder is regarded as a necessary condition for the diagnosis of compound schizophrenia. Had we an appropriate generalization to cover these three types of disorder, this difficulty would be overcome. Without it, one has to state that each of these singly is a sufficient condition for the diagnosis of compound schizophrenia and the presence of at least one of them is a necessary condition.

In all the remaining within-class differentiations, the circles representing the groups have been shown as overlapping. This implies that it is no longer possible to differentiate in terms of independently necessary and independently sufficient conditions.

The necessary and sufficient conditions for the distinction of catatonic from hebephrenic schizophrenia are the presence of stupor (particularly catalepsy), and/or a relative predominance of intropunitive over other types of delusion, and/or a relative absence of fatuousness.

The necessary and sufficient conditions for the distinction between catatonic and paranoid schizophrenia are the presence of stupor (particularly catalepsy), and/or gross intellectual impairment (a reversible, non-progressive type of intellectual deficit – Foulds & Dixon, 1962), and/or a relative predominance of intropunitive over extrapunitive delusions, and/or a relative predominance of visual over auditory hallucinations, and/or a relative predominance of imperception over gross perceptual distortion.

The necessary and sufficient conditions for the distinction between hebephrenic and paranoid schizophrenics are the presence of gross intellectual impairment and/or fatuousness, and/or a relative predominance of visual over auditory hallucinations, and/or a relative predominance of imperception over gross perceptual distortion.

The number of cases in the groups who have done the SSI is as yet too small to provide anything but the most tentative suggestions. It is possible that catatonic and paranoid schizophrenics complain of a larger number of symptoms on the SSI than do hebephrenic and simple schizophrenics. It is probable that intropunitive delusions appear more frequently in the catatonic group.

At the age of 14 Mark Twain thought his father was unbelievably stupid and ignorant; at the age of 19 he was astonished to find how much the old man had learnt in five short years. There is undoubtedly a growing, if somewhat shame-faced, awareness in the experimental literature that much information is lost through treating the schizophrenic class as a homogeneous group in all respects. It has become almost fashionable to compare groups who have and who have not got predominantly paranoid symptomatology. Shakow (1962), who has always been aware of the need to look at the sub-classes, reviews the vast number of studies which he and his associates have conducted and which demonstrate differences between paranoid and non-paranoid schizophrenics in the ability to maintain a set. Chapman & McGhie (1962) have shown similar differences in the ability to sustain attention in the face of distraction. Foulds, Dixon, McClelland & McClelland (1962) have shown differences between paranoid, catatonic, and hebephrenic schizophrenics in degree of intellectual impairment and in extent of recoverability. Foulds (1964) has shown that paranoid schizophrenics are better able to organize Thematic Apperception Test stories, on which they manifest more hostility; but that they produce more gross perceptual distortions, particularly in misperceiving the sex of a figure in the picture.

WITHIN THE INTEGRATED PSYCHOSIS CLASS

The paranoid schizophrenia circle in *Figure 3* should be shown as adjoining the paranoia circle in *Figure 4* to indicate the paranoid continuum. Strictly within the universe of discourse of integrated psychosis, the circles for paranoia, mania, and melancholia are shown as overlapping, and the same arguments apply here as for catatonic, hebephrenic, and paranoid schizophrenia.

The necessary and sufficient condition for the distinction of melancholia from mania is the presence in the former of the mood of depression, the predominance of intropunitive over other types of delusion, and retardation or agitation.

The necessary and sufficient condition for the distinction of melancholia from paranoia is the presence in the former of the same features as above and/or stupor.

The necessary and sufficient condition for the distinction of mania from paranoia is the presence in the former of a mood of elation, and/or psychomotor expansiveness, and/or pressure of talk, and/or stupor.

FIGURE 4 *Universe of discourse of integrated psychosis*

U = Integrated psychosis

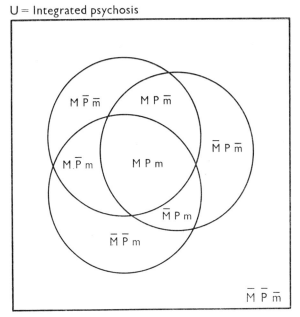

M = Melancholia
P = Paranoia
m = Mania

Psychiatrists have long debated whether or not to ascribe the extra-punitive delusions exclusively to the paranoid group and the intropunitive delusions to the melancholic group.

Stoddart (1921) apparently recognizes that extrapunitive delusions may be part of the melancholic picture. He says, 'There is another class of melancholics . . . who . . . develop delusions of persecution, they believe that other people are against them, even that there are world-wide conspiracies to do them harm.'

Séglas (1892), Ballet (1892), and Bleuler (1924), however, take a different view. Thus, Séglas states:

'The persecutory ideas found in deluded melancholics are not true ideas of persecution. Their foundation is not pride, but the peculiar humility of the melancholic; they bear the stamp of that peculiar

137

quality of resignation which is their own; for the patient finds his persecution justified by his unworthiness, and notwithstanding the "persecution" label we attach to his delusions, he remains first and foremost a self-accuser.'

Ballet argues, 'they are victims, but guilty victims, not as ordinary patients, innocent victims'. Bleuler's forthright comment is: 'Delusions of persecution do not belong to the depressive forms of delusion. The delusion of deserved punishment must not be classified with that of the unjust persecution.'

Lewis (1934) perhaps leans more to Stoddart's view. He says,
'. . . humility and resignation are by no means the only attitude the melancholic patient takes up, but . . . resentment and hostility may exist alongside these, or may even dominate the picture. . . . Resignation is certainly the commonest attitude towards the persecutory ideas, but it is not by any means the invariable one. It may be said that it is an admixture of other forms of reaction-types, which produces in some patients a resentful attitude towards the supposed discrimination, but where so small a number out of 61 patients are quite free from such features, one is more inclined to regard it as part of the depressive type of reaction.'

These authors have made the important point that ideas of reference or of persecution may be extrapunitive or intropunitive. This distinction is still frequently neglected.

The next point is to which class does each belong. If resentment and hostility occur in a majority of cases diagnosed on the basis of other criteria as paranoids, and resignation and humility occur in a minority, and if resentment and hostility occur in a minority of melancholics and resignation and humility in a majority, this association must be recognized even though it is not perfect. This presents no difficulty when the disease entity concept is abandoned. Unless it is abandoned, one of the grounds for making the respective allocations to the paranoid and melancholic classes is removed. It is not easy to see with what one is left, particularly in the case of paranoia. Even with melancholia this is difficult. A dominance of resentment and hostility seems rather incompatible with psychopathological depression. By what criteria, then, can one allocate such cases to the melancholic rather than to the paranoid class? The conclusion which Lewis rejects – that some cases are an admixture of other forms of reaction-types – seems the more acceptable one.

It is widely agreed that there is a continuum from paranoia through paraphrenia to paranoid schizophrenia. In the present system, paranoia or paranoid states would be regarded as those who fell into the class of integrated psychosis, but not of non-integrated psychosis; whereas paranoid schizophrenics would be those who fell into the class of non-integrated psychosis. Strictly, then, the diagnosis should be schizophrenia with paranoid features, or schizophrenia, paranoid type (see Chapter 12 below).

The manic group constitutes a difficulty from this point of view. It may be that cases of acute mania should be placed in the non-integrated psychotic category; but this remains to be seen. It might be argued that all manics are hypomanics, whereas not all hypomanics are manics; and that manics are non-integrated psychotics and hypomanics integrated. In practice the difficulty is largely resolved, since, in our age of conformity and pharmaco-dampening, scarcely anyone is allowed a full-blown mania.

One proceeds, therefore, to Level 6 and to the differentiation, by means of the SSI, within the universe of discourse of the integrated psychoses.

If, in any given period of time, only 10 non-integrated psychotics are admitted to hospital to every 40 integrated psychotics (such figures have been called 'the base-rates'), 80 per cent agreement with psychiatrists could be obtained by calling all cases integrated psychotics. One would probably do less well with a test. Because the base-rates for the non-integrated psychoses do, in fact, militate against the practical usefulness of the Non-integrated *v.* Integrated Psychotic split, the schizophrenics have been included here again at Level 6. When the paranoid schizophrenics have been assimilated into the non-integrated category, this may no longer be necessary. One is, therefore, in practice dealing with the differentiation within the universe of psychosis once more. Here the base-rates are still probably some way off a fifty-fifty split, but perhaps not so much as to vitiate practical usefulness.

Table 13 shows the distribution of scores on the Paranoid *v.* Schizophrenia (*Pa* v. *Sc*) scale. Treating scores of 0 and 1 as 'uncertain' as between paranoid and schizophrenic, 32 per cent remain unclassified; 68 per cent are in agreement with the psychiatric diagnosis and none is in disagreement.

Table 14 shows the percentages of paranoids and of schizophrenics who claim to have each of the symptoms on this scale.

TABLE 13   *Distribution of scores on the Paranoid v. Schizophrenia scale of paranoid, schizophrenic, melancholic, hysteric, anxiety, and depressive groups*

Pa-Sc score	Pa 30	Sc 20	Me 50	Hy 50	Ax 50	Dp 50
5	5					
4	9		1			
3	5		1	2		
2	4		1	6		1
1	2	2	4	13	4	6
0	5	7	12	9	14	14
−1		7	15	12	17	17
−2		4	6	4	10	9
−3			7	2	3	
−4			3	2	2	3

TABLE 14   *Percentages of paranoids and of schizophrenics claiming each symptom on the Paranoid v. Schizophrenic scale*

Item	Paranoids 30	Schizophrenics 20
D 1	63	30
D 3	67	25
D 6	60	20
D 7	63	15
D 10	50	20
G 6	37	10
A 6	10	40
A 9	20	30
B 3	7	40
B 10	7	40
F 2	10	35

The paranoid patient, in contradistinction to the non-paranoid schizophrenic, is characterized by the following symptoms:

D 1   People are talking about her and criticizing her through no fault of her own.

D 3   There are people who are trying to harm her through no fault of her own.

D 6   Someone, other than herself, is deliberately causing most of her troubles.

D 7 People are plotting against her through no fault of her own.
D 10 People can read her thoughts and make her do things against her will by a sort of hypnotism.
G 6 She has been in poor physical health during most of the past few years.

The schizophrenic, on the other hand, is characterized by the following symptoms:

A 6 She is afraid that she might be going insane.
A 9 She is afraid of going out alone.
B 3 She has attempted to do away with herself.
B 10 She has seriously thought of doing away with herself because she is no longer able to cope with her difficulties.
F 2 She sometimes sees visions, or people, animals, or things around her that other people don't seem to see.

Because many of the paranoid group used here were subsequently found to fall into the non-integrated psychotic class, although they did have paranoid characteristics, the items which differentiate the non-paranoid schizophrenic from the paranoid state are not, with the exception of the last, typical schizophrenic symptoms such as turn up in other comparisons. These items do, however, seem clinically apposite.

Table 15 shows the distribution of scores on the Melancholia *v.* Schizophrenia scale. Treating a score of 2 as indeterminate, 16 per cent remain unclassified; 7 per cent are allocated in disagreement and 77 per cent in agreement with the clinical diagnosis.

TABLE 15 *Distribution of scores on the Melancholia* v. *Schizophrenia scale of melancholic, schizophrenic, paranoid, hysteric, anxiety, and depressive groups*

Me-Sc score	Me 50	Sc 20	Pa 30	Hy 50	Ax 50	Dp 50
7	3			1		
6	9			3		4
5	13	1	1	5	3	4
4	6		4	6	7	13
3	8	1	1	12	15	9
2	8	3	4	7	13	11
1		5	13	8	8	5
0	2	10	5	7	4	4
−1	1		1	1		
−2			1			

A Quantitative Classification

Table 16 shows the percentages of melancholics and of schizophrenics who claim to have each of the symptoms on the scale.

TABLE 16 *Percentages of melancholics and of schizophrenics claiming each symptom on the Melancholia v. Schizophrenia scale*

Item	Melancholics 50	Schizophrenics 20
A 2	60	30
A 8	78	35
B 7	62	35
B 8	74	45
H 2	70	40
H 6	40	10
H 10	66	35
E 6	16	45
F 4	18	45
F 7	10	45

The melancholic, in contradistinction to the schizophrenic, is characterized by the following symptoms:

A 2 She sweats very easily, even on cool days.
A 8 She has difficulty in getting off to sleep.
B 7 The future seems pointless.
B 8 She is more absent-minded recently than she used to be.
H 2 She is an unworthy person in her own eyes.
H 6 Because of things she has done wrong, people are talking about her and criticizing her.
H 10 She sometimes goes to bed feeling she wouldn't care if she never woke up again.

The schizophrenic, on the other hand, is characterized by the following symptoms:

E 6 Distressing thoughts about sex or religion come into her mind against her will.
F 4 She sometimes has very strange and peculiar experiences.
F 7 She sometimes hears voices without knowing where they come from.

Again, the differentiating symptoms seem very consonant with clinical expectation.

142

Still at Level 6, data are insufficient for dealing with the manic group. A scale was, however, constructed for differentiating between the paranoid and melancholic groups. Here, as always, items were chosen which differentiated between these two groups at least at the 5 per cent level of significance in one sample and at least at the 10 per cent level in the other. The score on items given more frequently by melancholics was subtracted from the score on items given more frequently by paranoids.

Table 17 shows the distribution of scores on the Paranoid *v.* Melancholia scale. Treating scores of 0 to −4 as non-discriminating, 22 per cent remain uncertain; 76 per cent are classified in agreement with the psychiatric diagnosis and only 1 per cent in disagreement.

TABLE 17 *Distribution of scores on the Paranoid v. Melancholia scale of paranoid, melancholic, schizophrenic, hysteric, anxiety, and depressive groups*

Pa-Me score	Pa 30	Me 50	Sc 20	Hy 50	Ax 50	Dp 50
8						
7	1					
6	1					
5	5		1			
4	2					
3	4			1		
2	3			1		
1	4	1	1			
0	2	3	2	2	3	1
−1	2	2	2	9	3	1
−2	2	1	4	10	6	7
−3	2		2	3	8	4
−4	2	2	1	6	5	4
−5		6	2	1	6	5
−6		4	3	4	4	6
−7		6		2	6	9
−8		8	1	4	4	4
−9		2	1	1		4
−10		7		4		3
−11		2			3	1
−12		4		1	2	1
−13		2				
−14				1		

Table *18* shows the percentages of paranoids and of melancholics who claim to have each of the symptoms on the scale.

TABLE 18   *Percentages of paranoids and of melancholics claiming each symptom on the Paranoid v. Melancholia scale*

Item	Paranoids 30	Melancholics 50
D 1	63	28
D 2	17	0
D 3	67	8
D 4	30	2
D 5	27	8
D 6	60	14
D 7	63	6
D 8	30	4
D 9	50	26
D 10	50	20
F 7	40	10
A 2	23	60
A 6	10	56
A 8	43	78
A 9	20	52
B 2	33	64
B 3	7	40
B 4	23	60
B 7	27	62
B 10	7	36
H 2	30	72
H 4	20	44
H 5	33	66
H 8	10	30
H 9	17	56
H 10	30	66

The paranoid patient, in contradistinction to the melancholic, is thus characterized by all 10 symptoms in the *a priori* Paranoid scale, which consists of six extrapunitive persecutory delusions, two grandiose delusions, one delusion of influence, and one item hard to classify. In addition, she complains more frequently of auditory hallucinations.

D 1   People are talking about her and criticizing her through no fault of her own.

D 2   She has an important mission to carry out.

D 3   There are people who are trying to harm her through no fault of her own.

D 4   Someone is trying to poison her or make her ill in some way.

D 5   She has some special power, ability, or influence which is not recognized by other people.

D 6   Someone, other than herself, is deliberately causing most of her troubles.

D 7   People are plotting against her through no fault of her own.

D 8   She sometimes takes strong action against an evil person for the sake of a principle.

D 9   She sometimes sees someone do or say something which most people do not take much notice of, but which she knows has a special meaning.

D 10   People can read her thoughts and make her do things against her will by a sort of hypnotism.

F 7   She sometimes hears voices without knowing where they come from.

The melancholic, on the other hand, is characterized by 4 symptoms from the *a priori* Anxiety scale, 5 from the Neurotic Depressive, and 6 from the Melancholic. Summarily, she may be described as suffering from intropunitive delusions, despair, agitation, suicidal thoughts and attempts, sleep disturbance, and fear of insanity.

A 2   She sweats very easily, even on cool days.

A 6   She is afraid that she might be going insane.

A 8   She has difficulty in getting off to sleep.

A 9   She is afraid of going out alone.

B 2   She has lost interest in almost everything.

B 3   She has attempted to do away with herself.

B 4   The simplest task is too much of an effort.

B 7   The future seems pointless.

B 10   She has seriously thought of doing away with herself because she is no longer able to cope with her difficulties.

H 2   She is an unworthy person in her own eyes.

H 4   She is a condemned person because of her sins.

H 5   She is troubled by waking in the early hours and being unable to get off to sleep again.

H 8   She causes harm to people because of what she is.

H 9   She sometimes gets so worked up that she paces about the room wringing her hands.

H 10   She sometimes goes to bed feeling she wouldn't care if she never woke up again.

Once again the results are consonant with the hypothesized necessary and sufficient conditions for making the diagnoses.

WITHIN THE NEUROSIS CLASS

The circle for melancholia in *Figure 4* should be shown as adjoining the circles for anxiety states and for neurotic depressives, to indicate the affective disorder continuum. Strictly within the neurosis class, the circles for anxiety state, depression, hysteria, and obsessional are shown as overlapping, and once more the same argument applies.

FIGURE 5 *Universe of discourse of neurosis*

U = Neurosis

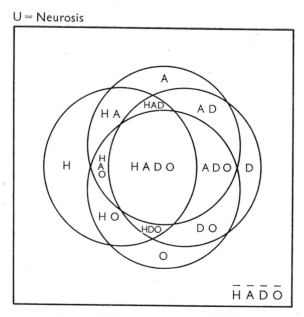

H = Hysteria   D = Depression
A = Anxiety state   O = Obsession

Still at Level 6, one has to attempt the differentiation within the neuroses. The various combinations are shown in *Figure 5*, but are so numerous as to be better left unstated. The fact of their being shown in the figure does not, of course, necessarily mean that there is class membership of all possible overlaps. With four circles not all the requisite overlaps can be drawn. This is the only reason for the omission of HD and AO.

Here, as with the integrated psychoses, there seems no question of an order of precedence, as it were, within the sub-classes. Where mixtures occur, the dominant diagnosis has to be determined by inferences about the most important symptoms.

Within the neuroses, the necessary and sufficient condition for the designation of hysteria is the unconscious simulation of some other illness, be it personal or organic. The term conversion hysteria might best be reserved for those who simulate a somatic illness. The pseudo-dementias (of which the Ganser state is a special instance – Enoch & Irving, 1962) and the pseudo-epilepsies are those who simulate a somato-psychological illness. The hysterical psychotics are those who simulate a psychosis, usually schizophrenia. It is probable that they do simulate other neurotic illnesses; but this is much harder to detect. It is claimed by some that depersonalization, though most often a symptom liable to occur in a number of syndromes, does occasionally appear in pure culture. It is usually referred to then as the depersonalization syndrome; but the writer would prefer to regard it as a hysterical dissociative phenomenon, whether it occur alone or as part of another dominant syndrome.

In the case of all the symptoms or signs named as necessary and sufficient conditions for any particular designation at this level, it is implicit that they are so only in the absence of symptoms at levels of classification which take precedence over this level. Thus the necessary and sufficient condition, within the neuroses, for the designation of obsessional is, of course, the presence of ruminations and/or compulsions. Schizophrenics may have these too; but, if there are other grounds for making the diagnosis of schizophrenia, the psychotic diagnosis would take precedence.

In the case of both anxiety states and neurotic depressives they must, of course, fulfil the necessary and sufficient condition for membership of the class, personal illness – namely, that there should be present affective disproportion, which provides presumptive evidence of displacement from the reason which is operative in bringing about the condition. The affect, which will constitute the necessary and sufficient condition for the designation of each group, will, of course, be anxiety and depression respectively.

A Quantitative Classification

It has already been intimated that the writer would wish to exclude many cases currently diagnosed as neurotic or reactive depression – cases in which the subject states the reason for his depression and we find no reason to doubt him. The criteria usually given for distinguishing a reactive from an endogenous depression are that the former should be reacting to a real loss (which is certainly not supported by the SSI), that it should be possible to distract him from his mood of depression, that the depressive reaction should have endured longer than the psychiatrist thinks it should have done (which is reminiscent of the Victorian periods of mourning – so much for a husband, so much for a father, a cousin, and so forth), and that the affect should be disproportionate to the loss. Only the last, we would argue, has validity. Too often professional, as well as lay, people speak of an individual being depressed when there is no evidence that he is other than grieved.

The same failure to distinguish between normal and psychopathological anxiety, despite the fact that Freud (1926, 1933) did so most clearly, has led to much loose thinking and to many profitless experiments by psychologists. The distinction is less likely to be lost sight of when one is confronted with a possible anxiety state; but what is meant when a patient is diagnosed as, say, a neurotic depression with anxiety features? It is still important to make the distinction between normal, or realistic, anxiety and psychopathological anxiety, as it is with the anxiety which has to be aroused in a hysteric before much progress can be made.

An additional dangerous confusion at this level is that of diagnosing, say, an anxiety state with hysterical features when the patient has, in fact, no hysterical symptoms or signs at all, but is of hysteroid personality – that is, he is histrionic in his behaviour, labile in his affect, attention-seeking, and so forth.

It is clear that there is no difficulty in stating the necessary and sufficient conditions for making each of the *designations* – hysteria, anxiety state, depression, and obsessional. The term designation has been used rather than diagnosis to suggest that it is equally clear that none of these conditions can be regarded as a necessary and sufficient condition for the class diagnosis of neurosis. This is probably a powerful reason for the relative unreliability of diagnosis within the neuroses.

Unconscious simulation of some other illness is only a necessary and sufficient condition for the *diagnosis* of hysteria. Conceivably, psychopathological anxiety or depression and ruminations or compulsions may be present in the same person. If any two or more occur together, the

148

dominant diagnosis has to be determined by inferences about the most important symptoms in the total picture. Thus, if the patient shows evidence of both anxiety and depression, the diagnosis might be either anxiety state with depressive features or neurotic depression with anxiety features. It is, of course, vital to distinguish between such diagnoses and, say, anxiety state with secondary depression (i.e. where the depression is reactive to the discomfort caused by the anxiety symptoms).

One could, of course, proceed from Level 6 to Level 7, at which one might seek to differentiate between, say, phobic anxiety states and free-floating anxiety; or between ruminative and compulsive obsessionals, and so forth, indeed until we are saying 'This is Tom Cobley'. As we proceed down the classificatory levels from main classes to groups, it becomes more and more likely that any one individual will at different times be a member of both classes. It should be noted also that we are proceeding more and more towards the dynamics of the individual case. For this purpose it may be vitally important to know that X is suffering from agoraphobia rather than claustrophobia. Indeed it will be important to be even more specific than this; but, even so, we never leave classification behind. Why so many dynamically orientated psychiatrists regard nosology as an insult to their art it is difficult to comprehend. Classification is the reverse of the Procrustean bed: it is a bed that can be made to accommodate as many or as few as we wish, or perhaps we should say it is a series of bunks arranged one above the other, and the sky is the limit.

At Level 6, data are insufficient for dealing with the obsessional neuroses; but scales have been worked out for differentiating between hysterics, anxiety states, and neurotic depressives.

Since here, as elsewhere, some pairs of diagnostic groups are more alike than others, it follows that there can be no fixed scale which will give optimal discrimination between one category and all others. Thus, instead of making up an Anxiety scale to distinguish anxiety states from all other groups, five scales were made up to distinguish anxiety states in turn from hysterics, depressives, melancholics, paranoids, and schizophrenics. In this chapter, concern is with the first two only.

Table 19 shows the distribution of scores on the Anxiety *v.* Hysteria scale. There is no point on the score distribution at which it seems unreasonable to make an allocation, so that we have 80 per cent of cases in agreement with the psychiatric diagnosis and the remaining 20 per cent in disagreement.

L   149

TABLE 19 *Distribution of scores on the Anxiety v. Hysteria scale of anxiety, hysteric, schizophrenic, paranoid, melancholic, and depressive groups*

Ax-Hy score	Ax 50	Hy 50	Sc 20	Pa 30	Me 50	Dp 50
6	2					
5	4					
4	7	2	1		1	1
3	16	2	1		6	6
2	11	6	2	5	13	10
1	6	13	7	6	14	21
0	4	14	9	6	12	11
−1		12		12	3	
−2				1	1	1
−3		1				

Table 20 shows the percentages of anxiety states and hysterics who claim to have each of the symptoms on the scale.

TABLE 20 *Percentages of anxiety states and of hysterics claiming each symptom on the Anxiety v. Hysteria scale*

Item	Anxiety states 50	Hysterics 50
A 1	66	46
A 4	80	58
A 5	52	24
A 9	66	36
C 2	14	0
C 4	32	10
D 1	12	44
G 6	16	50
G 9	12	30

Classification of Personal Illness – Groups

The anxiety state, in contradistinction to the hysteric, is characterize by the following symptoms:

A 1 Her hand often shakes when she tries to do something.
A 4 There are times when she feels anxious without knowing the reason.
A 5 She is afraid of being in a wide-open space or in an enclosed place.
A 9 She is afraid of going out alone.
C 2 She sometimes becomes very excitedly happy for no special reason.
C 4 There are times when exciting new ideas and schemes occur to her on e after the other.

The hysteric, on the other hand, is characterized thus:

D 1 People are talking about her and criticizing her through no fault of her own.
G 6 She has been in poor physical health during most of the past few years.
G 9 She sometimes does things in a dream-like state without remembering afterwards what she has been doing.

Six out of the 9 items came from the appropriate *a priori* scales.

Table 21 shows the score distribution on the Anxiety *v.* Depression scale. Treating scores of 2 as non-discriminating, 12 per cent remain unclassified; 72 per cent are in agreement and 16 per cent in disagreement with the clinical diagnosis.

TABLE 21 *Distribution of scores on the Anxiety v. Depression scale of anxiety, depressive, schizophrenic, paranoid, melancholic, and hysteric groups*

Ax-Dp score	Ax 50	Dp 50	Sc 20	Pa 30	Me 50	Hy 50
9						
8		1				1
7	2		1			1
6	8				1	
5	6		1	1	2	
4	9	1		3	4	4
3	7	3	5	1	2	6
2	7	5	4	7	11	9
1	8	22	2	10	9	15
0	3	8	4	4	11	9
−1		7	2	3	3	4
−2		3	1	1	5	1
−3					2	
−4						

Table 22 shows the percentages of anxiety states and of depressives who claim to have each of the symptoms on the scale.

TABLE 22 *Percentages of anxiety states and of depressives claiming each symptom on the Anxiety v. Depression scale*

Item	Anxiety states 50	Depressives 50
A 1	66	40
A 4	80	50
A 9	66	32
C 4	32	8
C 5	14	0
C 6	26	8
D 8	12	0
E 2	20	6
E 5	20	6
E 6	26	10
G 3	32	14
B 3	10	40
G 6	16	34
H 3	0	12
H 7	24	42

The anxiety state, in contradistinction to the depressive, is thus characterized by the following symptoms:

A 1   Her hand often shakes when she tries to do something.
A 4   There are times when she feels anxious without knowing the reason.
A 9   She is afraid of going out alone.
C 4   There are times when exciting new ideas and schemes occur to her one after the other.
C 5   She is sometimes so full of pep and energy that she could carry on doing things indefinitely.
C 6   She sometimes becomes so excited that her thoughts race ahead faster than she can express them.
D 8   She sometimes takes strong action against an evil person for the sake of a principle.
E 2   She is compelled to think over abstract problems again and again until she can't leave them alone.

152

E 5 She is afraid that she might do something seriously wrong against her will.

E 6 Distressing thoughts about sex or religion come into her mind against her will.

G 3 She sometimes loses her voice completely.

The depressive, on the other hand, is characterized by the following symptoms:

B 3 She has attempted to do away with herself.

G 6 She has been in poor physical health for most of the past few years.

H 3 There is some bodily condition which she finds disgusting.

H 7 She is sometimes so low in spirits that she just sits for hours on end.

Although only 4 out of the 15 items came from the appropriate *a priori* scales, for this particular differentiation the results do seem perfectly intelligible clinically.

Table 23 shows the distribution of scores on the Hysteria *v.* Depression scale. Treating scores of 0 and 1 as non-discriminating, as many as 40 per cent of the cases remain unclassified; 52 per cent are classified in agreement and 8 per cent in disagreement with the psychiatric diagnosis. This is the poorest differentiation in the whole series.

TABLE 23 *Distribution of scores on the Hysteria v. Depression scale of hysteric, depressive, schizophrenic, paranoid, melancholic, and anxiety groups*

Hy-Dp score	Hy 50	Dp 50	Sc 20	Pa 30	Me 50	Ax 50
8						
7			1			
6				1	1	
5	3				2	
4	9		1	3		1
3	8	2	1	3	5	4
2	8	2	8	7	7	11
1	8	11	4	6	8	9
0	10	11	3	8	15	14
−1	3	12	2	1	10	9
−2	1	10		1	2	1
−3		1				1
−4		1				

A Quantitative Classification

Table 24 shows the percentages of Hysterics and of Depressives who claim to have each of the symptoms on the scale. E 1, A 5, and E 3 just failed to reach the 5 per cent level of significance; but the lowest chi-

TABLE 24 *Percentages of hysterics and of depressives claiming each symptom on the Hysteria v. Depression scale*

Item	Hysterics 50	Depressives 50
C 6	22	8
D 1	44	16
D 8	10	0
E 1	30	14
E 5	30	6
F 3	16	6
F 5	36	16
G 2	40	18
G 9	30	12
A 5	24	42
B 3	20	40
E 3	16	30
E 9	12	28

square value was above 3·7. With this proviso, the hysteric, in contradistinction to the depressive, is characterized by the following symptoms:

C 6 She sometimes becomes so excited that her thoughts race ahead faster than she can express them.

D 1 People are talking about her and criticizing her through no fault of her own.

D 8 She sometimes takes strong action against an evil person for the sake of a principle.

E 1 She is distressed by silly, pointless thoughts that keep coming into her mind against her will.

E 5 She is afraid she will do something seriously wrong against her will.

F 3 She often wonders who she really is.

F 5 She thinks other people regard her as very odd.

G 2 She sometimes has fits, or difficulty in keeping her balance.

G 9 She sometimes does things in a dream-like state without knowing afterwards what she has been doing.

The depressive, on the other hand, is characterized by the following symptoms:

A 5   She is afraid of being in a wide-open space or in an enclosed place.
B 3   She has attempted to do away with herself.
E 3   She is unnecessarily careful in carrying out simple everyday tasks, like folding up clothes, reading notices, etc.
E 9   She is excessively concerned about cleanliness.

Only 3 out of 13 items were from the appropriate *a priori* scales. Here it is less apparent that the items are consonant with clinical expectation.

WITHIN THE PSYCHOPATH CLASS

There are, by definition, no symptoms or signs by means of which to make any further differentiation. There are, of course, innumerable possible personality dimensions. Two have been chosen – those involving extrapunitive and intropunitive attitudes on the one hand and hysteroid and obsessoid traits on the other. These characteristics are, of course, relevant to all who fall into the universe of discourse of personality. In effect, this will include virtually everyone, except possibly the most severely subnormal and those with extremely severe cerebral pathology, such as secondaries in the brain.

All extrapunitive and intropunitive must be either hysteroid or obsessoid, and conversely. The whole universe is, therefore, covered by the four classes – extrapunitive-hysteroids; intropunitive-hysteroids; extrapunitive-obsessoids; and intropunitive-obsessoids. Some evidence will be provided to show that the two dimensions are probably not orthogonal. Extrapunitiveness and hysteroidness appear to be associated, so that the *E-H* and the *I-O* classes will have higher membership.

SUMMARY

The necessary and sufficient conditions for distinguishing groups within the classes of schizophrenia, of integrated psychosis, and of neurosis have been described.

SSI scales for making these distinctions were shown for integrated psychosis and neurosis only. The distinctions within the psychoses were rather better than within the neuroses, though only the hysteria-depression differentiation could be said to be poor. The general conclusion would appear to be that agreement between the SSI and the clinical

A Quantitative Classification

diagnosis is about the same as between psychiatrists, which is all one can hope for.

The items which turned up in the empirical scales for the various differential diagnoses were rather congruent with clinical expectation. This was borne out to some extent by the frequency with which these items came from the appropriate *a priori* scale or an obviously neighbourly one.

REFERENCES

BALLET. (1892). Sur le caractère de certaines idées de persécution, etc. (Congrès de Blois.) *Le Mercredi Méd.*, **33**. (Quoted by A. J. Lewis, 1934.)

BLEULER, E. (1924). *Textbook of psychiatry.* (4th edn.) New York: Macmillan.

CHAPMAN, J. & MCGHIE, A. (1962). A comparative study of disordered attention in schizophrenia. *J. ment. Sci.*, **108**, 487.

ENOCH, D. & IRVING, G. (1962). The Ganser syndrome. *Acta Scandinavica*, **38**, 213.

FOULDS, G. A. (1964). Organization and hostility in the thematic apperception test stories of schizophrenics. *Brit. J. Psychiat.*, **110**, 64.

FOULDS, G. A., DIXON, P. M., MCCLELLAND, M. & MCCLELLAND, W. J. (1962). The nature of intellectual deficit in schizophrenia, II. A cross-sectional study of paranoid, catatonic, hebephrenic and simple schizophrenics. *Brit. J. soc. clin. Psychol.*, **1**, 141.

FOULDS, G. A. & DIXON, P. M. (1962). The nature of intellectual deficit in schizophrenia, III. A longitudinal study of the sub-groups. *Brit. J. soc. clin. Psychol.*, **1**, 199.

FREUD, S. (1926). *Inhibitions, symptoms and anxiety.* London: Hogarth Press, 1948.

FREUD, S. (1933). *New introductory lectures on psychoanalysis.* London: Hogarth; New York: Norton.

LEWIS, A. J. (1934). Melancholia: a clinical survey of depressive states. *J. ment. Sci.*, **802**, 77.

SÉGLAS. (1892). Idées de persécution. (Congrès de Blois.) *Le Mercredi Méd.*, **33**. (Quoted by A. J. Lewis, 1934.)

SHAKOW, D. (1962). Segmental set. *Arch. gen. Psychiat.*, **6**, 1.

STODDART, W. H. B. (1921). *Mind and its disorders.* (4th edn.) London: H. K. Lewis.

CHAPTER EIGHT

Comparisons between Psychotic and Neurotic Groups

Since there will be a percentage of cases in which no decision will be possible as between psychosis and neurosis, it is desirable to proceed to the nine possible comparisons between the psychotic and neurotic sub-groups.

The following scales involve comparisons between a psychotic and a neurotic group:

Schizophrenia v. Hysteria (Sc v. Hy) scale
Items given more frequently by schizophrenics:
  A 5
  E 6
  F 2, 4, 7, 9, 10

Items given more frequently by hysterics:
  A 8
  G 5, 6, 8

Schizophrenia v. Anxiety (Sc v. Ax) scale
Items given more frequently by schizophrenics:
  B 3
  F 2, 4, 5, 7, 9, 10
  G 9

Items given more frequently by anxiety states:
  A 1, 2, 3, 4, 8
  G 3, 5

Schizophrenia v. Depression (Sc v. Dp) scale
Items given more frequently by schizophrenics:
  D 3, 8, 10
  E 2, 5, 6
  F 2, 4, 5, 7, 9, 10
  G 9

157

Items given more frequently by depressives:

  A 8

  B 4

  G 5, 6

Paranoid v. *Hysteria (Pa* v. *Hy) scale*

Items given more frequently by paranoids:

  D 3, 4, 6, 7, 9, 10

  E 9

  F 4, 7

Items given more frequently by hysterics:

  A 2, 6, 7, 8

  B 4, 10

  G 5

Paranoid v. *Anxiety (Pa* v. *Ax) scale*

Items given more frequently by paranoids:

  D 1, 3, 4, 6, 7, 9, 10

  F 4, 7

Items given more frequently by anxiety states:

  A 1, 2, 3, 4, 6, 7, 8, 9

  B 1, 4

  C 2, 3, 4

  G 5

Paranoid v. *Depression (Pa* v. *Dp) scale*

Items given more frequently by paranoids:

  D 1, 2, 3, 4, 5, 6, 7, 8, 9, 10

  F 4, 5, 7, 8

Items given more frequently by depressives:

  A 6, 7, 8

  B 1, 2, 3, 4

Melancholia v. *Hysteria (Me* v. *Hy) scale*

Items given more frequently by melancholics:

  A 5

  B 2, 3

  F 8

  H 2, 3, 4, 5, 6, 7, 9, 10

Items given more frequently by hysterics:

A 7
C 1
E 1
G 5

Melancholia v. *Anxiety* (*Me* v. *Ax*) *scale*
Items given more frequently by melancholics:

B 3, 7
D 10
F 5, 8, 10
G 9
H 1, 2, 3, 4, 5, 6, 7, 8, 9, 10

Items given more frequently by anxiety states:

A 1, 3, 4, 7,
C 2, 4

Melancholia v. *Depression* (*Me* v. *Dp*) *scale*
Items given more frequently by melancholics:

A 6, 9
B 7, 10
D 10
F 5, 8, 10
G 9
H 1, 2, 4, 5, 6, 8, 9, 10

Items given more frequently by depressives:

A 7
B 1
E 3

Table 25 shows the distribution of scores on the Schizophrenia *v.* Hysteria scale. Cutting between 0 and 1, 91 per cent are classified in agreement with the psychiatric diagnosis and 9 per cent are in disagreement.

Table 26 shows the percentages of schizophrenics and of hysterics who claim to have each of the symptoms on this scale.

TABLE 25 *Distribution of scores on the Schizophrenia v. Hysteria scale of schizophrenic, hysteric, paranoid, melancholic, anxiety, and depressive groups*

Sc-Hy score	Sc 20	Hy 50	Pa 30	Me 50	Ax 50	Dp 50
6	2					
5			1	1		
4	3		1	1		
3	3		2	2		1
2	4	2	4	1	4	3
1	6	2	6	9	6	5
0	1	9	8	9	11	11
−1	1	13	7	16	20	16
−2		11	1	9	8	7
−3		10		2	1	5
−4		3				2
−5						

TABLE 26 *Percentages of schizophrenics and of hysterics claiming each symptom on the Schizophrenia v. Hysteria scale*

Item	Schizophrenics 20	Hysterics 50
A 5	60	24
E 6	45	12
F 2	35	4
F 4	45	12
F 7	45	2
F 9	55	22
F 10	30	4
A 8	35	72
G 5	20	60
G 6	10	50
G 8	20	40

Schizophrenics, in contradistinction to hysterics, are characterized thus:

A 5 They are afraid of being in wide-open spaces or in enclosed places.

E 6 Distressing thoughts about sex or religion come into their mind against their will.

F 2 They sometimes see visions, or people, animals, or things around them that other people don't seem to see.

F 4 They sometimes have very strange and peculiar experiences.

F 7 They sometimes hear voices without knowing where they come from.

F 9 They sometimes have very strange and peculiar thoughts.

F 10 There is something unusual about their body, like one side being different from the other and meaning something different.

The hysteric, on the other hand, is characterized by the following symptoms:

A 8 She has difficulty in getting off to sleep (without sleeping pills).

G 5 She sometimes has black-outs, dizzy spells, or faints.

G 6 She has been in poor health during most of the past few years.

G 8 She is often bothered with pains over her heart, in her chest, or in her back.

Thus 72 per cent of the items come from the appropriate *a priori* scales.

Table 27 gives the score distribution on the Schizophrenia *v.* Anxiety scale. Treating 0 and −1 as non-discriminating scores, 16 per cent of the schizophrenic-anxiety group remain unallocated and the other 84 per cent are classified in agreement with the psychiatric diagnosis.

TABLE 27 *Distribution of scores on the Schizophrenia v. Anxiety scale of schizophrenic, anxiety, paranoid, melancholic, hysteric, and depressive groups*

Sc-Ax score	Sc 20	Ax 50	Pa 30	Me 50	Hy 50	Dp 50
5	2					
4	1					
3	3			2		
2	2		4	4		2
1	6		5	3	2	1
0	2	3	7	9	5	6
−1	4	2	11	12	11	7
−2		10	2	4	7	11
−3		9	1	10	11	8
−4		11		4	10	9
−5		9		2	2	3
−6		6			2	3

Table 28 shows the percentages of schizophrenics and of anxiety states giving each of the symptoms on this scale.

TABLE 28 *Percentages of schizophrenics and of anxiety states claiming each symptom on the Schizophrenia v. Anxiety scale*

Item	Schizophrenics 20	Anxiety states 50
B 3	40	10
F 2	35	4
F 4	45	12
F 5	55	20
F 7	45	2
F 9	55	18
F 10	30	0
G 9	45	12
A 1	40	66
A 2	30	58
A 3	40	72
A 4	35	80
A 8	35	70
G 3	5	32
G 5	20	52

The schizophrenic is characterized thus:[1]

B 3   She has attempted to do away with herself.
F 2, 4, 7, 9, 10
F 5   She thinks other people regard her as very odd.
G 9   She sometimes does things in a dream-like state without remembering afterwards what she has been doing.

And the anxiety state by the following symptoms:

A 1   Her hand often shakes when she tries to do something.
A 2   She sweats very easily, even on cool days.
A 3   She suffers from palpitations or breathlessness.

[1] Items are given in full the first time that they occur in this chapter. Subsequently, to avoid undue repetition, they are referred to by number only.

A 4 There are times when she feels anxious without knowing the reason.
A 8
G 3 She sometimes completely loses her voice.
G 5

Thus 73 per cent of the items are from the appropriate *a priori* scales. Six of the items in the *a priori* Schizophrenia scale are given significantly more often by schizophrenics than by anxiety states, and the opposite holds for 5 of the items from the *a priori* Anxiety scale. Schizophrenics more often claim to have attempted suicide.

Table 29 gives the distribution of scores on the Schizophrenia *v.* Depression scale. Treating scores of 0 to +2 as uncertain, 67 per cent of schizophrenics and neurotic depressives are allocated in agreement with the clinical diagnosis, 26 per cent are uncertain, and 7 per cent are allocated in disagreement.

TABLE 29 *Distribution of scores on the Schizophrenia v. Depression scale of schizophrenic, depressive, paranoid, melancholic, hysteric, and anxiety groups*

Sc-Dp score	Sc 20	Dp 50	Pa 30	Me 50	Hy 50	Ax 50
10	2					
9						
8			2			
7	1		1	1		
6	1	1	2	1		1
5	4		2	1		
4	2		2	3	1	1
3	3	3	6	4	2	4
2	2	3	4	2	5	1
1	1	3	6	5	7	4
0	3	6	2	13	7	10
−1	1	12	2	13	11	18
−2		10	1	5	10	8
−3		5		2	6	3
−4		7		1		

163

A Quantitative Classification

Table 30 shows the percentages of schizophrenics and of depressives claiming each symptom on the Schizophrenia *v.* Depression scale.

TABLE 30 *Percentages of schizophrenics and of depressives claiming each symptom on the Schizophrenia v. Depression scale*

Item	Schizophrenics 20	Depressives 50
D 3	25	8
D 8	20	4
D 10	20	6
E 2	35	6
E 5	30	10
E 6	45	16
F 2	35	10
F 4	45	10
F 5	55	16
F 7	45	6
F 9	45	20
F 10	30	2
G 9	45	12
A 8	35	70
B 4	40	76
G 5	20	46
G 6	10	36

The schizophrenic:

D 3 There are people who are trying to harm her through no fault of her own.

D 8 She sometimes takes strong action against an evil person for the sake of a principle.

D 10 People can read her thoughts and make her do things against her will by a sort of hypnotism.

E 2 She is *compelled* to think over abstract problems again and again until she can't leave them alone.

164

E 5 She is afraid she might do something seriously wrong against her will.

E 6

F 2, 4, 5, 7, 9, 10

G 9

The depressive:

A 8

B 4 The simplest task is too much of an effort.

G 5, 6

Thirteen items are given significantly more often by schizophrenics, and of these 6 come from the *a priori* Schizophrenic scale and 3 from the Paranoid. All 4 symptoms given more often by depressives come from *a priori* neurotic scales.

Table 31 shows the distribution of scores on the Paranoid *v.* Hysteria scale: 88 per cent are in agreement with the psychiatric diagnosis, 8 per cent in disagreement, and 4 per cent (at score of 0) uncertain.

TABLE 31 *Distribution of scores on the Paranoid v. Hysteria scale of paranoid, hysteric, schizophrenic, melancholic, anxiety, and depressive groups*

Pa-Hy score	Pa 30	Hy 50	Sc 20	Me 50	Ax 50	Dp 50
6	2					
5	4					
4	8		1			
3	6		1	1		
2	2	1	1			
1	2		4	3	1	1
0	1	2	4	5	5	5
−1	3	11	3	10	7	8
−2	2	7	2	8	7	7
−3		7	4	7	12	14
−4		15		8	7	4
−5		5		7	7	9
−6		2		1	1	2
−7					3	

Table 32 shows the percentages of paranoids and of hysterics who claim to have each symptom on the Paranoid *v.* Hysteria scale.

TABLE 32.   *Percentages of paranoids and of hysterics claiming each symtom on the Paranoid v. Hysteria scale*

Item	Paranoids 30	Hysterics 50
D 3	67	14
D 4	30	4
D 6	60	6
D 7	63	4
D 9	50	16
D 10	50	6
E 9	30	12
F 4	33	12
F 7	40	2
A 2	27	50
A 6	10	42
A 7	13	40
A 8	43	72
B 4	23	62
B 10	7	28
G 5	27	60

The paranoid:

D 3, 10

D 4   Someone is trying to poison her or make her ill in some way.

D 6   Someone, other than herself, is deliberately causing most of her troubles.

D 7   People are plotting against her through no fault of her own.

D 9   She sometimes sees someone do or say something which most people do not take much notice of, but which she knows has a special meaning.

E 9   She is *excessively* concerned about cleanliness.

F 4, 7

166

The hysteric:

A 2, 8
A 6   She is afraid that she might be going insane.
A 7   She has a pain, or feeling of tension, in the back of her neck.
B 4
B 10 She has seriously thought of doing away with herself because she is no longer able to cope with her difficulties.
G 5

There are thus 9 symptoms given more frequently by paranoids and, of these, 6 come from the *a priori* Paranoid scale, and 2 from the Schizophrenia scale. All 7 of the items given more often by hysterics are from *a priori* neurotic scales.

Table 33 gives the score distribution on the Paranoid *v*. Anxiety scale for all groups: 90 per cent are allocated in agreement with the psychiatric diagnosis and 4 per cent in disagreement, leaving 6 per cent (at score −2) uncertain.

TABLE 33   *Distribution of scores on the Paranoid v. Anxiety scale of paranoid, anxiety, schizophrenic, melancholic, hysteric, and depressive groups*

Pa-Ax score	Pa 30	Ax 50	Sc 20	Me 50	Hy 50	Dp 50
6	1					
5	1					
4	3					
3	6		1			
2	4					
1	5		1			
0	3		1	1	1	
−1	3	1	7	1	4	3
−2	2	3	1	10	5	3
−3	1	3	5	7	2	3
−4	1	2	1	5	7	10
−5		8	2	12	9	7
−6		7		7	6	5
−7		4		5	9	5
−8		10	1	1	4	6
−9		2		1	1	7
−10		4			2	
−11		4				1
−12		2				

A Quantitative Classification

Table 34 shows the percentages of paranoids and of anxiety states claiming each symptom on the Paranoid *v.* Anxiety scale.

TABLE 34 *Percentages of paranoids and of anxiety states claiming each symptom on the Paranoid* v. *Anxiety scale*

Item		Paranoids 30	Anxiety states 50
D	1	63	12
D	3	67	4
D	4	30	0
D	6	60	6
D	7	63	0
D	9	50	12
D	10	50	4
F	4	33	12
F	7	40	2
A	1	23	66
A	2	27	58
A	3	40	72
A	4	47	80
A	6	10	44
A	7	13	50
A	8	43	70
A	9	20	66
B	1	47	66
B	4	23	60
C	2	0	14
C	3	0	16
C	4	3	32
G	5	27	52

The paranoid:

D 1 People are talking about her and criticizing her through no fault of her own.

D 3, 4, 6, 7, 9, 10

F 4, 7

168

The anxiety state:

A 1, 2, 3, 4, 6, 7, 8
A 9 She is afraid of going out alone.
B 1 She cries rather easily.
B 4
C 2 She sometimes becomes very excitedly happy for no special reason.
C 3 She is sometimes so cheerful that she wants to laugh and joke with *everyone*.
C 4 There are times when exciting new ideas and schemes occur to her one after another.
G 5

There are 9 symptoms given more frequently by paranoids, 7 of these being from the *a priori* Paranoid scale and the remaining 2 from the Schizophrenic scale. Of the 14 symptoms given more frequently by anxiety states, 8 are from the *a priori* Anxiety scale.

Table 35 shows the distribution of scores on the Paranoid *v.* Depression scale: 88 per cent are allocated in agreement with the psychiatric diagnosis, 4 per cent in disagreement, and 8 per cent (at score of 0) are uncertain.

TABLE 35 *Distribution of scores on the Paranoid v. Depression scale of paranoid, depressive, schizophrenic, melancholic, hysteric, and anxiety groups*

Pa-Dp score	Pa 30	Dp 50	Sc 20	Me 50	Hy 50	Ax 50
9	1					
8	2					
7	7					
6	2					
5	4		2			
4	4		2	1	1	1
3	2	1	2	3	2	
2	1		4	3	1	2
1	2		*1*	2	3	2
0	3	3		6	5	2
−1	1	6	4	9	10	5
−2	1	11	3	*13*	*14*	12
−3		7	1	8	4	*14*
−4		10	1	3	4	5
−5		8		2	5	5
−6		3				
−7		1				2

A Quantitative Classification

Table 36 shows the percentages of paranoids and of depressives giving each symptom on the Paranoid *v*. Depression scale.

TABLE 36 *Percentage of paranoids and of depressives claiming each symptom on the Paranoid* v. *Depression scale*

Item	Paranoids 30	Depressives 50
D 1	63	16
D 2	17	0
D 3	67	8
D 4	30	2
D 5	27	4
D 6	60	14
D 7	63	0
D 8	30	6
D 9	50	10
D 10	50	6
F 4	33	10
F 5	40	16
F 7	40	6
F 8	40	18
A 6	10	38
A 7	13	38
A 8	43	70
B 1	47	68
B 2	33	60
B 3	7	40
B 4	23	76

The paranoid:

D 1, 3, 4, 6, 7, 8, 9, 10
D 2 She has an important mission to carry out.
D 5 She has some special power, ability, or influence which is not recognized by other people.
F 4, 5, 7
F 8 She feels that she cannot communicate with other people because she doesn't seem to be on the same wave-length.

170

The depressive:

A 6, 7, 8
B 1, 3, 4
B 2 She has lost interest in almost everything.

There are thus 14 symptoms given significantly more often by paranoids – all 10 from the *a priori* Paranoid scale and 4 from the Schizophrenic. There are 7 symptoms given more frequently by the depressives, 4 being from the *a priori* Depressive scale and 3 from the Anxiety scale.

Table 37 shows the distribution of scores on the Melancholia *v.* Hysteria scale: 82 per cent are allocated in agreement with the psychiatric diagnosis, and 18 per cent in disagreement.

TABLE 37 *Distribution of scores on the Melancholia v. Hysteria scale of melancholic, hysteric, schizophrenic, paranoid, anxiety, and depressive groups*

Me-Hy score	Me 50	Hy 50	Sc 20	Pa 30	Ax 50	Dp 50
11	1					
10	1					
9	4	1	1			2
8	3	2	1	1	1	3
7	9	1	2			1
6	9	2	1	5	1	3
5	10	4	4	1	2	4
4	6	1	2	4	3	6
3	1	4	1	3	9	12
2	1	4	2	3	14	7
1	3	10	3	5	6	5
0	2	11	1	6	8	4
−1		7	2	2	4	2
−2		2			2	
−3						1
−4		1				

A Quantitative Classification

Table 38 shows the percentages of melancholics and of hysterics claiming each symptom on the scale.

TABLE 38   *Percentages of melancholics and of hysterics claiming each symptom on the Melancholia v. Hysteria scale*

Item		Melancholics 50	Hysterics 50
A	5	46	24
B	2	64	44
B	3	40	20
F	8	56	24
H	2	72	26
H	3	20	2
H	4	44	12
H	5	66	48
H	6	42	10
H	7	56	36
H	9	56	22
H	10	66	40
A	7	18	40
C	1	0	12
E	1	8	30
G	5	36	60

The melancholic:

A 5
B 2, 3
F 8
H 2   She is an unworthy person in her own eyes.
H 3   She has some bodily condition which she finds disgusting.
H 4   She is a condemned person because of her sins.
H 5   She is troubled by waking in the early hours and being unable to get off to sleep again.
H 6   Because of things she has done wrong, people are talking about her and criticizing her.
H 7   She is sometimes so low in spirits that she just sits for hours on end.
H 9   She sometimes gets so worked up that she paces about the room wringing her hands.
H 10   She sometimes goes to bed feeling she wouldn't care if she never woke up again.

172

The hysteric:

A 7
C 1 She sometimes feels so confident and successful that there is nothing she can't achieve.
E 1 She is *distressed* by silly, pointless thoughts that keep coming into her mind against her will.
G 5

There are thus 12 symptoms given more often by melancholics, and of these 8 come from the *a priori* Melancholic scale.

Table 39 gives the distribution of scores on the Melancholia *v*. Anxiety scale. Thus 88 per cent of cases are diagnosed in agreement with the clinical assessment, 9 per cent are in disagreement, and 3 per cent (at score 3) remain uncertain.

TABLE 39 *Distribution of scores on the Melancholia v. Anxiety scale of melancholic, anxiety, schizophrenic, paranoid, hysteric, and depressive groups*

Me-Ax score	Me 50	Ax 50	Sc 20	Pa 30	Hy 50	Dp 50
12	3					
11	3			1		
10	2		1	1	1	
9	3		1	1	1	1
8	4		2			2
7	6		2	1	1	3
6	7	1	3	3	3	
5	9		1	1	1	2
4	5	1	1	3	5	4
3	1	2	*1*	5	4	5
2		5	2	2	7	7
1	1	10	4	4	7	*10*
0	2	9		5	8	7
−1	4	12	2	2	8	2
−2		4		1	3	4
−3		5			1	2
−4						
−5		1				

Table 40 shows the percentages of melancholics and of anxiety states who claim to have each of the symptoms on this scale.

TABLE 40 *Percentages of melancholics and of anxiety states claiming each symptom on the Melancholia v. Anxiety scale*

Item		Melancholics 50	Anxiety states 50
B	3	40	10
B	7	62	38
D	10	20	4
F	5	50	20
F	8	56	22
F	10	20	0
G	9	30	12
H	1	42	24
H	2	72	20
H	3	20	0
H	4	44	6
H	5	66	44
H	6	42	10
H	7	56	24
H	8	30	8
H	9	56	36
H	10	66	26
A	1	42	66
A	3	42	72
A	4	46	80
A	7	18	50
C	2	2	14
C	4	10	32

The melancholic:

B 3
B 7 The future seems pointless.
D 10
F 5, 8, 10
G 9
H 1 She is worried about having said things that have injured others.
H 8 She causes harm to people because of what she is.
H 2, 3, 4, 5, 6, 7, 9, 10

The anxiety state:

A 1, 3, 4, 7
C 2, 4

There are 17 symptoms given significantly more often by melancholics than by anxiety states, including all 10 of the *a priori* Melancholic scale. Four out of the 6 symptoms given more often by anxiety states come from the *a priori* Anxiety scale.

Table 41 gives the distribution of scores on the Melancholia *v*. Depression scale. Treating scores of 3, 4, and 5 as non-discriminating, there are 19 per cent of cases about which no decision can be made, 66 per cent are allocated in agreement with the psychiatric diagnosis, and 15 per cent in disagreement.

TABLE 41 *Distribution of scores on the Melancholia* v. *Depression scale of melancholic, depressive, schizophrenic, paranoid, hysteric, and anxiety groups*

Me-Dp score	Me 50	Dp 50	Sc 20	Pa 30	Hy 50	Ax 50
14	1					
13	2					
12	4		1		1	
11	3	1		1	1	
10	5		1	1	2	
9	2	1			1	1
8	5	3	4	2	2	1
7	5	2	3	1	1	2
6	8	3	1	4	2	3
5	2	6	1	4	6	5
4	5	2	2	2	6	5
3	3	1		1	4	7
2		6	2	1	3	6
1	3	11	2	6	8	8
0	2	10	1	3	9	9
−1		2	2	3	3	3
−2		2		1	1	

A Quantitative Classification

Table 42 shows the percentages of melancholics and of depressives who claim to have each of the symptoms on the scale.

TABLE 42 *Percentages of melancholics and of depressives claiming each symptom on the Melancholia v. Depression scale*

Item	Melancholics 50	Depressives 50
A 6	56	38
A 9	52	32
B 7	62	40
B 10	36	24
D 10	20	6
F 5	50	16
F 8	56	18
F 10	20	2
G 9	30	12
H 1	42	16
H 2	72	22
H 4	44	12
H 5	66	40
H 6	42	4
H 8	30	6
H 9	56	30
H 10	66	38
A 7	18	38
B 1	48	68
E 3	12	30

The melancholic:

A 6, 9
B 7, 10
D 10
F 5, 8, 10
G 9
H 1, 2, 4, 5, 6, 8, 9, 10

The depressive:

A 7
B 1
E 3 She is *unnecessarily* careful in carrying out even simple everyday tasks, like folding up clothes, reading notices, etc.

176

Comparisons between Psychotic and Neurotic Groups

There are thus 17 symptoms given more commonly by psychotic than by neurotic depressives; of these 8 come from the *a priori* Melancholia scale. There are only 3 symptoms given more often by the neurotic depressives, one of which is from the *a priori* Depressive scale.

Table 43 shows the overall comparison of clinical and SSI diagnoses. To obtain the final SSI diagnosis for any individual, her score is assessed on each of the fifteen possible pairs resulting from the comparison between any two of the six groups: schizophrenia; paranoid; melancholia; hysteria; anxiety state; and depression. On each of these fifteen scales she is allocated to one or other of the pair, or recorded as 'uncertain' as between any particular pair. Her final SSI diagnosis is that of the group to which she is most frequently allocated. In the event of a tie, it is simply recorded that, on the basis of the SSI, the differential diagnosis lies between A and B, but between these no decision can be made.

TABLE 43 *Overall comparison of clinical and SSI diagnoses*

SSI	Sc	Pa	Me	Hy	Ax	Dp	Total		Agree %	Un-certain %	Dis-agree %
Sc	14	1			1	1	17	Sc	70	5	25
Pa		22	2	1			25	Pa	73	0	27
Me	3	1	39	9	2	9	63	Me	78	2	20
Hy	1	2		20	4	3	30	Hy	40	16	44
Ax	1	1	1	8	34	4	49	Ax	68	4	28
Dp		2	4	3	5	25	39	Dp	50	16	34
?+	1		1	8	2	8	20	Total	62	8	31
?−		1	3	1	2		7				
	20	30	50	50	50	50	250				

The column headers under *Clinical diagnosis* are: Sc, Pa, Me, Hy, Ax, Dp, Total.

?+ = Uncertain, but when the clinical diagnosis was one of the pair.
?− = Uncertain, but when the clinical diagnosis was *not* one of the pair.

It can be seen that the SSI diagnosis is more often in agreement with the clinical diagnosis when this is a psychotic diagnosis. The main weakness lies in the low level of agreement when the clinical diagnosis is one of depression or hysteria.

177

A Quantitative Classification

In relation to the psychiatric diagnosis, melancholics are being over-diagnosed by the SSI; anxiety states are about right; paranoids, schizophrenics, and depressives are very slightly under-diagnosed, and hysterics decidedly under-diagnosed. The excess of melancholics is almost entirely due to psychiatrically diagnosed hysterics and depressives. It may well be that the 'real' hysterics and depressives are in the main being correctly diagnosed by the SSI and that these misfits are, in fact, the depressives alias psychopaths discussed in Chapter 5, who produce pseudo-symptoms or who grossly exaggerate symptoms on admission in order to gain 'serious' attention. This is sufficiently familiar as to have been named the 'hello response'.

DISTINCTION BETWEEN FREQUENCY OF OCCURRENCE AND DIFFERENTIATING POWER OF SYMPTOMS

Students of psychiatry often complain that, after reading many text-books, they come away with the impression that everything occurs in everything. This confusion is generated because most authors fail to distinguish adequately between the frequency of occurrence of symptoms in a particular class and their differentiating power as between classes. The difficulty can be illustrated by the responses to certain items of the SSI. Consider the percentages of women complaining of the following symptoms in relation to the following scheme of classification:

A symptom is *very common* if it is given by 65 per cent or more of a particular class, and *common* if given by 40 to 64 per cent; it is *rare* if given by 15 to 39 per cent, and *very rare* if given by less than 15 per cent.

Differentiae are symptoms which distinguish at least at the 5 per cent level of significance between the class in question and any other single class. *Specific differentiae* are symptoms which distinguish at least at the 5 per cent level between the class in question and at least 67 per cent of all classes with which it is being compared.

Differentiae will be referred to as *positive* when the class in question is distinguished by a higher frequency of the symptom than the group or groups with which it is being compared. They will be referred to as *negative* when the class in question is distinguished by a lower frequency of the symptom than the group or groups with which it is being compared.

Comparisons between Psychotic and Neurotic Groups

B6   I have found it difficult to concentrate recently.

Hy 60; *Ax* 64; *Dp* 64; *Me* 64; *Pa* 57; *Sc* 50

This is a *common*, but – within the universe of the personally ill – *non-differentiating* symptom as between the six groups examined. All groups fall within the 40 to 64 percentage necessary for classification as a common symptom, and no one group is significantly different from any other one at the 5 per cent level of significance.

B5   I am depressed because of a particular loss or disappointment.

Hy 24; *Ax* 24; *Dp* 26; *Me* 24; *Pa* 27; *Sc* 35

This is a *rare* and *non-differentiating* symptom, in spite of what is usually written in textbooks about reactive depression.

H2   I am an unworthy person in my own eyes.

Hy 26; *Ax* 20; *Dp* 22; *Me* 72; *Pa* 30; *Sc* 40

This is a *very common* symptom in melancholia and a *positive specific differentia* in that it differentiates melancholics from all other groups. From the point of view of the other groups, it is a *rare negative differentia* in that it is the relative absence of this symptom that differentiates them from melancholics; but it does not differentiate any one of them from the others.

F2   I sometimes see visions, etc., that others don't seem to see.

Hy 4; *Ax* 4; *Dp* 10; *Me* 10; *Pa* 10; *Sc* 35

This is *rare* in schizophrenics; but it is *very rare* in the other five groups. It differentiates schizophrenics from all these groups. It is, therefore, a *rare positive specific differentia*. For the five groups it is a *very rare negative differentia*, since the absence of this symptom differentiates each of them from schizophrenics.

A8   I have difficulty in getting off to sleep.

Hy 72; *Ax* 70; *Dp* 70; *Me* 78; *Pa* 43; *Sc* 35

This symptom is *very common* in four groups, *common* in one, and *rare* in another one. Since it differentiates paranoids and schizophrenics from the other four groups, it is a *common* (or *rare*) *negative specific differentia*. For the other groups, it is a *very common positive differentia*, since each group significantly exceeds the paranoids and schizophrenics, but no other group.

B10   I have seriously thought of doing away with myself, etc.

Hy 28; *Ax* 22; *Dp* 24; *Me* 36; *Pa* 7; *Sc* 40

This symptom is *common* among schizophrenics, *very rare* among paranoids, and *rare* among the rest. For paranoids it is a *very rare negative specific differentia*.

179

A Quantitative Classification

Each group will be described only by symptoms which are specific differentiae, whether positive or negative, common or rare.

Schizophrenics

Positive common specific differentiae

F 4   I sometimes have very strange and peculiar experiences.

F 7   I sometimes hear voices without knowing where they come from.

Positive rare specific differentia

F 2   I sometimes see visions, etc., that others don't seem to see.

Negative rare specific differentia

A 8   I (do *not*) have difficulty in getting off to sleep.

Paranoids

Positive very common specific differentia

D 3   There are people who are trying to harm me through no fault of my own.

Positive common specific differentiae

D 1   People are talking about me and criticizing me through no fault of my own.

D 7   People are plotting against me through no fault of my own.

D 6   Someone, other than myself, is deliberately causing most of my troubles.

D 9   I sometimes see someone do or say something which most people do not take much notice of, but which I know has a special meaning.

D 10   People can read my thoughts and make me do things against my will by a sort of hypnotism.

F 7   I sometimes hear voices without knowing where they come from.

Positive rare specific differentia

D 4   Someone is trying to poison me or make me ill in some way.

Negative common specific differentia

A 8   I (do *not*) have difficulty in getting off to sleep.

Negative rare specific differentia

B 4   The simplest task is (*not*) too much of an effort.

Negative very rare specific differentia

A 6   I am (*not*) afraid that I might be going insane.

Comparisons between Psychotic and Neurotic Groups

Melancholics

Positive very common specific differentiae

H 2 I am an unworthy person in my own eyes.

H 5 I am troubled by waking in the early hours and being unable to get off to sleep again (though much of this is attributable to age).

H 10 I sometimes go to bed feeling I wouldn't care if I never woke up again

Positive common specific differentiae

B 7 The future seems pointless.

H 9 I sometimes get so worked up that I pace about the room wringing my hands.

H 4 I am a condemned person because of my sins.

H 6 Because of things I have done wrong, people are talking about me and criticizing me.

Positive rare specific differentia

H 8 I cause harm to people because of what I am.

Anxiety States

Positive very common specific differentiae

A 4 There are times when I feel anxious without knowing the reason.

A 1 My hand often shakes when I try to do something.

A 9 I am afraid of going out alone.

Positive rare specific differentia

C 4 There are times when exciting new ideas and schemes occur to me one after the other.

Positive very rare specific differentia

C 2 I sometimes become very excitedly happy at times for no special reason.

There were no specific differentiae at all for either hysterics or depressives.

These descriptions give a very fair indication of the ease or difficulty with which different groups can be identified by means of the SSI. The greater difficulty experienced with neurotics is in line with the much greater unreliability between psychiatrists in diagnosing them.

Consideration of the characteristics of paranoids in particular makes it manifest that common and rare can only be interpreted in relation to the items as they are worded in this inventory. Obviously many of the symptoms could be more widely classified under the heading of 'delusions of persecution'.

Of the 24 positive specific differentiae, 20 came from the scale originally intended to be associated with the diagnosis in question. This lends some credence to the belief that information acquired clinically is not entirely devoid of utility.

SUMMARY

It has been argued that the evidence for the unreliability of psychiatric diagnosis is based on studies that have been poorly designed, and that the issue is still an open one. It is clear, however, that the routine diagnoses used in psychiatry are quite inadequate as a basis for furthering our knowledge of personal illness and that they must give way to some more public and quantitative instrument. This does not imply that the observations of psychiatrists as brilliant as Kraepelin cannot be used for the development of such an instrument; quite the contrary. It does not mean that the clinical interview does not serve other very valuable functions, nor is it implied that the Symptom-Sign Inventory is fully adequate as a quantitative instrument. It is hoped, however, that it does illustrate some of the problems at issue, and that the distinction between symptoms and signs on the one hand and personality traits on the other will aid progress in this field.

The results obtained with this inventory for 100 psychotics and 150 neurotics (women) have been described. The overall agreement with the clinical diagnosis was 62 per cent in the main sample and 50 per cent in a small additional sample of 68. In 8 and 13 per cent respectively, the diagnosis on the SSI was uncertain and in 31 and 37 per cent respectively, the SSI diagnosis was at variance with the clinical diagnosis.

As would be expected, diagnosis among neurotics was more difficult than among psychotics or between neurotics and psychotics. The SSI tended to over-diagnose melancholics and to under-diagnose hysterics; but it was thought that the latter might be a benign error.

Frequency tables in the various groups were used to distinguish between frequency of occurrence of a symptom in a particular group and its differential power as between groups. Utilizing this distinction, a description was given of the characteristics of six groups of women – schizophrenics, paranoids, melancholics, hysterics, anxiety states, and depressives – as derived from responses on the Symptom-Sign Inventory. Psychotics were better differentiated than neurotics.

APPENDIX C

The Symptom-Sign Inventory

(giving the percentages in each group answering 'yes')

	A priori Anxiety State scale	50 Hy	50 Ax	50 Dp	50 Me	30 Pa	20 Sc
A 1	Does your hand often shake when you try to do something?	46	66	40	42	23	40
A 2	Do you sweat very easily, even on cool days?	50	58	46	60	27	30
A 3	Do you suffer from palpitations or breathlessness?	62	72	54	42	40	40
A 4	Are there times when you feel anxious without knowing the reason?	58	80	50	46	47	35
A 5	Are you afraid of being in a wide-open space or in an enclosed place?	24	52	42	46	37	60
A 6	Are you afraid that you might be going insane?	42	44	38	56	10	40
A 7	Have you a pain, or feeling of tension, in the back of your neck?	40	50	38	18	13	30
A 8	Have you difficulty in getting off to sleep (without sleeping pills)?	72	70	70	78	43	35
A 9	Are you afraid of going out alone?	36	66	32	52	20	30
A 10	Have you any particular fear not already mentioned?	46	34	48	46	40	55
	Group totals	476	592	458	486	300	395
	Overall total			2707			

Hy = Hysteric; *Ax* = Anxiety state; *Dp* = Depressive; *Me* = Melancholic; *Pa* = Paranoid; *Sc* = Schizophrenic.

183

	A priori Neurotic Depression scale	50 Hy	50 Ax	50 Dp	50 Me	30 Pa	20 Sc
B 1	Do you cry rather easily?	60	66	68	48	47	55
B 2	Have you lost interest in almost everything?	44	52	60	64	33	55
B 3	Have you ever attempted to do away with yourself?	20	10	40	40	7	40
B 4	Is the simplest task too much of an effort?	62	60	76	60	23	40
B 5	Are you depressed because of some particular loss or disappointment?	24	24	26	24	27	35
B 6	Have you found it difficult to concentrate recently?	60	64	64	64	57	50
B 7	Does the future seem pointless?	40	38	40	62	27	35
B 8	Are you more absent-minded recently than you used to be?	50	68	64	74	57	45
B 9	Are you slower recently in everything you do than you used to be?	70	74	78	74	57	60
B 10	Do you ever seriously think of doing away with yourself because you are no longer able to cope with your difficulties?	28	22	24	36	7	40
	Group totals	458	478	536	546	342	455
	Overall total			2815			

A priori Manic scale		50 Hy	50 Ax	50 Dp	50 Me	30 Pa	20 Sc
C 1	Do you ever feel so confident and successful that there is nothing you can't achieve?	12	2	2	0	10	5
C 2	Do you ever become very excitedly happy at times for no special reason?	0	14	4	2	0	10
C 3	Are you ever so cheerful that you want to laugh and joke with *everyone*?	10	16	4	6	0	15
C 4	Are there times when exciting new ideas and schemes occur to you one after another?	10	32	8	10	3	10
C 5	Are you ever so full of pep and energy that you carry on doing things indefinitely?	4	14	0	4	17	5
C 6	Do you ever become so excited that your thoughts race ahead faster than you can express them?	22	26	8	14	13	20
C 7	Are you ever so cheerful that you want to wear lots of gay things, like button-holes, flowers, bright ties, jewellery, etc.?	2	6	8	4	7	20
C 8	When you get bored, do you ever like to stir up some excitement?	4	8	2	6	7	20
C 9	Do you ever feel so full of energy that you don't want to go to bed?	2	6	2	2	7	20
C 10	Are you a much more important person than most people seem to think?	2	6	2	4	13	15
Group totals		68	140	40	52	77	145
Overall total				522			

A priori Paranoid scale	50 Hy	50 Ax	50 Dp	50 Me	30 Pa	20 Sc
D 1 Are people talking about you and criticizing you through no fault of your own?	44	12	16	28	63	30
D 2 Have you an important mission to carry out?	4	2	0	0	17	15
D 3 Are there people who are trying to harm you through no fault of your own?	14	4	8	8	67	25
D 4 Is someone trying to poison you or make you ill in some way?	4	0	2	2	30	10
D 5 Have you some special power, ability, or influence which is not recognized by other people?	8	2	4	8	27	10
D 6 Is someone, other than yourself, deliberately causing most of your troubles?	6	6	14	14	60	20
D 7 Are people plotting against you through no fault of your own?	4	0	0	6	63	15
D 8 Do you ever take strong action against an evil person for the sake of a principle?	10	12	6	4	30	20
D 9 Do you ever see someone do or say something which most people do not take much notice of, but which you know has a special meaning?	16	12	10	26	50	30
D 10 Can people read your thoughts and make you do things against your will by a sort of hypnotism?	6	4	6	20	50	20
Group totals	116	54	66	116	457	195
Overall total			1004			

A priori Obsessional scale	50 Hy	50 Ax	50 Dp	50 Me	30 Pa	20 Sc
E 1 Are you *distressed* by silly, pointless thoughts that keep coming into your mind against your will?	30	22	14	8	20	30
E 2 Are you *compelled* to think over abstract problems again and again until you can't leave them alone?	12	20	6	10	20	35
E 3 Are you *unnecessarily* careful in carrying out even simple everyday tasks, like folding up clothes, reading notices, etc.	16	18	30	12	23	15
E 4 Are you unable to prevent yourself from doing pointless things—like tapping lamp-posts, touching things, counting windows, uttering phrases, etc.?	6	14	12	14	10	15
E 5 Are you afraid you might do something seriously wrong against your will?	30	20	10	20	13	30
E 6 Do distressing thoughts about sex or religion come into your mind against your will?	12	26	16	14	23	45
E 7 Do you feel you just have to check things again and again – like turning off taps or lights, shutting windows at night, etc. – although you know there is really no need to?	28	34	22	28	27	35
E 8 Have you an *unreasonable* fear that some careless act of yours might have very serious consequences?	18	14	10	16	27	25
E 9 Are you *excessively* concerned about cleanliness?	12	16	28	18	30	10

187

A priori Obsessional scale	50 Hy	50 Ax	50 Dp	50 Me	30 Pa	20 Sc
E 10 Do you have an uneasy feeling that if you don't do something in a certain order, or a certain number of times, something might go wrong?	14	16	18	12	23	30
Group totals	178	200	166	152	216	270
Overall total			1182			

A priori Schizophrenia scale	50 Hy	50 Ax	50 Dp	50 Me	30 Pa	20 Sc
F 1 Do you feel that there is some sort of barrier between you and other people so that you can't really understand them?	26	26	22	40	40	45
F 2 Do you ever see visions, or people, animals, or things around you that other people don't seem to see?	4	4	10	10	10	35
F 3 Do you often wonder who you really are?	16	12	6	22	17	35
F 4 Do you ever have very strange and peculiar experiences?	12	12	10	18	33	45
F 5 Do you think other people regard you as very odd?	36	20	16	50	40	55
F 6 Do you often feel puzzled, as if something has gone wrong either with you or with the world, without knowing just what it is?	44	36	36	44	43	55
F 7 Do you ever hear voices without knowing where they come from?	2	2	6	10	40	45
F 8 Do you feel that you cannot communicate with other people because you don't seem to be on the same wave-length?	24	22	18	56	40	45
F 9 Do you have very strange and peculiar thoughts at times?	22	18	20	32	37	55
F 10 Is there something unusual about your body – like one side being different from the other and meaning something different?	4	0	2	20	10	30
Group totals	190	152	146	302	310	445
Overall total			1545			

A priori Hysteria scale	50 Hy	50 Ax	50 Dp	50 Me	30 Pa	20 Sc
G 1 Do you ever lose the use of an arm or leg or face muscle?	18	14	4	16	10	10
G 2 Do you ever have fits or have difficulty in keeping your balance?	40	32	18	18	20	25
G 3 Do you ever completely lose your voice (except from a cold)?	18	32	14	18	13	5
G 4 Do you ever lose all feeling in any part of your skin, so that you would not be able to feel a pin-prick; or do you ever have burning or tingling sensations under your skin?	46	30	28	22	30	35
G 5 Do you ever have black-outs, dizzy spells, or faints?	60	52	46	36	27	20
G 6 Have you been in poor physical health during most of the past few years?	50	16	36	32	37	10
G 7 Do you often suffer from blurring of vision or any other difficulty with your sight which no one seems able to put right?	32	32	16	24	20	35
G 8 Are you often bothered with pains over your heart, in your chest, or in your back?	40	32	28	32	28	20
G 9 Do you ever do things in a dream-like state without remembering afterwards what you have been doing?	30	12	12	30	27	45
G 10 Are you worried about your physical health?	34	30	34	40	33	40
Group totals	368	282	236	268	244	245
Overall total			1643			

A priori Melancholia scale	50 Hy	50 Ax	50 Dp	50 Me	30 Pa	20 Sc
H 1 Are you worried about having said things that have injured others?	24	24	16	42	27	40
H 2 Are you an unworthy person in your own eyes?	26	20	22	72	30	40
H 3 Have you some bodily condition which you find disgusting?	2	0	12	20	7	20
H 4 Are you a condemned person because of your sins?	12	6	12	44	20	30
H 5 Are you troubled by waking in the early hours and being unable to get off to sleep again (without sleeping pills)?	48	44	40	66	33	40
H 6 Because of things you have done wrong, are people talking about you and criticizing you?	10	10	4	42	27	10
H 7 Are you ever so low in spirits that you just sit for hours on end?	36	24	42	56	43	45
H 8 Do you cause harm to people because of what you are?	14	8	6	30	10	25
H 9 Are you ever so worked up that you pace about the room wringing your hands?	22	36	30	56	17	30
H 10 Do you ever go to bed feeling you wouldn't care if you never woke up again?	40	26	38	66	30	35
Group totals	234	198	222	494	244	315
Overall total			1707			

| GROUP GRAND TOTALS | 2088 | 2096 | 1870 | 2416 | 2190 | 2465 |

Empirical Studies utilizing the Distinction between Personality and Illness

CHAPTER NINE

Symptoms, Attitudes, Traits, and their Interrelationship

INTRODUCTION

It has now been established that various scales can be derived from the SSI to serve as criterion diagnostic measures and that the HOQ can serve as a criterion personality measure. Part III presents a number of studies utilizing the distinction between personality and illness. The plan is to work through the levels of classification previously described, where data are available.

Throughout it is predicted that those measures which are significantly associated with the criterion diagnostic measure will change significantly on re-testing for those cases regarded as much improved clinically, even after as short an interval as four to six weeks; whereas the criterion personality measure, and those measures significantly associated with it, will not change significantly. This follows from the earlier assertion that personality traits and attitudes are relatively more enduring than symptoms and signs of illness.

The present chapter describes a study in which nine other variables are related to the two criterion measures. The subjects were nearly all part of the second sample described in Chapter 6; those in Chapters 10, 11, and 12 were for the most part drawn from the 120 dealt with in this chapter.

PROCEDURE

Measurements

Eleven measurements from four tests are employed:

The criterion diagnostic measure from the SSI. There will, of course, be several of these, varying according to the particular study.

The hysteroid score derived from the HOQ, which serves as the criterion personality measure throughout.

The total number of symptoms on the SSI, excluding those given in the particular criterion diagnostic measure under consideration.

Seven measures derived from the Extrapunitive : Intropunitive scales:

General Punitiveness (E + I)
Direction of Punitiveness (E − I)

The five sub-scales of this test:

Acting-out Hostility (AH)
Criticism of Others (CO)
Delusional Hostility (DH)
Self-criticism (SC)
Delusional Guilt (DG)

Scatter of Tapping. Here the subject is provided with a quarto sheet of plain paper and a pencil, and is asked to tap as fast as he can for ten seconds. What, in fact, is measured is the scatter of tapping. This is done by placing over the sheet a transparent template marked off into half-inch squares. The score is the number of squares entered by dots (Foulds, 1961).

Subjects

The sample consisted of 120 women all falling within the personally ill class. This total was made up of 20 cases from each of the following groups, according to psychiatric diagnosis:

Schizophrenics (non-paranoid)
Paranoid states (including the whole range from paranoia to paranoid schizophrenia)
Melancholics (including all psychotic depressives)
Hysterics
Anxiety states
Neurotic depressives

All cases were new, though not always first, admissions. Schizophrenics were all within a two-year duration of hospitalization. Since all cases were tested within a week or so of admission, they were virtually untreated, except in so far as some may have been on drugs at outpatient clinics prior to admission; very occasionally, an inaccessible patient was tested after one, but never more than one, ECT.

All neurotics except three were sufficiently cooperative to be tested. Eight psychotics were unwilling or unable to cooperate and had to be excluded from the sample. Subjects falling below the 15th centile on the

Mill Hill Vocabulary scale were excluded from further testing. An additional five cases were excluded for this reason. Of the 120 cases, 88 were re-tested. The interval between testing was always from four to six weeks. Since we are concerned not with assessing the effects of treatment, but only with the relationship between clinical change, as rated by psychiatrists, and changes on test measures, any possible bias resulting from an incomplete re-test sample is not of major importance.

INITIAL TEST RESULTS

Personal Illness (or Neuroticism) v. Normal Scale

This scale was not significantly related to the HOQ, r being -0.147. *Table 44* shows the correlations between the diagnostic and personality criterion measures and the remaining nine measures for the total sample of 120 women. All subsequent results are also based on the 120 cases.

TABLE 44 *Correlations between the criterion measures (PI v. No and HOQ) and the nine remaining measures*

	Total SSI	E+I	E−I	Tapping	AH	CO	DH	SC	DG
PI v. No	·525	·392	−·187	−·210	·286	·170	−·007	·491	·403
p	·001	·001	n.s.	·05	·01	n.s.	n.s.	·001	·001
HOQ	−·138	−·017	·408	·160	·164	·163	·129	−·242	−·216
p	n.s.	n.s.	·001	n.s.	n.s.	n.s.	n.s.	·02	·05

Those who score high on Personal Illness have more non-specific symptoms than normals, and are high on General Punitiveness. This criterion diagnostic measure is not, however, significantly related to Direction of Punitiveness, and only just so to Scatter of Tapping. Three of the sub-scales of the Punitive scale are significantly related to the diagnostic measure: high scorers on Personal Illness are also high on Acting-out Hostility, Self-criticism, and Delusional Guilt.

The criterion personality measure, the HOQ, is not significantly related to the total number of non-specific symptoms on the SSI, nor to General Punitiveness; but it is quite strongly related to Direction of Punitiveness. Those who score towards the hysteroid end of the HOQ tend to score towards the extrapunitive end of the (E – I) scale. As would be expected the Extrapunitive sub-scales are all positively related to the HOQ (though not significantly), and both Intropunitive sub-scales are negatively and significantly related.

Self-criticism and Delusional Guilt are thus related to both the diagnostic and the personality criterion measures, though more markedly to the former. This means, therefore, that the highest scorers on these two scales are the highly personally ill subjects of obsessoid personality. They are followed in turn by the highly personally ill of hysteroid personality, the less personally ill of obsessoid personality, and, finally, by the less personally ill of hysteroid personality.

Psychotic v. Neurotic Scale

Since the Psychotic *v.* Neurotic scale was unrelated to the HOQ ($r = -0.015$), it was not necessary to partial out the effect of one when looking at the relationship between the other and the remaining nine scales.[1] *Table 45* shows the correlations.

TABLE 45   *Correlations between the criterion measures (P v. N and HOQ) and the nine remaining measures*

	Total SSI	E+I	E–I	Tapping	AH	CO	DH	SC	DG
P v. N	·393	·532	·134	·151	·273	·315	·568	·245	·522
p	·001	·001	n.s.	n.s.	·01	·01	·001	·02	·001
HOQ	−·185	−·017	·408	·160	·164	·163	·129	−·242	−·216
p	n.s.	n.s.	·001	n.s.	n.s.	n.s.	n.s.	·02	·05

Those who score towards the psychotic end of the Psychotic *v.* Neurotic scale tend to have more of the individually non-discriminating symptoms and to be more generally punitive. This greater degree of punitiveness applies throughout the five sub-scales, and most particularly in the case of the two Delusional scales.

Those who score towards the hysteroid end of the HOQ do not differ

[1] Since partial correlations are not being used, the correlations between the HOQ and all but the total SSI score are the same throughout the succeeding tables. They are, however, being repeated for convenience of comparison.

Symptoms, Attitudes, Traits, and their Interrelationship

from the obsessoids on total number of non-specific symptoms on the SSI, nor on General Punitiveness. These two measures may, therefore, once again be regarded as diagnostic, but not personality, measures. Hysteroids do, however, tend to be more extrapunitive, as has already been noted.

It was pointed out (Chapter 6) that most of the items in the Psychotic *v.* Neurotic scale are delusional items. It is not surprising, therefore, that the two highest correlations among the five sub-scales are with the Delusional Hostility and the Delusional Guilt scales. Since the procedure in the two tests is somewhat different, these correlations can be interpreted as useful confirmation of each other.

Again, SC and DG are related to both criterion measures, so that the highest scorers are the psychotics of obsessoid personality, followed by the psychotics of hysteroid personality, then the neurotics of obsessoid personality, and, finally, the neurotics of hysteroid personality.

Non-integrated Psychotic v. Integrated Psychotic Scale
The Non-integrated Psychotic *v.* Integrated Psychotic scale was not significantly related to the HOQ ($r = 0.039$). *Table 46* shows the correlations between each criterion measure and the remaining nine measures.

TABLE 46   *Correlations between the criterion measures (NIP v. IP and HOQ) and the nine remaining measures*

	Total SSI	E+I	E−I	Tapping	AH	CO	DH	SC	DG
NIP v. IP	·372	·396	·025	·145	·260	·196	·308	·225	·430
p	·001	·001	n.s.	n.s.	·01	·05	·01	·05	·001
HOQ	−·213	−·017	·408	·160	·164	·163	·129	−·242	−·216
p	·05	n.s.	·001	n.s.	n.s.	n.s.	n.s.	·02	·05

It can be seen that those who score towards the non-integrated end of the Non-integrated Psychotic *v.* Integrated Psychotic scale tend to have more of the individually non-discriminating symptoms and to be more generally punitive. This greater degree of punitiveness applies throughout the five sub-scales.

The fact that those who score high on the Non-integrated Psychotic *v.*

199

Integrated Psychotic scale also tend to score high on Delusional Hostility and on Delusional Guilt is of considerable interest. This high scoring on DH and DG does, in fact, apply equally to those psychiatrically diagnosed as non-paranoid schizophrenics. Clinically, this is not considered an important characteristic of non-paranoid schizophrenics – perhaps because they share these delusional beliefs with all other psychotics, and the clinician quite rightly looks beyond these delusions to the more specific differentiae. Nevertheless, for the purpose of constructing a logical classificatory system, it is vitally important to remember that non-integrated psychotics do admit to very many delusional items.

Those who score towards the hysteroid end of the HOQ tend to complain of slightly fewer symptoms than do obsessoids; but there is no difference in General Punitiveness. It has already been noted that hysteroids tend to be more extrapunitive; but they do not differ on Scatter of Tapping.

Interaction between diagnostic and personality type seems to account for scores on the five sub-scales of Punitiveness. On the Extrapunitive sub-scales it seems likely that non-integrated psychotics of hysteroid personality will score highest; whereas, on the Intropunitive sub-scales, non-integrated psychotics of obsessoid personality will score highest.

In sum, for these three main scales, obsessoid personalities tended to have more of the non-specific symptoms on the SSI, significantly so, if the Non-integrated Psychotic *v.* Integrated Psychotic scale is excluded. Hysteroids tended to be more extrapunitive, and obsessoids to be more self-critical and to have more delusional guilt.

Those who scored high on the Non-integrated Psychotic *v.* Integrated Psychotic scale also scored high on the non-specific symptoms of the SSI, on General Punitiveness, and on each of the sub-scales Acting-out Hostility, Criticism of Others, Delusional Hostility, Self-criticism, and Delusional Guilt. From this plethora of high scores it might be thought that non-integrated psychotics say 'yes' to everything. The response frequencies to individual items of the SSI (see Chapter 8, Appendix C, above) do not bear this out. One does not get the impression of lack of discrimination to any marked degree during the administration of the inventory. The commonest exception is among chronic burnt-out schizophrenics (not included here), and they say 'no' rather than 'yes'.

Those who scored high on the Psychotic *v.* Neurotic scale also scored high on the same measures.

Symptoms, Attitudes, Traits, and their Interrelationship

Those who scored high on the Personal Illness v. Normal scale also scored high on the same measures, except CO and DH; but they scored low on Scatter of Tapping.

These results lend some support to the view that non-integrated psychosis, integrated psychosis, and neurosis form a continuum. That this is not just an artifact of the SSI, divorced from clinical realities, is evidenced by *Table 47*, which shows the percentages of clinically diagnosed non-integrated psychotics, integrated psychotics, and neurotics who were diagnosed by the SSI as non-integrated psychotic, psychotic, or personally ill on these respective scales.

TABLE 47   *The relationship between clinical and SSI diagnoses*

Psychiatric diagnosis	SYMPTOM SIGN INVENTORY SCALES							
	Personally ill v. Normal		*Psychotic v. Neurotic*			*Non-integrated v. Integrated Psychotic*		
	PI	No	P	Uncertain	N	NIP	Uncertain	IP
	%	%	%	%	%	%	%	%
20 Schizophrenics	85	15	60	20	20	65	30	5
40 Integrated psychotics	87	12	75	17	7	25	25	50
60 Neurotics	97	3	17	7	77	5	22	73

Thus, on the Personal Illness v. Normal scale, 92 per cent were classified in agreement with the clinical diagnosis.

On the Psychotic v. Neurotic scale, 73 per cent were classified in agreement and 14 per cent in disagreement with the clinical diagnosis, 12 per cent remaining uncertain.

On the Non-integrated Psychotic v. Integrated Psychotic scale, 64 per cent were classified in agreement (assuming that neurotics would come out as integrated rather than as non-integrated psychotic in a forced choice) and 12 per cent in disagreement with the clinical diagnosis, 24 per cent remaining uncertain. Since, on this scale, a high percentage of correct hits could be obtained by calling every case an integrated psychotic, it was thought advisable to compare schizophrenics with paranoids and melancholics in turn. The base-rates would then be more nearly equal.

Empirical Studies

Let us now consider comparisons within psychosis:

Paranoid States v. *Schizophrenics*

The Paranoid *v.* Schizophrenic scale was not significantly related to the HOQ ($r = 0.166$). *Table 48* shows the correlations between the two criterion measures and the nine remaining measures.

TABLE 48 *Correlations between the criterion measures (Pa v. Sc and HOQ) and the nine remaining measures*

	Total SSI	E+I	E−I	Tapping	AH	CO	DH	SC	DG
Pa v. *Sc*	−·121	·010	·411	·069	·171	·161	·340	−·255	−·152
p	n.s.	n.s.	·001	n.s.	n.s.	n.s.	·001	·01	n.s.
HOQ	−·187	−·017	·408	·160	·164	·163	·129	−·242	−·216
p	n.s.	n.s.	·001	n.s.	n.s.	n.s.	n.s.	·02	·05

Paranoids do not differ from schizophrenics on the total SSI score, on General Punitiveness, or on Tapping. They do, however, differ very significantly on Direction of Punitiveness, paranoids being much more extrapunitive. From this it would be expected that the Extrapunitive sub-scales would show positive correlations with the *Pa* v. *Sc* scale and that the Intropunitive sub-scales would show negative correlations. This is, in fact, the case; but only the Delusional Hostility and Self-criticism scales achieve an acceptable level of significance.

Since the total SSI and General Punitiveness were related to the criterion diagnostic measure and not to the criterion personality measure at the main class level used (namely Non-integrated Psychotic *v.* Integrated Psychotic), these measures must be expected to change in an improved group, despite the fact that they do not differentiate at the group level of paranoid *v.* schizophrenic.

Melancholic v. *Schizophrenic Scale*

The criterion diagnostic and personality measures are significantly related at the 5 per cent level ($r = -0.218$). Melancholics, therefore, tend to be somewhat more obsessoid than schizophrenics. The association is not, however, very strong, and partial correlations have not been used. *Table 49* shows the correlations between the two criterion measures and the nine remaining measures.

TABLE 49   *Correlations between the criterion measures (Me v. Sc and HOQ) and the nine remaining measures*

	Total SSI	E+I	E−I	Tapping	AH	CO	DH	SC	DG
Me v. *Sc*	·350	·227	−·233	−·153	·181	−·055	−·097	·536	·412
p	·001	·05	·02	n.s.	n.s.	n.s.	n.s.	·001	·001
HOQ	−·155	−·017	·408	·160	·164	·163	·129	−·242	−·216
p	n.s.	n.s.	·001	n.s.	n.s.	n.s.	n.s.	·02	·05

Melancholics tend to have more non-discriminating symptoms on the SSI and to be more generally punitive than schizophrenics. These scales are unrelated to personality type. Tapping is again unrelated to the criterion diagnostic measure.

With regard to Direction of Punitiveness, the tendency to score predominantly in the extrapunitive direction is associated with being hysteroid and schizophrenic.

On the Self-criticism and Delusional Guilt scales, melancholics score highest, particularly if they are of obsessoid personality, which they tend to be.

Paranoid v. Melancholic Scale

The Paranoid *v.* Melancholic scale is significantly related to the HOQ ($r=0·278$). Paranoids, therefore, tend to be more hysteroid than melancholics. *Table 50* shows the correlations between the two criterion measures and the remaining nine measures.

TABLE 50   *Correlations between the criterion measures (Pa v. Me and HOQ) and the nine remaining measures*

	Total SSI	E+I	E−I	Tapping	AH	CO	DH	SC	DG
Pa v. *Me*	−·316	−·193	·423	·149	−·171	·088	·272	−·434	−·358
p	·01	n.s.	·001	n.s.	n.s.	n.s.	·01	·001	·001
HOQ	−·154	−·017	·408	·160	·164	·163	·129	−·242	−·216
p	n.s.	n.s.	·001	n.s.	n.s.	n.s.	n.s.	·02	·05

Paranoids tend to have fewer non-discriminating symptoms on the SSI, and to be somewhat less generally punitive than melancholics.

There is no significant relationship between the Paranoid *v.* Melancholic scale and Tapping, although the difference is in the direction found by Caine (1960, 1962[1]) in studies at Runwell and Claybury Hospitals. In both of his studies paranoids scattered their tapping significantly more than melancholics. It had been noted in the present studies that the melancholic group contained an unusually high proportion of agitated as opposed to retarded melancholics. It seems reasonable to speculate that agitated melancholics would scatter their tapping more than retarded melancholics. The same explanation might account for the unexpectedly high score on Acting-out Hostility of the present melancholics as compared with those used for the original work on the Extrapunitive : Intropunitive scales (Foulds, Caine & Creasy, 1960).

The highest scorers in the extrapunitive direction tend to be paranoids of hysteroid personality.

Melancholics tend to be the highest scorers on SC and DG, particularly if they are of obsessoid personality; whereas paranoids are significantly higher on DH.

We now turn to the within-neuroses scales:

Anxiety State v. *Hysteria Scale*
The two criterion measures are unrelated ($r = -0.065$). *Table 51* shows the correlations between the two criterion measures and the nine remaining measures.

TABLE 51   *Correlations between the criterion measures (Ax* v. *Hy and HOQ) and the nine remaining measures*

	Total SSI	E+I	E−I	Tapping	AH	CO	DH	SC	DG
Ax v. *Hy*	·128	·075	·146	−·163	·043	·118	−·270	·245	·028
p	n.s.	n.s.	n.s.	n.s.	n.s.	n.s.	·01	·02	n.s.
HOQ	−·186	−·017	·408	·160	·164	·163	·129	−·242	−·216
p	n.s.	n.s.	·001	n.s.	n.s.	n.s.	n.s.	·02	·05

[1] Personal communication.

Symptoms, Attitudes, Traits, and their Interrelationship

Delusional Hostility scores tend to be higher among those scoring at the hysteria end of the Anxiety *v.* Hysteria scale; whereas the reverse is true for the SC scale, anxiety states of obsessoid personality being the highest scorers.

Anxiety State v. *Depression Scale*

The two criterion measures are unrelated ($r = 0.050$). *Table 52* shows the correlations between the two criterion measures and the nine remaining measures.

TABLE 52   *Correlations between the criterion measures (Ax* v. *Dp and HOQ) and the nine remaining measures*

	Total SSI	E+I	E−I	Tapping	AH	CO	DH	SC	DG
Ax v. *Dp*	·233	·273	·029	·040	·149	·338	·038	·288	·057
p	·02	·01	n.s.	n.s.	n.s.	·001	n.s.	·01	n.s.
HOQ	−·162	−·017	·408	·160	·164	·163	·129	−·242	−·216
p	n.s.	n.s.	·001	n.s.	n.s.	n.s.	n.s.	·02	·05

Four measures are significantly related to the criterion diagnostic measure – the total SSI score, General Punitiveness, Criticism of Others, and Self-criticism all being associated positively with anxiety state.

Hysteria v. *Depression Scale*

The two criterion measures are unrelated ($r = 0.072$). *Table 53* shows the correlations between the two criterion measures and the nine remaining measures.

TABLE 53   *Correlations between the criterion measures (Hy* v. *Dp and HOQ) and the nine remaining measures*

	Total SSI	E+I	E−I	Tapping	AH	CO	DH	SC	DG
Hy v. *Dp*	·447	·418	·020	·141	·204	·259	·320	·342	·360
p	·001	·001	n.s.	n.s.	·05	·01	·01	·001	·001
HOQ	−·170	−·017	·408	·160	·164	·163	·129	−·242	−·216
p	n.s.	n.s.	·001	n.s.	n.s.	n.s.	n.s.	·02	·05

The Hysteria *v.* Depression scale was the poorest of all in the SSI and yet, within the neurotic scales, it has quite unexpectedly produced a large number of correlations with other measures. Thus hysterics tend to have more non-discriminating symptoms on the SSI than depressives and to be more generally punitive. This General Punitiveness is borne out in all five sub-scales. The explanation for these findings is far from clear.

With the six groups in this study there are fifteen possible comparisons between pairs consisting of one neurotic and one psychotic group. It is not, however, proposed to set out these comparisons. The results may be crudely summarized by showing, in *Table 54*, from which end of the diagnostic criterion scale or of the personality criterion scale high scorers on the remaining scales come. A group is shown in the table only when the two scales in question correlate significantly at least at the 5 per cent level or better.

TABLE 54 *High scorers on ten scales in terms of diagnostic category (as assessed by the SSI) or personality type (as assessed by the HOQ)*

	NIP v. IP	P v. N	PI v. No	Pa v. Sc	Me v. Sc	Pa v. Me	Ax v. Hy	Ax v. Dp	Hy v. Dp	HOQ
Total SSI	NIP	P	PI		Me	Me		Ax	Hy	
E+I	NIP	P	PI		Me			Ax	Hy	
E−I				Pa	Sc	Pa				Hysteroid
Tapping			PI							
AH	NIP	P	PI						Hy	
CO	NIP	P						Ax	Hy	
DH	NIP	P		Pa		Pa			Hy	
SC	NIP	P	PI	Sc	Me	Me	Ax	Ax	Hy	Obsessoid
DG	NIP	P	PI		Me	Me			Hy	Obsessoid
HOQ					Sc	Pa				

The table brings out clearly the fact that one cannot strictly and in any absolute sense speak of a particular scale being a diagnostic or a personality measure. This depends upon the population to which the scale is being applied. Thus (E+I) is a diagnostic measure when melancholics and schizophrenics constitute the test population; but it is not so when anxiety states and hysterics are being compared.

Symptoms, Attitudes, Traits, and their Interrelationship

Rather than work through the whole range of criterion diagnostic measures and the total SSI minus each of these criterion scales, it was decided simply to use the total SSI for purposes of test and re-test comparison. This score would be expected to change significantly on re-test, at least in any group rated as much improved clinically. The General Punitive scale (E + I) should also change; whereas (E − I), Tapping, and HOQ should not change.

Subjects

Of the original 120 cases, 88 were re-tested. Of the 88, 37 were rated on an improvement scale as either 3 or 2 on a scale from 0 to 3, the remaining 51 being rated as 0 or 1. The former are designated as the improved group and the latter as the unimproved group (although many of the second group were thought to have shown slight improvement).

Ratings were made by an independent psychologist from the case notes. He was given the date of re-testing in each case and was asked to rate any change between admission and that date. He agreed exactly with a second independent rater on 26 cases out of 30, differed by only one on the remaining 4, and never crossed from the 3 : 2 to the 1 : 0 category. The subsequent ratings were therefore made by the one rater only.

Table 55 compares the mean scores for the improved and unimproved groups on the ten measures – the five mentioned above, plus the five sub-scales of the Extrapunitive : Intropunitive scale.

TABLE 55 *Comparison of the mean differences for test and re-test on the total SSI, HOQ, Tapping, and the Extrapunitive: Intropunitive scales*

	37 Improved				51 Unimproved			
	Mean	s.d.	t	p	Mean	s.d.	t	p
Total SSI	12·65	10·86	7·08	·001	4·88	7·85	4·44	·001
E + I	6·89	8·32	5·03	·001	0·82	5·71	1·03	n.s.
E − I	−1·00	4·47	1·36	n.s.	0·18	3·88	0·33	n.s.
HOQ	−1·38	4·13	2·03	·05	0·37	4·60	0·57	n.s.
Tapping	−0·15	0·34	2·68	·02	0·05	2·80	0·13	n.s.
AH	0·84	1·69	3·02	·01	0·14	2·16	0·46	n.s.
CO	1·14	2·71	2·56	·02	0·39	1·90	1·47	n.s.
DH	0·86	1·84	2·84	·01	−0·10	1·50	0·48	n.s.
SC	1·92	3·12	3·74	·001	0·02	2·38	0·06	n.s.
DG	2·14	2·29	5·68	·001	0·25	1·58	1·13	n.s.

Empirical Studies

The prediction would be, of course, that none of the measures would change significantly in the unimproved group. In fact, one did so – the total SSI declined very significantly; but, as was mentioned above, the group contained many cases rated as slightly improved.

In the improved group all measures, except Direction of Punitiveness (E – I), changed significantly. The criterion personality measure (HOQ) was, however, only just significant at the 5 per cent level. This was mainly due to the depressives, both psychotic and neurotic, who moved somewhat from the obsessoid to the hysteroid end of the scale.

Scatter of Tapping was inclined to increase with clinical improvement, despite the lack of any significant association with diagnosis in most comparisons.

The total SSI declined more markedly in the improved than in the unimproved group, and General Punitiveness declined very significantly only in the improved group. It would appear, therefore, that General Punitiveness may be a 'deeper' measure of clinical change.

All five sub-scales of the Extrapunitive : Intropunitive scale changed significantly in the improved group, but not in the unimproved group.

Re-test correlations were next run within the improved and unimproved groups on the five main measures. These are shown in *Table 56*.

TABLE 56 *Re-test correlations within the improved and unimproved groups on the five main measures*

Measure	37 Improved	51 Unimproved
Total SSI	·520	·716
E+I	·528	·663
E−I	·540	·761
HOQ	·710	·699
Tapping	·750	·735

The prediction would be that the correlations for the two diagnostic measures in the improved group would be lower than all the others. This, in fact, they are; but none of the differences between groups is significant and the (E−I) correlation is unexpectedly low. These re-test correlations might in general be thought to be on the low side; but when it is remembered that many of the subjects were very disturbed people who had undergone a variety of treatments, and that even the group

Symptoms, Attitudes, Traits, and their Interrelationship

referred to here as 'unimproved' included many who were thought to have changed slightly, the figures are not too discouraging. Indeed, altogether some support has been obtained for acceptance of a difference between signs and symptoms of illness on the one hand and personality traits and attitudes on the other in respect to stability.

SUMMARY

A group of 120 women, made up of 20 of each of the following sub-groups: non-paranoid schizophrenics, paranoid states (including paranoid schizophrenics), melancholics, hysterics, anxiety states, and neurotic depressives, was examined on the SSI, the HOQ, the Extrapunitive and Intropunitive scales, and Scatter of Tapping.

The main findings were that those who scored high on the Non-integrated Psychotic v. Integrated Psychotic scale tended to have more non-specific symptoms on the SSI and to be more generally punitive. Those who scored high on the Psychotic v. Neurotic scale tended to have high total SSI and general punitive scores. Those who scored high on the Personal Illness v. Normal scale also tended to score high on the total SSI and General Punitive scales. These results lent some support to the view that there is a continuum from non-integrated psychotic through psychotic to personally ill categories.

Hysteroidness of personality tended to be associated with extra-punitiveness.

When improved and unimproved groups were compared on re-testing with their previous results, changes were much more marked in the former group and on measures which tended to be closely associated with diagnosis rather than with personality. Some support was, therefore, given to the view that personality traits and attitudes are relatively more enduring than signs and symptoms of illness.

REFERENCES

CAINE, T. M. (1960). The expression of hostility and guilt in melancholic and paranoid women. *J. consult. Psychol.*, 24, 18.

FOULDS, G. A. (1961). Scatter of tapping among mental patients. *J. clin. Psychol.*, 17, 168.

FOULDS, G. A., CAINE, T. M. & CREASY, M. A. (1960). Aspects of extra- and intro-punitive expression in mental illness. *J. ment. Sci.*, 106, 599.

CHAPTER TEN

The Melancholic-Depressive Continuum

INTRODUCTION

The previous chapter showed the relationship between the criterion diagnostic measures (from the SSI) and a criterion personality measure (the HOQ), and the relationship between each of these and Scatter of Tapping and various scales derived from the Extrapunitive : Intropunitive scale. For this purpose a sample of 120 women was used. This sample was made up of 20 cases from each of the following groups: non-paranoid schizophrenics; paranoid states (including paranoid schizophrenics); melancholics; hysterics; anxiety states; and neurotic depressives – all these as psychiatrically diagnosed. Correlations were run between, say, the Paranoid v. Schizophrenic scale and Criticism of Others on all subjects, 80 of whom were neither paranoiacs nor schizophrenics. From the seemingly meaningful results and from their consonance with results obtained when only the clinically relevant groups are used, as in this and the two succeeding chapters, it would appear that the scores obtained by any particular group even on an alien scale are meaningful and of significant interest.

Chapters 10, 11, and 12 deal with specific diagnostic groups as psychiatrically diagnosed, and in particular with the three continua to which reference has already been made. These are the melancholic-depressive, the paranoid-melancholic, and the paranoia-paraphrenia-paranoid schizophrenia continua.

Some reasons for rejecting the endogenous-exogenous split in depression have already been stated. Suddenly to burgeon forth into an aetiological mode of classification within the framework of a predominantly phenomenological mode of classification is confusing. Even the most staunch advocates of this distinction admit that evidence is almost entirely lacking. To hazard a present differentiation on the basis of future hopes is a curious procedure. That the writer seeks to examine only the possible psychological grounds for distinction does not mean that he rejects the contributions that biochemistry, for example, may eventually make. What is denied is that any such contributions can make putative psychological distinctions irrelevant. Probably a larger proportion of psychiatrists than of biochemists look to biochemistry for the production of single causes.

It has been suggested that a double classificatory scheme, which takes account of both the more unstable symptom variables and the rather more enduring and stable personality variables, should increase the reliability of psychiatric diagnosis. The task undertaken in this chapter is to determine whether this double classificatory scheme is valid and useful within the depressive illnesses. More specifically, it is to ascertain the degree to which a person's place on a hysteroid : obsessoid dimension of personality is independent of his place on a psychotic : neurotic scale of depressive illness.

This is not an attempt to decide the question of whether psychotic and neurotic depression are continuous or discrete. Psychologists can produce continua like rabbits out of a hat by an artifactual sleight of mensuration. What it is hoped to show is that people at or towards one end of a given continuum are very different from those at or towards the other end, and that the differences which they manifest do or do not bear a close resemblance to the descriptions of psychotic and neurotic depression offered by clinical psychiatrists. It is further hoped to show that any such differences found have or have not predictive value.

Measurement of a hysteroid : obsessoid typology, originally worked out on normal and neurotic groups, may prove extremely difficult among non-integrated psychotics because of the shattering effect of the illness on the possibly poorly individuated basic personality. The hypothesis is, however, that it can be measured among the psychopathologically integrated psychotics, such as the paranoid and melancholic groups. Traits may nevertheless be more difficult to distinguish from symptomatology among those groups than among the neuroses, since the psychotic patient tends to emphasize, or overemphasize, particular aspects of the personality to the virtual exclusion of others which were perhaps equally prominent before the illness.

Although many writers, including Kraepelin, have drawn attention to the difference between pre-illness personality patterns and the more flagrant and transient symptomatology of illness, this question has received little attention in the systematic research on depression. Mayer-Gross, Slater & Roth (1954) do state that 'affective psychosis can occur in persons without a noticeably cycloid temperament'. They go on to describe the 'constitutional depressive', who, when they are not simply arguing backwards from factors which we would prefer to call symptoms, sounds not unlike the obsessoid personality type. Their 'constitutional hypomanic' is not unlike the hysteroid personality type. Yet it is never clear how the clinician is supposed to separate data used to make inferences about pre-illness personality from data involving criteria for diagnosis. Thus, 'the depressive mood of the reactive patient is much more responsive to the immediate environment than an endogenous depression'. It is evident that the data from which such an inference is derived may in practice as easily lead to the inference of the emotional lability of the hysteroid personality. There is a very common tendency in present systems of classification to apply different labels to the same trait when it appears in the company of a different complex of symptoms.

The study reported here, designed to disentangle certain aspects of depressive symptomatology from a hysteroid : obsessoid dimension of personality, was guided by the following specific hypotheses:

1. The first concerned the nature of the correlation to be expected between the Melancholia scale and the Hysteroid : Obsessoid Questionnaire.

Guilford (1934) has called attention to 'the very troublesome situation found by those who construct tests of $E - I$ [Extraversion–Introversion] and of "neurotic tendency", a difficulty in keeping the two types of tests from correlating significantly with one another'. This is a genuine difficulty; but it is important to keep in mind that even very high correlations between two measures administered on a single occasion reflect only the degree of covariance under those particular conditions. They may be found to go quite different ways under different conditions (thus, hypothesis 3 below). It was thought to be very likely, for example, that a significant correlation would be found between the Melancholia scale (*Me*) and the Hysteroid : Obsessoid Questionnaire (HOQ) on the initial testing before treatment. It should be negative, because psychotic depression in an obsessoid personality is widely regarded as a more likely occurrence than psychotic depression in a hysteroid personality; but it should also be fairly low, since it would seem from earlier work (Foulds, 1961a) that dysthymic neurotics divide rather evenly between hysteroid and obsessoid personalities, or even, when the HOQ is used, lean towards the obsessoid side.

2. The second set of hypotheses concerned relationships between particular measures at the time of initial testing:

(a) Certain measures (specified below) would be more closely related to the diagnostic than to the personality dimension.

(b) Certain test measures would be more closely related to the personality than to the diagnostic dimension.

(c) Certain test measures would not be related to either diagnosis or personality.

3. The following predictions related to results of re-testing:

(a) Diagnostic measures would change significantly after effective treatment.

(b) Personality measures and those under 2 (c) would not change significantly.

PROCEDURE

Subjects

The subjects of this study were 37 women between the ages of 30 and 59, diagnosed by two psychiatrists as having illnesses falling within the 'depression' category. The sample contained 17 psychotic and 20 neurotic depressives. The psychotic group was made up of ten manic-depressives, one involutional melancholic, five 'other' psychotic depressives, and one 'uncertain as between psychotic and neurotic'. Only one subject could be said to be severely retarded, and she was testable. Previous research samples have usually contained a much higher proportion of such cases, which makes comparison with earlier work hazardous.

A minimum score of 14 on the Definitions half of the Mill Hill Vocabulary scale was required. All patients in fact achieved this level; but three out of forty successive admissions had to be excluded as otherwise untestable.

Of the 17 psychotic depressives, 16 were re-tested. Of the 20 neurotic depressives, 15 were re-tested.

Tests

Each patient was given the following tests:

Mill Hill Vocabulary scale (Definitions)
Progressive Matrices (1947, Part I, 12 items)

P   213

Symptom-Sign Inventory (SSI)
Scatter of Tapping
Extrapunitive : Intropunitive scales
Porteus Mazes
Hysteroid : Obsessoid Questionnaire.

From these tests fourteen measures were derived in all. These can be grouped according to whether they were expected to be predominantly diagnostic or predominantly personality measures, or neither.

Diagnostic Measures

Two measures – the Melancholia scale (*Me*) and the Delusional Guilt scale (DG) – should be more closely related to diagnosis than to personality.

The *Me* scale is not identical with that finally derived from the complete standardization sample (see p. 159 above), since this investigation was in fact carried out earlier. The items used here were:

A 6 Are you afraid that you might be going insane?
B 10 Do you ever seriously think of doing away with yourself because you are no longer able to cope with your difficulties?
H 1 Are you worried about having said things that have injured others?
H 2 Are you an unworthy person in your own eyes?
H 4 Are you a condemned person because of your sins?
H 5 Are you troubled by waking in the early hours and being unable to get to sleep again?
H 6 Because of things you have done wrong are people talking about you and criticizing you?
H 8 Do you cause harm to people because of what you are?
H 9 Are you ever so worked up that you pace about the room wringing your hands?
H 10 Do you ever go to bed feeling you wouldn't care if you never woke up again?

It can be seen that eight out of the ten items came from the *a priori* Melancholia scale, one from the Neurotic Depression scale (*Dp*), and one from the Anxiety scale (*Ax*). There were no items on which neurotic depressives significantly exceeded all other groups. This finding raises the possibility that neurotic depressives receive their label through diagnosis by exclusion. There may exist other symptoms which they possess with greater frequency than other diagnostic groups, but the list was rather extensive; it is likely that the only group from which they differ in this way is a normal group.

With a cutting score between 4 and 5 on the SSI *Me* scale, 78 per cent of depressives were allocated to the neurotic or psychotic categories in agreement with the clinical diagnosis in the first sample described in Chapter 6. The scale was, therefore, included here as the criterion diagnostic measure.

In a previous study (Foulds, Caine & Creasy, 1960), the Delusional Guilt scale was found to differentiate psychotic depressive women from neurotic depressive women. Only the neurotics had been typed as of hysteroid or obsessoid personality. Since these two neurotic groups differed somewhat, there may be a significant relationship with personality, but of a lower order than with the criterion diagnostic measure.

Personality Measures
The HOQ was again used as the criterion personality measure.

Of the Extrapunitive : Intropunitive sub-scales, only Acting-out Hostility (AH) and Criticism of Others (CO) would, on the basis of the results obtained in the original investigation referred to above, be expected to relate significantly to personality.

The time taken to complete Progressive Matrices (1938) was found to be significantly related to personality type, but not to diagnostic type among neurotics (Foulds & Caine, 1958). In the present study the twelve items of the Progressive Matrices (1947, Part I) were substituted, in the hope that this measure would serve as well as the longer test. Diagnostic differences might have been expected to emerge too, had the sample contained more truly retarded cases.

The Porteus Mazes administration was as described in earlier experiments (Foulds, 1951). The scoring categories were Total Time (TT) and number of Lifted Pencils (LP). The modification used in a later experiment (Foulds, 1956) was again used, namely that all wrong channels were marked off with a red line. The intellectual problem was, therefore, reduced to a minimum. These two measures (TT and LP) were found to be related to personality type, but not to diagnostic type, among neurotics when the unblocked mazes were used (Foulds & Caine, 1958).

Measures related to neither Diagnosis nor Personality
The Mill Hill Vocabulary scale (Definitions) was not expected to differentiate between diagnostic or personality groups.

Scores on the Progressive Matrices (1947, Part I) were not expected to differentiate either way, since psychotic depressives do not generally show any marked intellectual impairment.

Empirical Studies

Scatter of Tapping was previously found not to differentiate significantly between psychotic depressives and dysthymics (Foulds, 1961b). The test was included for comparison with other groups to be collected later.

The Self-criticism (SC) and Delusional Hostility (DH) scales were not, on the basis of previous results, expected to show significant differences, though there might be some tendency for obsessoids to score higher than hysteroids on the former and lower on the latter.

RESULTS

Criterion Diagnostic Measure

Only 5 of the 17 psychiatrically diagnosed psychotic depressives scored 4 or less on the Melancholia scale of ten items. Of the 20 neurotic depressives only 3 scored 5 or more. Thus, 29 out of 37 (or 78 per cent) were correctly allocated, as in the original sample (chi-square $= 14\cdot15$; $p < \cdot001$). This cross-validation provides additional justification for the use of this scale as the criterion diagnostic measure.

Criterion Personality Measure

It was possible to have only 19 of the 37 subjects rated by observers on the hysteroid : obsessoid rating scale. Nine were classified as hysteroid and 10 as obsessoid. Eight of the 9 hysteroids fell at or above the median and 7 of the 10 obsessoids fell below the median on the HOQ. Thus 79 per cent of the scores were in agreement with the ratings, as compared with the 80 per cent found by Caine (chi-square $= 4\cdot54$; $p < \cdot05$). The HOQ was accordingly used as the criterion measure for the personality dimension.

The correlation between the two criterion scales was $-0\cdot343$. Thus a high score on the *Me* scale is associated with a low score on the hysteroid scale. In consequence of this association, all subsequent correlations reported are partial correlations, with melancholia and hysteroid score held constant in turn.

Other Diagnostic Measures

DG and *Me* (HOQ): $r = 0\cdot685$; $t = 5\cdot48$; $p < \cdot001$
DG and HOQ (*Me*): $r = -0\cdot380$; $t = 2\cdot39$; $p < \cdot05$

Both relationships were, therefore, significant; but the relationship with diagnosis, as predicted, was the paramount one.

Other Personality Measures

AH and *Me* (HOQ): $r = 0.327$; $t = 2.02$; n.s.

AH and HOQ (*Me*): $r = 0.051$; n.s.

The relationship of Acting-out Hostility with diagnosis was, therefore, almost significant and was considerably greater than the relationship with personality. Since, in an earlier study (Foulds & Caine, 1958), the total Extrapunitive scale differentiated between personality types and since the AH alone failed to differentiate between two psychotic groups, viz. paranoids and melancholics (Foulds *et al.*, 1960), it was thought likely that AH would prove to be a personality measure in this study. This finding was, therefore, contrary to prediction. The failure of AH to differentiate melancholics from paranoids and the higher scores of melancholics in this study could possibly be due to a 'psychosis' factor and concomitant feelings of loss of control. This would certainly seem more likely in a group composed very largely of agitated rather than retarded depressives, as was the case in the present study. It does not, however, explain the lack of correlation with personality.

CO and *Me* (HOQ): $r = 0.134$; n.s.

CO and HOQ (*Me*): $r = 0.127$; n.s.

Contrary to prediction, Criticism of Others was not related significantly to personality. It was not expected to be related to diagnosis. This, together with the AH finding, suggests the possibility that hysteroid and obsessoid depressives have equally extrapunitive attitudes when these are considered in isolation from their intropunitive attitudes.

Progressive Matrices time and *Me* (HOQ): $r = 0.081$; n.s.

Progressive Matrices time and HOQ (*Me*): $r = -0.088$; n.s.

Contrary to prediction, Progressive Matrices time was related to neither personality nor diagnosis. The change from the sixty-item Progressive Matrices to the twelve-item form appears to have effected a marked change. Certainly in the 1958 study most of the difference in speed was because obsessoids took very much longer on the final twelve items. This shorter version does not apparently tax the patience and persistence of hysteroids sufficiently. The longer test may be more a measure of persistence than of speed. In fact, an experiment by Lynn & Gordon (1961) showed that even the most extreme introverts were no slower than the most extreme extraverts on the first six problems of the

Progressive Matrices; only in the latter stages of the task did introverts become slower.

Neither Porteus Mazes Total Time nor Lifted Pencils came near to showing a significant relationship with either diagnosis or personality. Here the change from open to blocked mazes may have effected the difference in results. In the open mazes the subject is presented with a speed/accuracy preference situation; whereas, in the blocked mazes, accuracy is a minimal consideration. It may be that, in these circumstances, hysteroids and obsessoids do not differ. Obsessoids may be slower only where they fear the possibility of going wrong.

Lifting of the Pencil is probably related, among other variables, to stopping to think where to go next. This, of course, is also reduced to a minimum in the blocked maze version. This measure has, at any rate, suffered a sad change.

Measures predicted as being related to neither Diagnosis nor Personality

Mill Hill Vocabulary and *Me* (HOQ): $r =$ 0·118; n.s.

Mill Hill Vocabulary and HOQ (*Me*): $r =$ 0·036; n.s.

Progressive Matrices and *Me* (HOQ): $r = -$0·167; n.s.

Progressive Matrices and HOQ (*Me*): $r =$ 0·000; n.s.

Scatter of Tapping and *Me* (HOQ): $r =$ 0·233; n.s.

Scatter of Tapping and HOQ (*Me*): $r =$ 0·335; $t = 2·07$; $p < ·05$

SC and *Me* (HOQ): $r =$ 0·431; $t = 2·79$; $p < ·01$

SC and HOQ (*Me*): $r = -$0·247; n.s.

DH and *Me* (HOQ): $r =$ 0·263; n.s.

DH and HOQ (*Me*): $r =$ 0·036; n.s.

The predicted absence of relationships was found in eight out of ten instances. Scatter of Tapping was found to be positively related to hysteroid personality. This seems eminently reasonable and was, indeed, the prediction made in the original study with neurotics; but it was not confirmed at that time (Foulds & Caine, 1958).

Self-criticism, in this study, is significantly related to degree of melancholia. In the original study melancholics did score higher than the neurotic groups, but not by very much (Foulds, Caine & Creasy, 1960).

The Melancholic-Depressive Continuum

Measures for which no Prediction was made

Inspection of the sub-scale results suggested that examination of the General Punitive score (E + I) and of the ratio of E to I might be of interest:

(E + I) and *Me* (HOQ): $r =$ 0·497; $p < ·001$

(E + I) and HOQ (*Me*): $r =$ 0·086; n.s.

(E/I × 100)[1] and *Me* (HOQ): $r = -0·232$; n.s.

(E/I × 100) and HOQ (*Me*): $r =$ 0·425; $p < ·01$

General Punitiveness correlated 0·421 ($p < ·01$) with the total SSI, but less than 0·1 with Direction of Punitiveness and with Scatter of Tapping; whereas Direction of Punitiveness was positively associated with wide Scatter of Tapping ($r = 0·341$; $p < ·05$), but only $-0·158$ with the total SSI. General Punitiveness (E + I) is, therefore, a diagnostic measure, and Direction of Punitiveness (E − I) a personality measure.

DISCUSSION

Several findings of possible importance emerge from this section of the study, the first of which concerns the cross-validation of the two criterion measures. The Melancholia scale seems to be fairly adequate as a substitute for clinical diagnosis for some purposes. It has, of course, the advantage of enabling the number of symptoms scored to be related to other variables in which the investigator is interested, and this in a quantitative fashion. Similarly, the HOQ has been cross-validated against observer ratings, although on a very small sample, and it has stood up well as in the original study (Chapter 3), correctly classifying 79 per cent of the obsessoids and hysteroids. It may be said to serve as a reasonably adequate substitute for clinical ratings of personality type. A quantitative scale of this sort makes it possible to investigate whether the *degree* to which a person is hysteroid or obsessoid on the scale is related to other variables.

The correlation of $-0·343$ between these two criterion measures is consistent with the first hypothesis. Melancholics describe themselves as more obsessoid than do neurotic depressives. The tendency is not, however, extremely marked. Psychoses are more disruptive than neuroses, which may make disentanglement of transient from permanent characteristics more difficult.

[1] The final version of the relationship between E and I is the one used in Chapters 13 and 14, viz. (2 SC+DG)−(AH+CO+DH).

Empirical Studies

The second set of hypotheses concerned the relationship between variables at the time of testing initially. Four of the nine predictions of a significant relationship between two variables were confirmed: the association of each of the two criterion measures with their respective external criterion, and the association of DG with both diagnosis and personality. Its association with diagnosis (i.e. the *Me* scale) may be taken as confirmatory evidence of the 'construct validity' of the *Me* scale, since the two scales have some similar content, but different methods of administration. In the *Me* scale questions are asked orally; whereas in the DG scale the subject is left to sort cards into true and false categories. The presence of severe self-reproach and guilt is usually taken to be a good criterion in our culture for psychotic depression. The *Me* scale, of course, unlike the DG scale, contains additional items which seem to have more to do with depth of depressive affect.

It is difficult to say whether the negative correlation between DG and HOQ – i.e. the relationship between guilt and obsessoid personality – involves a distortion of the self-report on the HOQ due to the psychosis or a real association. Again, we are dependent on the re-test data for further clarification.

Five of the nine measures predicted to correlate significantly did not do so. Three out of these five – the Progressive Matrices time, and the Porteus Mazes Lifted Pencils and Total Time – have already been discussed and the results attributed to ill-judged interference with the administration of the tasks. The other two were sub-scales of the Extrapunitive scale, AH and CO, which were expected to correlate positively with scores on the HOQ, since Caine found that total E score and HOQ correlated 0.26 ($p < .01$). Our sample had generally slightly lower HOQ scores than Caine's sample of neurotics, which is not surprising in view of the association between psychotic depression and obsessoidness. The depressives were rather more homogeneous with regard to HOQ score, which would make the relationship with E more difficult to demonstrate. In any case, a measure for which no prediction was made – Direction of Punitiveness – did correlate significantly with HOQ ($r = 0.425$; $p < .01$). Thus, among depressed patients, regardless of whether they are psychotic or neurotic, it is apparently the relationship between tendency to place the blame on others and tendency to disparage oneself that is most closely related to the hysteroid: obsessoid dimension.

Of the sixteen correlations predicted to be non-significant, two were

The Melancholic-Depressive Continuum

significant and one nearly so. Self-criticism correlated with the *Me* scale; it was not expected to do so, since a previous study found no differences between melancholics and neurotic depressives. Unexpectedly, therefore, SC is behaving like a diagnostic measure.

Scatter of Tapping was not expected to correlate with personality, since a previous study found no difference between hysteroid and obsessoid personalities among dysthymics on this measure. The prediction made in the earlier study was that it should relate to personality. It appears on the face of it to have some connection with expansiveness and extrapunitiveness. In any event, the results are inconsistent, for the present study found that there was a significant correlation between Scatter of Tapping and HOQ, and Scatter of Tapping and Direction of Punitiveness. Possibly this measure is over-determined and both symptoms and personality traits play a part. Extreme agitation in an obsessoid personality may cause the individual to throw caution to the winds and spread all over the page; whereas depressive or anxious inhibitions may severely restrict a usually expansive hysteroid personality. An investigation of the reliability of this measure over well-spaced intervals seems to be necessary. Earlier estimates are based on re-tests administered at the same session. In fact, the test : re-test rank-order reliability coefficient on the 31 patients in the present study was only 0·545, though this, of course, with treatment intervening.

It is also to be noted that the AH measure correlated almost significantly with *Me*. There was only one severely retarded woman in the whole group, however, and agitated depressives may be more susceptible to feelings of loss of control over impulses. Several said, for example, blushing with shame, 'Sometimes I feel like smashing things'. The melancholics in an earlier study, which included more retarded patients, had a somewhat lower mean AH score.

RE-TEST STUDY

Subjects

Sixteen of the original 17 cases diagnosed as psychotic depressives were re-tested, and 15 of the 20 diagnosed as neurotic depressives. All cases were re-tested just before or shortly after discharge at outpatient clinics.

Tests

The Porteus Mazes, Progressive Matrices, and Mill Hill Vocabulary were not included in the re-test programme. The total score on the SSI,

221

Empirical Studies

excluding those items on the *Me* scale, was included, with the expectation that it would behave as a diagnostic measure. Its individual items have not been found to differentiate between melancholics and depressives; but the total scale, as a measure of symptoms and signs of illness, could be expected to alter with treatment. In fact, the total scale was found to correlate with *Me*, with HOQ held constant, at 0·410. The correlation with HOQ, with *Me* held constant, was only −0·165.

Results

Eighteen of the 31 subjects who were re-tested were rated clinically at the time as much improved, and 13 as having limited improvement or no improvement. Since the third set of predictions applied only to those patients who psychiatrists felt had benefited from treatment, the results for the two groups were analysed separately. It was predicted that measures of personality could be demonstrated to have greater stability after treatment than measures of symptomatology. The first question to be answered was whether the HOQ showed any consistent directional change, i.e. a group effect. The prediction would be that the group should become neither more nor less hysteroid or obsessoid; but that it should report fewer symptoms on the *Me* scale.

Table 57 shows the difference scores between test and re-test for the *Me* scale and for the HOQ. With the much improved group, the diagnostic measure changed very significantly; with the relatively unimproved group it also changed significantly, but to a lesser degree. Hypothesis 3 (*a*) was therefore confirmed. The 'limited' improvement ascribed to some of the patients in the second group may account for the improvement that occurred on the *Me* scale.

TABLE 57 *Mean differences between test and re-test scores on criterion diagnostic and personality measures of improved and unimproved depressives*

Measures	18 Much improved				13 Unimproved			
	Mean	s.d.	t	p<	Mean	s.d.	t	p<
Me	3·50	2·35	6·32	·001	1·38	1·71	2·91	·02
HOQ	−1·72	4·87	1·50	n.s.	−2·69	4·52	2·15	n.s.

HOQ scores, on the other hand, did not change either for improved or for unimproved patients. Thus there is no apparent tendency for depressed patients to become either more hysteroid or more obsessoid

222

as a group on experiencing alleviation of their depressive symptomatology.

The theoretical position outlined here has implications, however, not only for the stability of a whole group on the hysteroid : obsessoid dimension, but also for the stability of the positions of individuals on this dimension relative to the other members of the group. The finding of no difference in mean HOQ score from test to re-test could have been caused by large numbers of subjects becoming more hysteroid while an equal number became more obsessoid. It follows from earlier statements that patients who have been labelled hysteroid by the HOQ on initial testing should again be labelled hysteroid on re-test; the same should hold for obsessoids. The same degree of consistency would not be expected to hold for the psychotic : neurotic dichotomy. Whereas of 14 initially classified as psychotic (i.e. *Me* score of 5 or over) only 2 were so classified on re-test, of 17 classified as non-psychotic initially, 16 were again so classified on re-test. There was thus no significant association between diagnostic classification on first testing and on re-testing (for $n = 1$, chi-square $= 0.01$).

All 12 initially classified as hysteroid (i.e. HOQ score of 18 or over) were again so classified on re-test; whereas of 19 initially classified as obsessoid, 7 were classified as hysteroid on re-test. The association between personality classification on first and second testing was nevertheless very significant (for $n = 1$, chi-square $= 9.85$; $p < 0.01$). Since 5 of the 7 patients who changed class had been diagnosed as psychotics, it was decided to investigate the mean HOQ change for improved psychotics. *Table 58* shows the mean HOQ changes for 11 improved psychotics and for the remaining 20 cases.

TABLE 58   *Changes between test and re-test scores on criterion personality measure for improved psychotics and for the remaining cases*

Measure	11 Improved psychotics				Remaining 20 cases			
	Mean	*s.d.*	*t*	*p<*	*Mean*	*s.d.*	*t*	*p<*
HOQ	−3.00	3.35	2.97	.02	−1.55	5.20	1.34	n.s.

Thus in this instance a significant group effect has been found, an effect which is no doubt related to the original correlation of -0.343 between the HOQ measure and the *Me* scale. Psychotic depressives

223

tended on initial testing to be more obsessoid than neurotic depressives. It would appear that after treatment there is a tendency for them to become more like the neurotics on the *Me* scale and somewhat more like the neurotics on the personality scale. The latter finding is true, however, only in so far as some psychotic depressives become more hysteroid – only 7 to a sufficient degree to lose their original obsessoid classification. It appears, therefore, that the illness was affecting the validity of self-description on the initial testing for these patients. The HOQ may not be entirely free of symptom variables at its lowest level; the change in scores for the improved psychotics may be a function of their initial starting-point. The initial mean for melancholics was 17·2; whereas for neurotic depressives it was 20·0. Their respective means on re-test were 20·0 and 20·5. If the scale is not an equal interval scale, and there is no reason why it should yet have attained this degree of dis-criminatory power, changes at one level may mean very much less psychologically than changes at another level. What is important psycho-logically at this stage is that the original hysteroid : obsessoid dichotomy held up in 78 per cent of cases. There is also some evidence to suggest that under certain conditions the scale has at least ordinal value, since the test : re-test correlation coefficient for the 18 improved patients is 0·744 ($p < ·001$). Thus, although some of these improved patients changed their absolute score, there was very little change in their position relative to other improved patients. It is not possible adequately to compare this finding with a similar coefficient on the *Me* scale, since there were so many zeros on re-test; but a comparison of frequencies above and below the cutting point for diagnosis on initial testing with frequencies above and below the group re-test median shows that only 5 out of 11 originally scoring above the cutting point on the *Me* scale did score above the re-test median, and that 6 out of 7 scoring below the cutting point initially did score below the re-test median. There is, therefore, no association between position on the diagnostic scale on first and on second testing (for $n = 1$, chi-square $= 0·73$).

It now remains to discuss the results obtained for measures other than the criterion measures. *Table 59* indicates that the improved patients showed a mean decrease of 2·50, significant at the 0·1 per cent level, on the DG scale. DG correlated with *Me* on first testing at $r = 0·685$. The mean change for unimproved patients was only 0·85, and non-significant.

Two other diagnostic measures were examined on re-test: one was the SC scale, which was found on initial testing to correlate with diagnosis,

The Melancholic-Depressive Continuum

but not with personality. If it is an expression of transient symptomatology among depressives rather than an expression of personality, it should change on re-test. The third diagnostic measure was the total score on the SSI (excluding *Me*), which correlated significantly with *Me* on initial testing and which, in any event, would be expected, as a symptom measure, to change on re-test. A fourth measure was General Punitiveness (E+I), which correlated significantly with the *Me* scale and with the total SSI, but not with any of the personality measures. *Table 59* shows the test : re-test means for these four measures. It can be seen that DG, SC, the total SSI, and General Punitiveness all hold up as diagnostic measures, since all change significantly among improved patients and not among unimproved patients.

TABLE 59 *Mean differences between test and re-test scores on additional diagnostic measures on improved and unimproved depressives*

| | 18 Much improved | | | | 13 Unimproved | | | |
Measures	Mean	s.d.	t	p<	Mean	s.d.	t	p
DG	2·50	2·15	4·93	·001	0·85	1·86	1·65	n.s.
SC	3·11	3·18	4·15	·001	1·00	2·92	1·24	n.s.
SSI	15·83	12·23	2·88	·01	7·08	7·79	2·16	n.s.
E+I	9·17	9·22	4·23	·001	3·15	7·60	1·49	n.s.

Since the criterion measure of personality changed for improved psychotics, but not for the other three groups, two other personality measures were also examined for their behaviour on re-test. These are Direction of Punitiveness and Scatter of Tapping, the only two tests found to correlate with the personality criterion measure rather than the diagnostic one on initial testing. *Table 60* gives the mean changes for improved psychotics on these two measures, compared with unimproved psychotics and all neurotics. Both tests changed in the same way as the HOQ.

Improved psychotic depressives, in addition to becoming more hysteroid with clinical improvement, become more extrapunitive in their attitudes and more expansive in their tapping. It was noted above that only 7 out of 31 patients actually exchanged one personality type for the other. The association between Direction of Punitiveness on first and second testing was significant (for $n=1$, chi-square$=4·01$; $p<·05$). Fourteen out of 15 originally classified as predominantly extrapunitive

Empirical Studies

were again so classified; but 6 out of 16 originally classified as intro-punitive became extrapunitive.

The association between high and low Scatter of Tapping on first and second testing was significant (for $n=1$, chi-square$=7.60$; $p<.01$). Of 15 originally scored as high for Scatter, 13 were high on re-test; of 16 originally low, 11 remained low on re-test.

TABLE 60 *Mean differences between test and re-test scores on additional personality measures of improved psychotics compared with the remaining cases*

Measures	11 Improved psychotics				Remaining 20 cases			
	Mean	s.d.	t	p<	Mean	s.d.	t	p
Tapping	−0·38	0·48	2·62	·05	0·03	0·35	0·38	n.s.
E−I×100	−47·55	52·46	3·01	·02	−10·15	57·81	0·79	n.s.

Thus these two personality measures are behaving in a similar fashion: (i) they are tending not to correlate with the diagnostic measure; (ii) they are tending to correlate with each other; (iii) whereas diagnostic measures are altering for improved patients on re-test, these are not; (iv) whereas the diagnostic dichotomies are disappearing on re-test, these 'personality' tests are generally classifying people in the same way on re-test; and (v) all three personality measures are showing directional changes for one particular group, the improved psychotics. Psychotics had lower scores than neurotics on all three personality measures on initial testing, but were no lower on re-test. Only limited success has, therefore, been achieved in constructing measures of habitual personality patterns which are free from psychotic symptom variables. The present measures do not appear to have been entirely free of them at the lower levels, that is, at the more obsessoid, intropunitive, and restricted ends of the three scales. This does not mean that the more crude two-category classification does not withstand the impact of psychotic symptomatology; this it apparently does.

SUMMARY

An investigation of psychotic and neurotic depressives has attempted to demonstrate the utility of a double classificatory system which takes account of both symptom variables and personality variables.

The Melancholic-Depressive Continuum

The three hypotheses: that certain test measures would be more closely related to the diagnostic than to the personality dimension; that certain test measures would be more closely related to the personality than to the diagnostic dimension; and that certain test measures would relate to neither, were confirmed in general; but predictions about the particular measures were less accurate. The number of correct predictions was, however, well beyond what would be expected by chance.

None of the three personality measures showed mean changes for all improved patients; whereas all four diagnostic measures did. Whereas the diagnostic test classifications disappeared on re-test, the personality tests continued to classify people in the same categories. Personality measures thus appeared to have much greater stability than diagnostic measures.

The scales used in this investigation have stretched depressive subjects out along various continua. It seems quite clear that subjects at or towards one end of the main continuum can best be differentiated from those at or towards the other end by the presence of delusions of an intropunitive kind. It does not seem unreasonable to describe the ends as 'psychotic' and 'neurotic'. Among improved subjects, different things happen according to which end of the scale the individual occupies. There is, therefore, some practical value in being able to identify the continuum and whereabouts people fall on it.

From Appendix C (Chapter 8 above) it can be seen what percentages of depressives and melancholics answered each question affirmatively. The 'depressive' items may be grouped thus: failing function: B 2, 4, 6, 8, 9; mood: B 1, 3, 5, 7, 10; H 7, 9, 10; guilt: H 1, 6; shame: H 2, 3, 4, 8. To equate for the different number of items in each category, the average percentages for each category for each group are quoted:

	Function	Mood	Guilt	Shame
Depressives	49	38	10	13
Melancholics	48	48	42	41

In the depressives as a whole, the entire range of self-critical attitudes can be observed. The neurotic depressive emphasizes her failing powers first, fairly closely followed by her mood of depression, she rarely expresses feelings of guilt or shame. The psychotic depressive, on the other hand, emphasizes her feelings of guilt and shame almost as much as her failing powers and depressed mood. Even though she goes to the limit, as it were, in expressing shame, she rarely, if ever, admits just what is the real content of her shame. She confesses some peccadillo of twenty years ago, protests her masturbation guilt, proclaims that she has committed the unforgivable sin (which can never be elicited), that she is vile and unclean and will contaminate all who come into contact with her, even that she feels an unworthy person in her own eyes. She resists reassurance and, at least indirectly, pleads for condemnation, for punishment to expiate her guilt and thus liquidate her shame, her profound and private conviction that she really is worthless. It may be that only those who love and are loved deeply can withstand the naked light of shame and, as Lynd would suggest, can turn it to positive account by strengthening the sense of their own identity. It may be that the melancholic, tormented by her ambivalence towards those with whom she is most intimate, is denied this hope of regeneration by a feeling that she has lost the capacity to love.

REFERENCES

FOULDS, G. A. (1951). Temperamental differences in maze performance. *Brit. J. Psychol.*, **42**, 209.

FOULDS, G. A. (1956). Distraction and affective disturbance. *J. clin. Psychol.*, **12**, 291.

FOULDS, G. A. (1961a). Personality traits and neurotic symptoms and signs. *Brit. J. med. Psychol.*, **34**, 263.

FOULDS, G. A. (1961b). Scatter of tapping among mental patients. *J. clin. Psychol.*, **17**, 168.

FOULDS, G. A. & CAINE, T. M. (1958). Psychoneurotic symptom clusters, trait clusters and personality tests. *J. ment. Sci.*, **104**, 722.

FOULDS, G. A., CAINE, T. M. & CREASY, M. A. (1960). Aspects of extra- and intro-punitive expression in mental illness. *J. ment. Sci.*, **106**, 599.

GUILFORD, J. P. (1934). Introversion-extraversion. *Psychol. Bull.*, **31**, 331.

LYND, H. M. (1958). *On shame and the search for identity.* London: Routledge & Kegan Paul.

LYNN, R. & GORDON, I. E. (1961). The relation of neuroticism and extraversion to intelligence and educational attainment. *Brit. J. educ. Psychol.*, **31**, 194.

MAYER-GROSS, W., SLATER, E. & ROTH, M. (1954). *Clinical psychiatry.* (2nd edn., 1960). London: Cassell; Baltimore: Williams & Wilkins, 1955.

CHAPTER ELEVEN

The Paranoid-Melancholic Continuum

INTRODUCTION

In this chapter two psychotic groups are examined from the point of view of personality and symptomatological dimensions. It is conceivable that illnesses as devastating and widespread in their effects as the psychoses may complicate and blur relationships that seem rather clear-cut among neurotics. Our thesis is, however, that the Hysteroid : Obsessoid Questionnaire will continue to behave reliably and to account for much of the variance of other measures among the partially integrated psychotics, such as the paranoid and melancholic subjects to be examined here.

The paranoid and depressive psychoses aptly illustrate Frenkel-Brunswick's contention (1954) that, owing to the work of mechanisms such as denial and reaction-formation, opposites are more alike in psychology than are similars. 'Realization of the possibility that apparent opposites . . . may be psychologically closer together and more apt to combine with each other in the same subject than any of them with an intermediate position along the same scale may be traced back to psychoanalysis.' Most people 'stick to the more obvious policy of naïve dichotomizing in which opposite extremes are conceived of as true polarities'. The first view may be traced still further back to Hegel and the latter to Plato. One important respect in which paranoids and depressives are similar, and in which they differ from people suffering from other forms of mental illness, is that they cling to rather well-organized delusional belief systems. It is not characteristic of neurotics to have such delusional beliefs, and those of the other psychotic groups are, at least in their expression, much more fragmentary and episodic.

Rokeach (1960) distinguishes two types of primitive belief:

'One definition of primitive belief is any belief that virtually everyone is believed to have also. For example, I believe that this object I write with is a pencil, and I believe that my name is so-and-so. I also believe that all persons in a position to know (this excludes infants, strangers, etc.) would agree with me on both counts. All such persons could be said to be external referents or authorities for those beliefs. When this is the case, my belief is primitive. It is rarely, if ever, challenged. . . .'

'A second kind of primitive belief is the converse of the above. Instead of virtually everyone serving as external referents or authorities, there is no one. Suppose I suffer from claustrophobia. I have been told many times that my fear is groundless, unrealistic. But it does not help. I go on believing that dreadful things will happen to me in closed rooms. The belief is a primitive one because there exist no external reference, persons or authorities who can disconfirm it' [presumably for the sufferer].

Rokeach does not relate his views to the problem of delusional beliefs; but it could be argued that the absence of referents who can disconfirm the belief is at least one indication that the belief is psychopathological. Other considerations are needed to enable us to distinguish between the neurotic's primitive belief about closed rooms and the psychotic's belief about the influence of Japanese x-rays: the neurotic recognizes that his belief is unshared and therefore primitive, and worries about this; the psychotic has no reason to be concerned – he has left the world of men and has no need to adjust his beliefs to theirs. The neurotic may know intellectually that what he knows emotionally is groundless; but the psychotic brings his conceptualizations into line with his feelings and thus need pay little heed to the lack of confirmation. One wonders whether either person would ever be able to gain much solace from confirmation. Possibly one claustrophobic will be able to understand the feelings of another, but one paranoid schizophrenic will in all probability give no indication that he is able to understand the situation and feelings of a fellow-sufferer from Japanese rays. In this sense, the old psychiatric dictum that a delusion is a belief that is *shared* by *no* other member of the same race, colour, or creed seems justified. The converse, as Nivelle de la Chausée so clearly saw, is also true: *Quand tout le monde a tort, tout le monde a raison.*

The well-organized character of these psychotic belief systems – as opposed to the fragmented and patchy ideas appearing in non-paranoid schizophrenia – has provided the clinician with a source of information which is not available in the case of other diagnostic splits, i.e. the *content* of these belief systems. One important dimension on which the paranoids and depressives differ from each other is the direction of blame associated with their delusional beliefs. No clearer summary of the earlier discussion (see Chapter 7 above) can be given than the statement by Bleuler (1924): 'Delusions of persecution do not belong to the depressive forms of delusion. The delusion of deserved punishment must not be classed with that of the unjust persecution.'

The authors cited in that discussion were, of course, considering the extremes of the dimension. In practice, a small proportion of patients are encountered – perhaps 10 to 15 per cent – who seem, as it were, not to have made up their minds whether to blame themselves or others. They adopt a somewhat indeterminate attitude or alternate between the two attitudes. It might be expected that during the course of an illness the balance would shift to predominantly one side or the other. This appears, however, to be the exception rather than the rule. Patients from this minority group are often readmitted on a subsequent breakdown in just the same ambiguous position on this dimension, so that they have to be regarded as belonging to both classes.

With a few exceptions, members of these classes are motivated to reveal their delusional beliefs, the paranoids to convince the listener of their innocence despite what 'they' are saying about them, the melancholics to convince him of their unparalleled wickedness. Because of this predominant motivation to reveal beliefs and attitudes, and because the original boundaries between the two classes appear to have been drafted so as to take account of the type of ideational content, it was predicted that the groups would be relatively easily differentiated by means of symptoms and subjective signs. It was expected that items regarding direction of delusional blame would play a prominent part in a Paranoid-Melancholic scale extracted on an empirical basis from the Symptom-Sign Inventory.

The next question concerns the relationship to be expected between the hysteroid : obsessoid personality dimension and the paranoid-versus-melancholic diagnosis. There is some experimental work which would suggest the possibility of a mild association between paranoid and hysteroid – if delusional blame were, indeed, prominent among the diagnostic criteria. Direct measures of delusional blame were found in one study at least (Foulds, Caine & Creasy, 1960) to correlate positively with non-psychotic measures of extrapunitive and intropunitive attitudes. Yet these latter measures were found, among neurotics, to be associated with hysteroid and obsessoid personality type rather than with diagnosis (Foulds & Caine, 1958). They could thus in the present situation be expected conceivably to forge a link between symptoms and personality that might not exist in diagnostic groups which are not differentiated on the basis of the content of their interpersonal attitudes. Nevertheless, it was predicted that the hysteroid : obsessoid dimension would not be entirely engulfed by the paranoid-melancholic one. At least some of the hysteroid : obsessoid traits intended to be measured by the Hysteroid : Obsessoid Questionnaire – e.g. tendency to display emotions and degree of emotional lability – are probably relatively independent of habitual direction of blame-attribution.

The third issue of concern is the degree to which test variation among a battery of tests used in earlier studies can be accounted for by personality rather than diagnosis. Among neurotics, most of the variation was due to personality (Foulds & Caine, 1958); but, among psychotic and neurotic depressives, the balance shifted more in favour of diagnostic differences. Personality, however, still had some independent part to play. It was anticipated that personality would again emerge with some independence in the present investigation; but that, because of the predicted closer relation between personality and diagnosis, few measures could be expected to be found which would go with personality alone. Excluding the two criterion measures, three of the four additional measures were found in earlier work to be related to personality. The particular nature of the present two diagnostic groups suggests an additional relationship with diagnosis.

The following predictions were made for the initial testing prior to the administration of treatment:

1. A Paranoid-Melancholic scale (*Pa-Me*), empirically derived from the SSI to maximize differences between paranoids and psychotic depressives, and probably found to contain many items concerned with delusional thought content, would correlate positively and strongly with a measure of direction of delusional blame (DH-DG).

2. The (*Pa-Me*) scale would show a mild positive association with the Hysteroid : Obsessoid Questionnaire (HOQ). Paranoids would tend to be more hysteroid than melancholics.

3. Three measures, (DH-DG), (AH+CO)−SC, and Scatter of Tapping, would bear a significant relation to personality regardless of diagnosis, but would also bear a significant relation to diagnosis when the effect of personality was controlled.

The Paranoid-Melancholic Continuum

The second half of the study concerned changes to be expected following treatment for paranoid and depressive symptomatology. Although a correlation was expected between diagnosis and personality on initial testing, such correlations between two measures administered on a single occasion can easily be reflecting a degree of covariance which is peculiar to that occasion. A variation in a third factor, exposure to treatment aimed at affecting symptoms, could be expected to alter this relation and to permit the two measures to part company. If the HOQ measures a relatively enduring set of personality characteristics, and if treatment effects some symptomatic change, then diagnostic differences between paranoids and melancholics would be reduced and the following predictions could be made:

4. The HOQ would show greater stability after treatment than would the (Pa-Me) scale and certain other measures to be described later.

5. Changes in measures found on initial testing to be associated with both personality and diagnosis would be greater than changes in measures associated with personality alone.

6. Melancholics, on the basis of their better prognosis (Henderson & Gillespie, 1950), would show a greater degree of symptom change than paranoids.

PROCEDURE

Subjects

The subjects were all women between the ages of 29 and 59. Twenty out of 24 successive admissions who had been diagnosed clinically as paranoid psychoses (including paranoid schizophrenia) and 20 out of 23 diagnosed as psychotic depressives comprised the two groups. The latter group was made up predominantly of agitated rather than retarded cases. Four paranoids and 3 melancholics were found to be untestable and had to be excluded from the study.

Of the 40 cases, 30 were re-tested either shortly before or shortly after discharge. Of the ten who were not re-tested, one committed suicide, two left the country, and the remainder either refused testing while in hospital or failed to appear for the outpatient appointment. Six were paranoids and four melancholics.

233

Empirical Studies

Tests

Each patient was given the following tests:

Mill Hill Vocabulary scale (Definitions)
Progressive Matrices (1947, Part I, 12 items)
Symptom-Sign Inventory (SSI)
Scatter of Tapping
Extrapunitive-Intropunitive scales
Hysteroid : Obsessoid Questionnaire (HOQ)

The (*Pa-Me*) scale (see Chapter 7) was the sum of positive responses to eleven items given significantly more often by the first 15 paranoids (D 1 to 10; F 7) minus the sum of positive responses to fifteen items given significantly more often by the first 30 melancholics (A 2, 6, 8, 9; B 2, 3, 4, 7, 10; H 2, 4, 5, 8, 9, 10). For this earlier sample, cutting between 0 and 1, 89 per cent were allocated in agreement with the psychiatric diagnosis. The same cutting point was therefore used in the present study. It should be noted that this measure does not include symptoms which the two groups have in common, nor necessarily those which distinguish either or both from other groups, but only those which best differentiate each from the other.

The HOQ was again used as the criterion personality measure.

The (*Pa-Me*) scale was cross-validated: two clinically diagnosed melancholics and four paranoids were misclassified out of the 40 cases (85 per cent were thus correct). This scale was, therefore, used as the criterion diagnostic measure.

RESULTS

In the neurotic and psychotic depression comparison the HOQ correlated $-·343$ with the *Me* scale that differentiated between the two depressive groups (see p. 214 above). Psychotic depression was associated with the obsessoid personality. In the present study the (*Pa-Me*) scale correlated ·347 ($p < ·05$) with the HOQ. Again, therefore, and to about the same extent, psychotic depression was associated with the obsessoid personality. Paranoid psychosis was associated with a personality relatively more hysteroid than that of melancholics, but not more than that of normal subjects.

None of the following measures was related to (*Pa-Me*) with HOQ held constant, or to HOQ with (*Pa-Me*) held constant: age; Mill Hill Vocabulary; Progressive Matrices; total symptoms on the SSI; and Scatter of Tapping (*Table 61*).

TABLE 61   *Partial correlations between certain variables and the diagnostic and personality criterion measures*

	Pa-Me (HOQ)		HOQ (Pa-Me)	
	r	p<	r	p<
Age	−0·310	n.s.	−0·114	n.s.
Mill Hill Vocabulary	−0·246	n.s.	0·100	n.s.
Progressive Matrices	−0·060	n.s.	0·020	n.s.
Total SSI	−0·202	n.s.	−0·106	n.s.
Tapping	−0·059	n.s.	0·020	n.s.
(DH-DG)	0·693	0·001	0·386	0·02
(AH+CO)−SC	0·397	0·02	0·417	0·01

The total extrapunitive-intropunitive difference (E − I) tended in the depression study to be more highly related to personality than to diagnosis (see p. 219 above). It also met the second criterion for being a personality measure in that it remained relatively stable after treatment. It was necessary in the present study to correct for the expected diagnostic value of the two delusional sub-scales, and thus to examine separately the non-psychotic, (AH+CO)− SC, difference. This was almost equally related to both diagnosis and personality. That Direction of Delusional Punitiveness (DH-DG) should correlate even more highly with (*Pa-Me*) than with HOQ is not surprising since (*Pa-Me*) was found to contain, among its twenty-six items, eight which had to do with type of delusional blame (five persecutory ideas and three ideas of guilt or unworthiness).

DISCUSSION OF INITIAL TEST RESULTS

Age, Mill Hill Vocabulary, and Progressive Matrices scores were correlated with the criterion diagnostic and personality measures so that their effects could be held constant in the event of their being significantly related. Since none of them was so related, they are of no further interest.

With regard to the first hypothesis, the importance of the patient's thought content for the differential diagnosis of paranoid and melancholic illnesses was demonstrated by a high relationship between (*Pa-Me*) and (DH-DG). Paranoids were more delusionally extrapunitive and melancholics more intropunitive.

The second hypothesis, that there would be a low positive correlation between diagnosis and personality, was also confirmed. The association was sufficiently low to suggest that the HOQ continues, even with two psychotic groups, to measure variables which function somewhat independently of diagnosis.

The third hypothesis concerned three measures which were expected to correlate independently with both the diagnostic criterion and the personality criterion. (DH-DG) was strongly related to both diagnosis and personality. Thus, hysteroid paranoids had the highest and obsessoid melancholics the lowest scores. While the non-psychotic difference, (AH + CO) − SC, is also associated with both diagnosis and personality, the correlation with diagnosis is a good deal lower and with personality somewhat higher than in the case of the psychotic (DH-DG) measure. This might suggest that the non-psychotic direction of blame is a measure of rather more habitual attitudes; whereas the psychotic difference reflects a somewhat transient and exaggerated deviation from, or possibly even reaction against, the patient's usual attitudes.

That Scatter of Tapping failed to differentiate between paranoids and melancholics was surprising in view of the marked differences found by Caine (1960). His melancholic group did, however, contain a majority of rather severely retarded cases, whereas the present sample was composed mainly of agitated cases. If the test is in part an expressive movement measure of expansiveness, agitated melancholics would be expected to scatter more than retarded cases. This is not, however, an entirely satisfactory explanation of the differences in the results, since the paranoids in this study did not scatter nearly as much as did Caine's. Caine, however, took care to include no 'mixed' cases, whereas in this study the only criterion for inclusion was agreement between at least two clinicians on the dominant category. Scatter of Tapping also failed to relate significantly to HOQ, although in the study comparing the neurotic and psychotic depressives it did so. No explanation for this finding can be offered.

The total number of symptoms complained of on the SSI (excluding the (*Pa-Me*) scale) was also examined. No particular prediction was made for the initial testing, although it was expected to behave as a symptom measure in the sense that it would change after treatment. It was in fact not significantly related to either diagnosis or personality in this study, although it was significantly related to diagnosis when the two depressive groups were compared. Thus the two psychotic groups have given more non-specific symptoms than has the one neurotic group. Subsequent research suggests that this finding is in fact generally characteristic of psychotics and neurotics.

RE-TEST FINDINGS AND DISCUSSION

Correlations tell us very little about the existence of functional dependencies – i.e. whether changes in one variable are a function of changes in another. It is always possible that both are varying because of some third factor and that the correspondence between them will disappear when this third factor varies still more. The hypothesis was made that there would be some divergence of symptoms from traits and attitudes after the entrance of a third factor in the form of treatment directed at removal of symptoms. It was predicted that the personality measures would show greater stability in this situation than would the diagnostic. In fact, the fourth prediction did hold up: whereas the criterion diagnostic measure did change significantly on re-test for both the 13 (SSI diagnosed) paranoids and for the 17 (SSI diagnosed) melancholics, the criterion personality measure did not change significantly for either group (see *Table 62*). Both paranoids and melancholics moved slightly towards the hysteroid end; but the re-test means of 21·92 and 20·06 respectively are still below the mean for normals, which Caine gives as 24·07 (see p. 46 above). Melancholics in particular still fell rather definitely on the obsessoid side.

Paranoids scored significantly lower on (*Pa-Me*) after treatment, whereas melancholics scored significantly higher. The two groups thus became more alike after treatment. The two sides of the (*Pa-Me*) scale were also analysed separately. Paranoids should change significantly on the items on which they exceed melancholics, and conversely. *Table 62*, which gives the significance of the mean differences between first and second testing, confirms this expectation.

The total SSI score, excluding (*Pa-Me*), though not diagnostic in the sense of differentiating between these two groups, is clearly a symptom measure and would thus be expected to change. This, in fact, it did, and in both groups. Thus even paranoids have improved considerably, at least in respect of the less specific and perhaps secondary symptoms.

237

TABLE 62   *Mean differences between test and re-test scores of paranoid and melancholic subjects*

Measures	13 Paranoids				17 Melancholics			
	Mean	s.d.	t	p<	Mean	s.d.	t	p<
(Pa-Me)	1·46	1·86	2·84	0·02	−1·76	1·68	4·29	0·001
Pa	2·00	1·96	3·68	0·01	0·29	0·92	1·30	n.s.
Me	0·23	0·73	1·14	n.s.	2·12	1·87	4·68	0·001
Total SSI	11·31	9·23	4·42	0·001	16·71	13·54	4·94	0·001
(DH-DG)	−0·54	1·95	1·00	n.s.	−1·82	2·28	3·29	0·01
(AH+CO)−SC	−0·08	0·52	0·56	n.s.	−1·47	2·90	2·09	n.s.
Tapping	−0·03	0·31	0·35	n.s.	−0·15	0·54	1·18	n.s.
HOQ	−2·15	4·10	1·89	n.s.	−1·76	4·07	1·78	n.s.

(AH+CO)−SC was the only measure to have a higher correlation with personality than with diagnosis and the difference was extremely slight. This is nevertheless the only measure besides the criterion HOQ itself which did not change significantly for either paranoids or melancholics, although for melancholics the change was close to significance at the 5 per cent level. Among depressed patients, regardless of whether they were neurotic or psychotic, it was the relationship between the tendency to place the blame on others and the tendency to disparage oneself that was most closely related to the hysteroid: obsessoid dimension. The measure was also relatively stable after treatment in that study as in this.

The second measure related to both diagnosis and personality was the psychotic direction of blame score (DH-DG). While the non-psychotic direction of blame changed for neither group on re-test, (DH-DG) did change for melancholics. They had less delusional hostility and still less delusional guilt, so that (DH-DG) showed a shift in the extrapunitive direction.

The fifth prediction could not be examined because there was no measure which related to personality but not to diagnosis. In general, however, diagnostic and symptomatic changes can be seen to be more marked than personality changes. It was impossible to predict the degree of change for individual measures expected to relate to both diagnosis and personality, since the two criteria would be expected to pull in opposite directions over re-test change.

The Paranoid-Melancholic Continuum

The sixth hypothesis, concerning the greater predicted change for melancholics, was confirmed. Although they changed significantly on only one more measure than the paranoids, the differences were considerably greater.

CONCLUSIONS

Illnesses with effects as widespread as those of the psychoses may be expected to complicate the symptom-trait relations partially disentangled in studies of neurotics. This probably has some bearing on the results for Scatter of Tapping and the total SSI score, where a psychosis factor, or severity of illness, appears to be playing some part. The measures are probably over-determined.

Considerable evidence has thus been collected which suggests that the total score on the Extrapunitive : Intropunitive scales, that is General Punitiveness, distinguishes between neurotics and psychotics, and that Direction of Punitiveness is rather closely associated with the HOQ. The association of Direction of Punitiveness with both diagnosis and personality in this study is the exception rather than the rule, and was adumbrated by the opening remarks about the unusual features of these particular groups. Nevertheless, even in these groups, these measures remain fairly stable. Hysteroid extrapunitive paranoids and hysteroid extrapunitive melancholics remain relatively more hysteroid and extrapunitive than their more obsessoid intropunitive paranoid and melancholic fellows, even when both have been exposed to hospitalization and to treatment for the paranoia and the melancholia.

REFERENCES

BLEULER, E. (1924). *Textbook of psychiatry.* (4th edn.) New York: Macmillan.

CAINE, T. M. (1960). The expression of hostility and guilt in melancholic and paranoid women. *J. consult. Psychol.* **24**, 18.

FOULDS, G. A. & CAINE, T. M. (1958). Psychoneurotic symptom clusters, trait clusters and psychological tests. *J. ment. Sci.*, **104**, 722.

FOULDS, G. A., CAINE, T. M. & CREASY, M. A. (1960). Aspects of extra- and intro-punitive expression in mental illness. *J. ment. Sci.*, **106**, 599.

FRENKEL-BRUNSWICK, E. (1954). Intolerance of ambiguity as an emotional and perceptual personality variable. In H. Brand (Ed.), *The study of personality*. New York: Wiley; London: Chapman & Hall.

HENDERSON, D. K. & GILLESPIE, R. D. (1950). *Textbook of psychiatry*. (7th edn.) London: Oxford University Press.

ROKEACH, M. (1960). *The open and closed mind*. New York: Basic Books.

CHAPTER TWELVE

Analysis of Results in terms of the Clinical Diagnosis

I. PSYCHOTICS

INTRODUCTION

In Chapter 9 the relationship was shown between various scales on a sample of 120 cases; for this purpose clinical diagnosis was ignored. In Chapters 10 and 11 clinical diagnosis was brought in to look at the continua of melancholia-depression and of melancholia-paranoia. Much of the emphasis in the first part of the present chapter is on the third continuum which has already been mentioned, the paranoia-paraphrenia-paranoid schizophrenia continuum. To complete the picture of available psychotics and to further the argument, melancholics are again included. In the second part of the chapter, the groups of neurotics are compared. Finally, in the third part, all available groups of the personally ill are compared with normals.

It has long been recognized that there is a continuum from paranoia through paraphrenia to paranoid schizophrenia. About this there has been little argument. What has been in dispute is whether the whole continuum belongs inside, outside, or part inside and part outside the class of schizophrenia.

Kraepelin (1919, 1921), classifying by terminal state, recognized three groups – dementia praecox of paranoid type, paraphrenia, and paranoia. Patients in the first group were usually hallucinated as well as deluded. The majority of the remainder were paraphrenics, who showed a better level of personality integration. At the end of this continuum was a small group of paranoiacs, who showed little personality disintegration and who were characterized by highly systematized delusions and an absence of hallucinations.

The basis of paranoia, he considered, was 'the morbidly transformed expression of natural emotions of the human heart'. This he deemed understandable in term sof the morbidly self-conscious person's resisting the realization of failure at a time when youthful optimism has evaporated. In order for the delusions to form and for the illness to develop, he presupposed that the thinking of the paranoiac was undeveloped, egocentric, and superstitious. The thought processes of the schizophrenic, on the other hand, were not so much primitive as subject to some inner destruction which unhinged the thought process itself.

The ideas of late onset, preserved personality, and relative absence of dementia are part of all subsequent concepts of paranoia; but to Kraepelin we also owe three other ideas: that paranoia is a distortion more than a morbid process; that it is related to the time of life of the patient (and not necessarily to chronological age); and that the patient is resisting his failure.

Bleuler (1924) considered that the true paranoia was a rare case and that a separate class was not warranted. He did, however, note that where a case did occur, the schizophrenic symptoms did not appear unless suspected from the start. He therefore recognized a differentia and turned away from it. The in-between states appeared so frequently in so many transitional forms, and 'on the other hand a closer study of our cases showed so much that was identical' that he put them all in with dementia praecox (by now schizophrenia) and held that they all manifested a particular sort of disturbance in the associative process.

Henderson & Gillespie (1950) adhered to the school of Kraepelin in regarding paranoiacs as a distinct and homogeneous group, characterized by late onset, circumscribed symptomatology, and freedom from the gross intellectual deterioration prevalent in schizophrenia; but they took the whole range of paranoid cases, including paraphrenia and paranoid schizophrenia, out of the schizophrenic and into a separate class. They followed Meyer in believing that 'the crux of the situation from the standpoint of differential diagnosis is determined by the underlying type of personality' (Fraser Steele, 1948).

Fraser Steele, after an intensive clinical investigation of a series of cases, distinguished paranoiacs by the following characteristics:

(i) the paranoid personality traits: although successful and conscientious, paranoiacs are touchy, hypersensitive, ill-adaptive, suspicious-minded, ambitious, proud, irritable, defensive, with a tendency to misrepresent innocent circumstances and fall prey to ideas ill-founded in fact;

(ii) a greater degree of maturity and general adjustment than schizophrenics;

Analysis of Results in terms of the Clinical Diagnosis

(iii) later age of onset;

(iv) dominant and long-lasting delusions;

(v) absence of dementia;

(vi) paranoid reactions throughout their history.

Mayer-Gross, Slater & Roth (1954) trace the paranoid reaction in two ways: it can develop into the classical paranoid psychosis or it can characterize a form of schizophrenia. Thought disorder in these latter cases may not be easily detectable, but is 'rarely absent'. In fact the true paranoid psychosis without schizophrenic symptoms is only an 'idealized picture' and can more or less be disregarded. The real differential sign of paranoid psychosis is the primary delusion, or the experience that there is something directly significant in the patient's situation for which the delusions are brought in as an explanation. Delusions of persecution or of grandiosity are common to all paranoid reactions (neurotic and psychotic), which can occur in any breakdown of function (e.g. deafness), so that separation of paranoid states from paranoid schizophrenia on the criterion of delusions is not successful: for instance, a co-worker of Kraepelin, they point out, found that 50 per cent of 78 patients diagnosed as paraphrenic by Kraepelin himself had developed into typical schizophrenics. Kolle followed 66 patients diagnosed as paranoid and, in 62, primary delusions were found. Mayer-Gross *et al.* do not comment on the other 50 per cent who did not turn out to be typical schizophrenics. The implication may presumably be that eventually they would have done so; but, meantime, they would have been living their lives in a state not identifiable as schizophrenic.

The idea that delusions can occur, and occur commonly, in a neurotic condition is, of course, incompatible with the view advanced in Chapter 6.

Cameron (1959) voices what seems perhaps to be the predominant opinion, distilled from sixty years of psychiatric experience. He separates paranoia on the basis of a distinctive dynamic picture (after Freud). The extreme of this paranoid reaction is the rare paranoid state in which a rigid delusional system exists without impairment of the rest of the thought processes or of personality. The intermediate paranoid states may be 'complicated by schizophrenic factors' and, following current American practice, can be separated out only relatively from schizophrenia.

243

There are thus essentially three main theories:

1. Kraepelin: Paranoia is separate from dementia praecox of paranoid type, and there are intermediate states, paraphrenics.

2. Bleuler: Pure paranoia, if it exists at all, is so rare as to be disregardable. Schizophrenia includes in-between states. ·

3. Henderson & Gillespie: Paranoia is separate from schizophrenia and includes in-between states.

Most authors, regardless of their standpoint on the relationship between paranoid states and schizophrenia, would agree that those falling very close to the paranoia end of the continuum are characterized by:

(*a*) Dominant and persistent delusions which are highly systematized and usually involve ideas of persecution and/or grandiosity.

(*b*) A particular type (or types) of personality, which sounds like a watered-down paranoid psychosis (Arieti, 1959; Cameron, 1959; Fraser Steele, 1948), and a long-term history of paranoid reactions.

(*c*) A relatively late age of onset, at which characteristically different problems are encountered.

(*d*) A relative absence of dementia or thought disorder.

(*e*) A greater resistance to change, possibly, than paranoid schizophrenics, but a better prognosis in the sense that they are more likely to spend a greater proportion of their lives outside mental hospitals, functioning at a socially more or less acceptable level.

There seems to be most support in the literature for widening the concept of schizophrenia to include all paranoid manifestations, except the neurotic ones (which are regarded here as extrapunitive, but neither neurotic nor paranoid) and pure paranoia, which can be swept under the carpet. In the present study, however, group comparisons between non-paranoid schizophrenics, and integrated and non-integrated paranoiacs show up differences quite clearly.

PROCEDURE

Subjects

The sample in this inquiry, part of the larger sample described in Chapter 9, consisted of 20 melancholics, 26 paranoid states, and 20

Analysis of Results in terms of the Clinical Diagnosis

schizophrenics. Eight of the 20 schizophrenics overlapped with the original SSI sample; they are therefore kept separate for cross-validation purposes.

All the subjects were women recently admitted to hospital, though not necessarily for the first time. The schizophrenics were all acute cases, with less than two years' total time in hospital. The melancholic group included manic-depressives in the depressive phase, involutional melancholics, and other psychotic depressives. The paranoid group included all cases diagnosed as paranoid psychosis, paraphrenia, or paranoid schizophrenia.

Approximately 10 per cent of all successive admissions among the psychotics had to be rejected either because they were unwilling or unable to cooperate or because their Mill Hill Vocabulary score fell below the 15th centile. Cases of 60 or more years of age were also excluded.

Measures

All subjects completed the Symptom-Sign Inventory (SSI), the Hysteroid : Obsessoid Questionnaire (HOQ), and the Punitive scales. From the SSI the following scales were used:

Personal Illness *v.* Normal (PI *v.* No)
Psychotic *v.* Neurotic (P *v.* N)
Non-integrated Psychotic *v.* Integrated Psychotic (NIP. v IP)
Paranoid *v.* Schizophrenic (*Pa.* v. *Sc*)
Melancholic *v.* Schizophrenic (*Me* v. *Sc*)
Paranoid *v.* Melancholic (*Pa* v. *Me*)
Anxiety *v.* Hysteria (*Ax* v. *Hy*)
Anxiety *v.* Depression (*Ax* v. *Dp*)
Hysteria *v.* Depression (*Hy* v. *Dp*)

From the Punitive scales the following measures were used:

Acting-out Hostility (AH)
Criticism of Others (CO)
Delusional Hostility (DH)
Self-criticism (SC)
Delusional Guilt (DG)
General Punitiveness (E + I)
Direction of Punitiveness (E − I)

The final measure was the hysteroid score from the HOQ.

R   245

TABLE 63 Mean scores of non-integrated and integrated psychotics

Scale	Schizophrenics				Paranoids				Melancholics			
	15 NIP		5 IP		10 NIP		16 IP		8 NIP		12 IP	
	Mean	s.d.	Mean	s.d.	Mean	s.d.	Mean	s.d.	Mean	s.d.	Mean	s.d.
P v. N	2·73	2·26	1·60	1·02	6·00	2·05[a]	3·50	2·60	3·75	1·85	2·17	1·28
PI v. No	9·27	4·02	6·40	4·67	9·70	4·82[b]	5·31	3·12	12·00	2·91	10·67	3·62
Me v. Sc	1·47	2·09	1·00	1·41	1·80	2·09	1·31	1·45	3·62	2·12	4·75	1·74
Pa v. Sc	0·53	1·41	0·80	1·33	3·00	1·26	3·75	1·89	−0·25	1·48	0·42	1·93
Pa v. Me	−3·53	3·16	−2·20	2·23	−0·40	3·88	1·87	2·31	−7·88	3·82	−7·92	4·13
Ax v. Hy	0·87	1·02	0·20	0·75	0·70	1·10	−0·06	1·09	1·00	1·58	0·50	1·32
Ax v. Dp	2·67	2·57[a]	0·00	1·41	2·40	1·56[d]	0·44	1·00	1·75	2·28[a]	−0·42	1·89
Hy v. Dp	2·53	1·82[a]	0·60	1·20	2·00	1·38	0·75	1·09	1·62	2·39	0·42	1·38
HOQ	23·00	6·40	20·80	6·11	22·50	4·76	21·94	5·27	17·50	4·47	18·58	6·17
E+I	26·13	7·99	23·80	5·78	27·10	6·39[d]	15·62	6·42	25·87	6·83	21·67	7·09
E−I	2·53	5·99	3·00	8·32	1·80	6·72	5·12	4·81	0·62	5·09	−1·65	6·34
AH	5·47	2·45	3·80	1·47	5·80	2·48[c]	3·06	1·71	4·25	1·30	4·42	2·40
CO	5·53	2·75	5·80	2·76	5·40	2·37	3·81	2·13	5·75	2·77[a]	3·08	2·43
DH	3·33	2·39	3·80	2·14	3·40	2·50	3·50	2·23	3·25	1·92	1·58	1·38
SC	7·47	2·73	7·80	2·32	8·00	1·61[d]	3·69	1·96	7·50	2·18	8·33	2·54
DG	5·43	1·99	2·60	2·33	4·50	1·91[d]	1·56	1·54	5·12	1·96	4·25	2·49

[a] $p < ·05$; [b] $p < ·02$; [c] $p < ·01$; [d] $p < ·001$.

Italics denote the groups between which the differences are statistically significant.

Analysis of Results in terms of the Clinical Diagnosis

Since the Non-integrated Psychotic *v.* Integrated Psychotic scale was to be crucial in the study, cross-validation with the new sample was looked at first. Eight of the 12 schizophrenics scored 2 or more. Thus 67 per cent were classified as non-integrated as against 75 per cent in the first sample (p. 126 above). Sixteen out of 26 paranoids were classified as integrated (62 per cent as against 67 per cent). Only 12 of the 20 melancholics were classified as integrated (60 per cent as against 80 per cent); four of the recalcitrants, however, scored just immediately above the cutting point. A further 15 melancholics (not otherwise in this study) were looked at and 11 of these (or 73 per cent) fell into the integrated category. It was decided that these results justified the use of the scale for the present purpose, although the overall cross-validation shrinkage was from 74 to 62 per cent.

RESULTS

The three groups – 20 schizophrenics, 26 paranoids, and 20 melancholics – were each divided on the basis of a score of 2 or more being non-integrated and a score of 1 or less being integrated.

Table 63 shows the mean scores of non-integrated and of integrated schizophrenics, paranoids, and melancholics. The significance of the difference between the means of paranoids, schizophrenics, and melancholics was not examined, but only the difference between non-integrated and integrated schizophrenics, and similarly between non-integrated and integrated paranoids and melancholics.

Within schizophrenia, there are only two significant differences out of sixteen measures; within melancholics, there are again only two; but within the paranoid class there are seven differences which are significant, and these mostly at higher levels of significance. It would appear, therefore, that there are four readily distinguishable groups: melancholics, schizophrenics (non-paranoid), paranoid schizophrenics, and paranoiacs. This grouping is accomplished by re-combining the non-integrated and the integrated schizophrenics and melancholics. The means for these four groups are shown in *Table 64*.

TABLE 64 *Mean scores of melancholics, schizophrenics, paranoid schizo-phrenics, and paranoiacs on the SSI, HOQ, and E : I scales*

Scale	20 Melancholics		20 Schizophrenics		10 Paranoid schizophrenics		16 Paranoiacs	
	Mean	s.d.	Mean	s.d.	Mean	s.d.	Mean	s.d.
P v. N	2·80	1·72	2·45	2·09	6·00	2·05	3·50	2·60
PI v. No	11·20	3·41	8·55	4·38	9·70	4·82	5·31	3·12
Me v. Sc	4·30	1·95	1·35	1·96	1·80	3·88	1·31	1·45
Pa v. Sc	0·15	1·80	0·60	1·39	3·00	1·26	3·75	1·89
Pa v. Me	−7·90	4·01	−3·20	2·93	−0·40	3·88	1·87	2·31
Ax v. Hy	0·70	1·45	0·70	1·00	0·70	1·10	−0·06	1·09
Ax v. Dp	0·45	2·31	2·00	2·61	2·40	1·56	0·44	1·00
Hy v. Dp	0·90	1·95	2·05	1·88	2·00	1·38	0·75	1·09
HOQ	18·15	5·57	22·45	6·40	22·50	4·76	21·94	5·27
E+I	23·35	7·42	25·55	7·57	27·10	6·39	15·62	6·42
E−I	−1·95	6·62	2·65	7·02	1·80	6·72	5·12	4·81
AH	4·35	2·03	5·05	2·26	5·80	1·71	3·06	1·71
CO	4·15	2·89	5·60	2·76	5·40	2·37	3·81	2·13
DH	2·25	1·85	3·45	2·33	3·40	2·50	3·50	2·23
SC	8·00	2·41	7·55	2·64	8·00	1·61	3·69	1·96
DG	4·60	2·33	4·05	2·25	4·50	1·91	1·56	1·54

When those groups which do not differ significantly are combined into one group, and this group is compared with any from which it does differ, the results emerge that are shown in *Table 65*.

This rather complicated table may be crudely summarized and presented as in *Table 66* (p. 250). It can be seen that paranoid schizo-phrenics really do belong most clearly with schizophrenics, and that they differ as much on these measures from paranoiacs as they do from melancholics.

TABLE 65 *Means, t, and p values of groups that differ on the measures in Table 64*

Scale	Mean	s.d.	n	Mean	s.d.	n	t	p
P v. N	Paranoid schizophrenics			Rest				
	6·00	2·05	10	2·87	2·19	56	2·70	·01
PI v. No	Paranoiacs			Rest				
	5·31	3·12	16	9·84	4·05	50	4·57	·001
Pa v. Sc	Paranoid schizophrenics and Paranoiacs			Schizophrenics and Melancholics				
	3·46	1·76	26	0·37	1·62	40	7·07	·001
Me v. Sc	Melancholics			Rest				
	4·30	1·95	20	1·43	1·84	46	5·57	·001
Pa v. Me	Paranoiacs			Melancholics				
	1·87	2·31	16	−7·90	4·01	20	8·88	·001
Ax v. Hy	No significant differences							
Ax v. Dp	Melancholics and Paranoiacs			Paranoid schizophrenics and Schizophrenics				
	0·44	1·94	36	2·13	2·09	30	3·61	·001
Hy v. Dp	Melancholics and Paranoiacs			Paranoid schizophrenics and Schizophrenics				
	0·83	1·63	36	2·03	1·74	30	2·83	·01
HOQ	Melancholics			Rest				
	18·15	5·57	20	22·28	5·70	46	2·70	·01
E+I	Paranoiacs			Rest				
	15·62	6·42	16	24·98	7·39	50	4·78	·001
E−I	Paranoiacs			Melancholics				
	5·12	4·81	16	−1·95	6·62	20	3·61	·001
AH	Paranoid schizophrenics			Paranoiacs				
	5·80	2·48	10	3·06	1·71	16	3·97	·001
CO	Schizophrenics and Paranoid schizophrenics			Melancholics and Paranoiacs				
	5·53	2·64	30	4·00	2·65	36	2·32	·05
DH	Melancholics			Rest				
	2·25	1·85	20	3·46	2·38	46	2·18	·05
SC	Paranoiacs			Rest				
	3·69	1·96	16	7·82	2·38	50	6·78	·001
DG	Paranoiacs			Rest				
	1·56	1·54	16	4·36	2·23	50	5·50	·001

TABLE 66 *High, medium, and low scorers relative to each other on the same measures*

Scale	Melancholics	Schizophrenics	Paranoid schizophrenics	Paranoiacs
P v. N	low	low	high	low
PI v. No	high	high	high	low
Pa v. Sc	low	low	high	high
Me v. Sc	high	low	low	low
Pa v. Me	low		high	very high
Ax v. Hy				
Ax v. Dp	low	high	high	low
Hy v. Dp	low	high	high	low
HOQ	low	high	high	high
E+I	high	high	high	low
E—I	low			
AH			high	low
CO	low	high	high	low
DH	low	high	high	high
SC	high	high	high	low
DG	high	high	high	low

The foregoing results would have been substantially the same had the SSI scales of *Pa* v. *Sc*, *Me* v. *Sc*, and *Pa* v. *Me* been used to allocate patients to the groups of schizophrenia, paranoia, and melancholia instead of the clinical diagnosis, since agreement was high. The relationship between the SSI and the clinical diagnoses is shown in detail in *Table 67*.

TABLE 67 *Relationship between clinical and SSI diagnoses in allocating psychotics to three categories*

Clinical diagnosis	Symptom-Sign Inventory		
	Schizophrenia	Paranoia	Melancholia
Schizophrenia	14	3	3
Paranoia	5	20	1
Melancholia	2	1	17
	77% agreement		

It is possible, on the basis of the present study, to consider three of the five crucial criteria for differentiation listed above (p. 244), namely: (i) prognosis or prediction of clinical change, (ii) age of onset, and

Analysis of Results in terms of the Clinical Diagnosis
(under Conclusions, p. 254 below) (iii) dominance of systematized delusions.

(i) Clinical change was assessed by psychiatrists after five to seven weeks. *Table 68* shows the number of cases in each of the four diagnostic categories who were rated as much improved or as unimproved (including slightly improved). The frequency of marked clinical change is, therefore, highest among melancholics, with schizophrenics and paranoid schizophrenics very close together in an intermediate position, and paranoiacs much the lowest.

TABLE 68   *Relationship between clinical category and clinical improvement*

	Schizophrenics	Paranoid schizophrenics	Paranoiacs	Melancholics
Much improved	7	4	3	12
Unimproved	13	6	13	8
% improved	35	40	19	60

It should perhaps be emphasized again that prediction or assessment of the future course of the illness has not been studied, but rather the degree of change in the clinical picture after a short period of time. The commonly used rating of recovered, much improved, slightly improved, unimproved, in fact illustrates the difference. A paranoid state may be classified as recovered in the sense that he is able to return home, do his job, and generally lead a fairly normal life; yet he may be only slightly improved. A hebephrenic patient who was only slightly improved would still be a long way from home. Recovered is not a logical extension of the improvement continuum.

Even with these small numbers the results would at least seem to hold out some hope that the division into paranoid schizophrenic and paranoid state on the basis of the Non-integrated Psychotic scale of the SSI is a useful one, in that the two groups have a different short-term reaction to treatment and to hospitalization. Whether this short-term reaction has a close relationship with long-term reaction remains to be seen. The fact that the trends are as they would be expected to be clinically suggests that this relationship might be a fairly close one.

Since paranoiacs had changed the least and melancholics the most, the Paranoia *v.* Melancholia scale was examined for its predictive value.

Table 69 shows the relationship between this scale and improvement, both within diagnostic categories and overall. If the prediction were made that melancholics would do well and that the rest would do badly, 44 out of 66 (or 67 per cent) would be correct. The *Pa* v. *Me* scale correctly predicts 49 (or 74 per cent).

Table 70 shows the relationship between the total intropunitive score (SC+DG) and improvement, both within diagnostic categories and overall. Scores of 16 and over and of 9 and under are almost faultless; whereas the middle range is much more uncertain. No better result is obtained by combining *Pa* v. *Me* and Intropunitiveness, since the two scales are highly correlated.

(ii) However closely age may be related to an illness category, even within a particular universe of discourse such as psychotic illness, it is never an objective sign of that illness category. It is never a necessary or a sufficient condition for the occurrence of that illness. It can help to account for the form that the illness has taken; but it cannot constitute that illness.

Within the non-paranoid schizophrenic group, age was not significantly related to the Non-integrated Psychotic *v.* Integrated Psychotic scale, the Psychotic *v.* Neurotic scale, the Personal Illness *v.* Normal scale, or the General Punitive scale. The correlation between age and non-integrated Psychosis was, however, -0.403, and was close to the 5 per cent level of significance.

Within the melancholic group, age was not significantly related to any of the four scales; but, again, much the highest correlation was with non-integrated psychosis, r being -0.303.

Within the paranoiac group, age was significantly related to non-integrated psychosis (-0.488; $p < 0.01$); to personal illness (-0.409; $p < 0.05$); and to General Punitiveness (-0.429; $p < 0.05$). These results again support the need to regard the distinction between paranoid schizophrenics and paranoiacs.

Within the total psychotic class, age was significantly related to the Non-integrated Psychotic *v.* Integrated Psychotic scale (-0.529; $p < 0.001$), but was not at all related to the Psychotic *v.* Neurotic scale (0.051) or to the Personal Illness *v.* Normal scale (-0.072). The relationship between age and General Punitiveness was of borderline significance (-0.238).

That those who break down with a psychotic illness in their youth

TABLE 69 Relationship between the Paranoid v. Melancholia scale and improvement within diagnostic categories and overall

Pa v. Me	Schizophrenics Imp.	Unimp.	Paranoid schizophrenics Imp.	Unimp.	Paranoiacs Imp.	Unimp.	Melancholics Imp.	Unimp.	All Imp.	Unimp.
Melancholics	3	1	4	1	3		12	5	15	7
Paranoids	2	8		5		12		3	9	28
% correct	79		50		80		75		73	

TABLE 70 Relationship between Intropunitive scale and improvement within diagnostic categories and overall

Intropunitive scale	Schizophrenics Imp.	Unimp.	Paranoid schizophrenics Imp.	Unimp.	Paranoiacs Imp.	Unimp.	Melancholics Imp.	Unimp.	All Imp.	Unimp.
16+	2		2				6		10	
15/10	2	6	2	5		2	4	3	8	16
9−	1	3		1	3	10	1	6	5	20

should tend to be relatively non-integrated is not at all surprising. The adolescent search for identity is aided or hindered by increasing contact with the adult world. Those who fail by a wide margin to assume adult roles and responsibilities are halted in mid-stream. Having abandoned hope of achieving an integrative solution, they adopt a highly punitive attitude, oscillating between blaming themselves and blaming others. Lacking a sense of identity, and therefore of self-control, their aggression, when expressed overtly, tends to be unbridled. This presumably evokes the fear of unbridled retaliation, and so they retreat into fantasy.

Those who break down in middle age with a psychotic illness have already acquired, with, of course, varying degrees of success, adult roles and responsibilities. They meet their increasing responsibilities, declining skills, and accumulated failings with more crystallized attitudes. They are more discriminating in their attribution of blame.

CONCLUSIONS

When each of the clinically diagnosed groups of non-paranoid schizophrenia, paranoid states (including paranoid schizophrenia), and melancholia was split on the Non-integrated Psychotic *v.* Integrated Psychotic scale, very few differences were found within the non-paranoid schizophrenic and within the melancholic groups; but many differences were found within the paranoid group.

It is, therefore, useful to recognize four groups – non-paranoid schizophrenics, paranoid schizophrenics, paranoiacs, and melancholics. Paranoid schizophrenics were much closer to non-paranoid schizophrenics than to paranoiacs. This finding has relevance to the three main views that have been discussed. One group takes all the paranoid illnesses out of the schizophrenic group, another leaves them all in. The present results suggest that non-integrated paranoids belong with the schizophrenic group, and that integrated paranoids should be regarded as a distinct group. It is, therefore, the third view – that of Kraepelin – which is best supported.

The Paranoid *v.* Melancholic scale and the total intropunitive score each predicted with fair accuracy what psychiatrists would say about changes in the clinical state of patients five to seven weeks later.

Within the psychoses, age is strongly related to the Non-integrated Psychotic *v.* Integrated Psychotic scale (-0.529), but not to the Psychotic *v.* Neurotic scale (0.051). It has some relation also to General

Analysis of Results in terms of the Clinical Diagnosis

Punitiveness (−0·238). Younger patients are much less well integrated and tend to be somewhat more generally punitive.

II. NEUROTICS

As indicated in Chapter 4, the reliability of psychiatric diagnosis within the neuroses is poor. It is more or less inevitable, therefore, that the results from psychological tests based on clinical criteria will also be poor. For the sake of completeness, however, the results for the neurotics are analysed in the same way as those of the psychotics. The measures and scoring are as before. The subjects are the same 60 neurotics described in Chapter 9.

RESULTS

Since the Non-integrated Psychotic v. Integrated Psychotic scale is largely irrelevant, the neurotic groups have not been split on this basis. Otherwise *Table 71*, showing the mean scores of clinically diagnosed anxiety states, hysterics, and depressives, corresponds to *Table 64*, which shows the means for psychotics.

TABLE 71 *Mean scores of hysterics, anxiety states, and depressives on the SSI, HOQ, and E : I scales*

Scale	20 Hysterics Mean	s.d.	20 Anxiety states Mean	s.d.	20 Depressives Mean	s.d.
NIP v. IP	0·10	0·71	0·70	1·14	0·25	1·34
P v. N	0·00	1·84	−0·85	1·28	−0·05	1·53
PI v. No	9·95	4·42	10·75	2·72	12·55	3·01
Pa v. Sc	1·00	1·30	0·30	1·23	0·55	1·50
Me v. Sc	2·35	1·73	2·70	1·00	3·05	1·32
Pa v. Me	−4·10	3·53	−4·95	2·97	−5·95	3·20
Ax v. Hy	0·65	1·32	2·10	1·70	1·55	1·28
Ax v. Dp	1·05	1·57	2·70	2·12	0·75	1·45
Hy v. Dp	1·40	1·91	0·85	1·32	−0·35	1·71
HOQ	24·00	7·08	21·40	4·73	20·20	5·08
E+I	16·60	7·62	16·35	7·26	19·15	6·28
E−I	−0·20	4·41	0·00	4·52	0·65	4·30
AH	3·80	2·18	3·20	1·96	3·70	1·55
CO	3·10	2·26	4·15	2·74	4·70	2·87
DH	1·30	1·42	0·85	0·73	1·50	1·02
SC	6·20	2·00	6·10	2·95	6·85	2·56
DG	2·20	1·60	1·95	1·40	2·40	1·16

Hysterics differed from anxiety states only on the *Ax* v. *Hy* scale, which was, of course, made up specifically for this purpose, and on the *Ax* v. *Dp* scale. The respective values were $t = 2.94$, $p < 0.01$; and $t = 2.70$, $p < 0.02$.

Anxiety states differed from depressives on the *Ax* v. *Dp* scale ($t = 3.31$; $p < 0.01$); on the *Hy* v. *Dp* scale ($t = 2.40$; $p < 0.05$); and on Delusional Hostility ($t = 2.24$; $p < 0.05$).

Hysterics differed from depressives on the *Hy* v. *Dp* scale ($t = 2.97$; $p < 0.01$); on the *Ax* v. *Hy* scale ($t = 2.14$; $p < 0.05$); and on the Personal Illness *v.* Normal scale ($t = 2.11$; $p < 0.05$).

Apart from the scales which were specifically constructed to differentiate between the various groups, the number of differences is very small. There seems little point on this evidence in attempting to differentiate between the neurotic groups. No prognostic indicators were found, and age was of no significance.

III. SCHIZOPHRENICS, PARANOIACS, MELANCHOLICS, AND NEUROTICS COMPARED WITH NORMALS

Since, on the measures used here, paranoid schizophrenics and paranoiacs were so similar as to be combinable, four groups remain – schizophrenics, paranoiacs, melancholics, and neurotics.

No normal group has been examined on all measures together; but reference will be made to results obtained with different groups on each of the measures. Results are available for 88 normals on the HOQ (see p. 46 above), 73 have done the SSI (p. 110 above), and 32 have done the Punitive scales (p. 94). The samples are composed largely of various grades of mental hospital staff, members of the Friends of the Hospital, and patients recuperating on medical and surgical wards in a general hospital. They are probably reasonably comparable to the patients in intellectual level. Exact matching was not employed since none of the measures is consistently related to intellectual level. Most of the subjects were from Social Classes III and IV, but with a slight bias in the upward direction among normals. The major difference between the normal subjects and the patients would, however, consist in the fact that the normal subjects were all volunteers examined in an entirely different setting, having a quite different significance for the individual.

Analysis of Results in terms of the Clinical Diagnosis

Table 72 shows the mean scores of 30 schizophrenics, 16 paranoiacs, 20 melancholics, 60 neurotics, and 32–88 normals.

TABLE 72 *Mean scores of schizophrenics, paranoiacs, melancholics, neurotics, and normals on the SSI, HOQ, and E : I scales*

Scale	30 Schizophrenics		16 Paranoiacs		20 Melancholics		60 Neurotics		$N = 32$ to 88 Normals	
	Mean	s.d.	Mean	s.d.	Mean	s.d.	Mean	s.d.	Mean	s.d.
NIP v. IP	3·63	2·18	−0·31	0·92	1·00	2·17	0·35	1·12	0·97	1·08
P v. N	3·63	2·66	3·50	2·60	2·80	1·72	−0·30	1·62	0·29	0·70
PI v. No	8·93	4·56	5·31	3·12	11·20	3·41	11·08	3·61	1·80	1·28
HOQ	22·47	5·90	21·94	5·27	18·15	5·57	21·90	5·94	24·07	5·51
E+I	26·07	7·23	15·62	6·42	23·35	7·42	17·37	7·23	12·31	5·16
E−I	2·37	6·69	5·12	4·81	−1·95	6·62	0·15	4·40	2·00	3·92
AH	5·30	2·30	3·06	1·71	4·35	2·03	3·57	1·89	3·34	1·86
CO	5·53	2·64	3·81	2·13	4·15	2·89	3·98	2·74	3·25	2·00
DH	3·43	2·59	3·50	2·23	2·25	1·85	1·22	1·21	0·56	0·66
SC	7·70	2·35	3·69	1·96	8·00	2·41	6·38	2·69	3·84	2·22
DG	4·20	2·15	1·56	1·54	4·60	2·33	2·18	1·41	1·31	1·29

Table 73 deals with the significance of the difference between normals and each of the four abnormal groups in turn. The two comparisons in Table 73 marked with an asterisk are not in fact 'not significant'; they are actually significant in the opposite direction. Paranoiacs scored significantly lower than normals on non-integrated psychoticism ($t = 4·35; p < 0·001$). This paranoiac group was, however, selected on the basis of this scale. In addition, there are three 'manic' items in this scale whose abnormality is dependent on their being accepted in a mental hospital setting, and two items given more often by integrated than by non-integrated psychotics, which normals tend not to give.

Neurotics scored significantly lower on the Psychotic scale ($t = 2·46; p < 0·02$). This is mainly due to the fact that there were two items given more often by neurotics than by psychotics, and these were subtracted from the total number of 'psychotic' items. Normals tended to give neither the 'psychotic' nor the 'neurotic' items, and were thus penalized.

If these two scales were being used for screening purposes in a normal population, the two items going against the main stream should be eliminated to make the scale completely unidirectional. The Personal Illness v. Normal scale is unidirectional and could, therefore, be used for this purpose without modification.

TABLE 73   *Significance of the difference between normals and each of the four abnormal groups on the principal measures*

Scale	30 Schizophrenics		16 Paranoiacs		20 Melancholics		60 Neurotics	
	t	*p*	*t*	*p*	*t*	*p*	*t*	*p*
NIP *v.* IP	6·07	·001 H	n.s.*	L	n.s.		n.s.	
P *v.* N	6·68	·001 H	4·86	·001 H	6·24	·001 H	n.s.*	L
PI *v.* No	8·29	·001 H	4·33	·001 H	11·85	·001 H	18·05	·001 H
HOQ	n.s.		n.s.		4·29	·001 L	n.s.	
E+I	8·60	·001 H	n.s.		5·84	·001 H	3·89	·001 H
E−I	n.s.		2·24	·05 H	2·44	·02 L	2·06	·05 L
AH	3·70	·001 H	n.s.		n.s.		n.s.	
CO	3·80	·001 H	n.s.		n.s.		n.s.	
DH	6·38	·001 H	5·16	·001 H	3·93	·001 H	3·40	·01 H
SC	6·66	·001 H	n.s.		6·21	·001 H	4·88	·001 H
DG	6·57	·001 H	n.s.		5·77	·001 H	3·00	·01 H

H=high; L=low.

Direction of Punitiveness seems to be more related to the amount of clinical change to be expected within the personally ill. The most extrapunitive group is the psychopathic, followed by paranoiacs, schizophrenics, neurotics, and, finally, melancholics.

It is important to point out that most of the findings here have been anticipated by Trouton & Maxwell (1956), although they have not drawn all the conclusions from their results which are drawn here. Trouton & Maxwell carried out a factor analysis of items from the Maudsley Medical Questionnaire. They concluded that psychosis and neurosis were independent dimensions, and noted that, while neurotics scored high on neuroticism and low on psychoticism, psychotics scored high on both. McGuire (1962) also found that psychotics scored as high as neurotics on the Maudsley Personality Inventory Neuroticism scale.

Eysenck (1960) plotted the Trouton & Maxwell results on the two dimensions, using factor scores. If the NIP *v.* IP and the P *v.* N scales are added to give a scale more equivalent to their psychoticism, and the mean scores of each group are plotted against the mean scores on the PI *v.* No scale, the positions are almost identical to those shown by Eysenck. In his diagram all the schizophrenic groups are higher on psychoticism than the psychotic depressive and paranoid groups. The paranoiacs are relatively low on neuroticism, and the paranoid schizo-

Analysis of Results in terms of the Clinical Diagnosis

phrenics are in among the other schizophrenics and well away from the paranoiacs. All of this is found here. The fact that, in both studies, schizophrenics score appreciably higher on psychoticism lends additional support to the contention that it is useful to think in terms of non-integrated and integrated psychotics. The former category consists largely of non-paranoid and of paranoid schizophrenics; whereas the latter category consists largely of melancholics and paranoiacs.

The virtual identity between the results of the two studies is the more striking in that Trouton & Maxwell were using questionnaires filled in by psychiatrists (albeit some of their answers would result from questioning the patients); whereas the present results are derived solely from the replies of patients to standard questions. The comparison is shown in *Table 74*.

TABLE 74 *Mean scores on NIP v. IP plus P v. N and on PI v. No for seven psychiatric groups, compared with a rough approximation to the Trouton & Maxwell factor scores*

	NIP v. IP + P v. N	PI v. No	Psychotic	Neurotic
10 Paranoid schizophrenics	10·50	9·70	15½	9½
20 Non-paranoid schizophrenics	5·65	8·55	13	9
20 Melancholics	3·80	11·20	10	9
16 Paranoiacs	3·19	5·31	10	4½
20 Hysterics	0·10	9·95	6	10
20 Anxiety states	−0·15	10·75	5	9
20 Depressives	0·20	12·55	4	6½

For a more accurate and detailed comparison see Eysenck (1960, p. 15).

From these rough comparisons it is clear that there is only one serious discrepancy. The present neurotic depressives are, relative to other groups, much higher on neuroticism than are those of Trouton & Maxwell. As their study was *ex post facto*, they were presumably unable to avoid the extraordinary diagnostic huggermugger. Some of their oddments, which have been ironed out here, might have found their way into the depressive group of the present study and thus raised the mean somewhat. On the other hand, the present results perhaps look the less likely clinically and may be corrected in a larger sample.

CONCLUSIONS

The four groups that can be identified may thus be described, with some confidence, in the following way:

Schizophrenics score abnormally high on all scales, except the two main personality measures – the HOQ and Direction of Punitiveness. All these differences are significant at the 0·1 per cent level. They have almost as many 'neurotic' symptoms as neurotics; they have as many 'psychotic' symptoms as integrated psychotics, plus additional ones of their own. They are highly punitive in their attitudes and are as likely to have intropunitive as extrapunitive delusions. Consideration of the frequency table in Appendix C (Chapter 8 above) makes it clear that they do not just answer 'yes' indiscriminately to all items or to all types of items.

Paranoiacs do not have as many 'neurotic' symptoms as neurotics or as other psychotics (manics apart); but they do have far more than normal people, and they do have as many 'psychotic' symptoms as other psychotics. They are the least generally punitive of the abnormal groups and do not quite differ significantly in this respect from normals. They are, however, significantly more extrapunitive than normals, particularly as a result of the frequency of their delusions of hostility. These results, therefore, reflect very well the clinical picture of highly encapsulated delusions with very little carry-over into other areas, at least as measured here. In the sense that they often persist almost indefinitely in their abnormal state, the cost of *not* having more widespread symptomatology may be said to be very high.

Melancholics are abnormally high in their scores on both 'neurotic' and 'psychotic' symptoms. They are much more obsessoid than any other group. They are abnormally punitive, and intropunitiveness is the direction in which their punitiveness is usually expressed. Although they have significantly more delusions of hostility than normal people, it is in their self-criticism and delusions of guilt that they are most markedly different.

Neurotics are, pleasingly, more 'neurotic' than normals; but they do not differ from them on the two psychotic scales. They are abnormally punitive, and are rather more intropunitive than normals. Like the melancholics, they have more delusions of hostility (but these are not the unequivocally delusional items) than normals, and they are abnormal in their scores on both intropunitive scales.

REFERENCES

ARIETI, S. (1959). Schizophrenia: the manifest symptomatology, the psychodynamic and formal mechanisms. In S. Arieti (Ed.), *American handbook of psychiatry*, Vol. 1. New York: Basic Books.

BLEULER, E. (1924). *Textbook of psychiatry*. (4th edn.) New York: Macmillan.

CAMERON, N. (1959). Paranoid conditions and paranoia. In S. Arieti (Ed.), *American handbook of psychiatry*, Vol. 1. New York: Basic Books.

EYSENCK, H. J. (1960). Classification and the problem of diagnosis. In H. J. Eysenck (Ed.), *Handbook of abnormal psychology*. London: Pitman Medical Publishing Co.

HENDERSON, D. K. & GILLESPIE, R. D. (1950). *Textbook of psychiatry*. (7th edn.) London: Oxford University Press.

KRAEPELIN, E. (1919). *Dementia praecox*. Edinburgh: Livingstone.

KRAEPELIN, E. (1921). *Manic-depressive insanity and paranoia*. Edinburgh: Livingstone.

MAYER-GROSS, W., SLATER, E. & ROTH, M. (1954). *Clinical psychiatry*. (2nd edn., 1960.) London: Cassell; Baltimore: Williams & Wilkins, 1955.

MCGUIRE, R. J. (1962). A study of the MPI used with psychiatric patients. *Bulletin of the Brit. Psychol. Soc.*, **47**, 56.

STEELE, G. D. FRASER (1948). The place of paranoid states in psychiatric classification with special reference to paranoid schizophrenia. *Edinburgh med. J.*, **55**, 362.

TROUTON, D. & MAXWELL, A. E. (1956). The relation between neurosis and psychosis. *J. ment. Sci.*, **102**, 1.

CHAPTER THIRTEEN

Changes in Symptom, Attitude, and Trait Measures among Chronic Neurotics in a Therapeutic Community[1]

INTRODUCTION

One of the criticisms levelled at psychotherapists is that their published accounts of therapeutic results usually lack an adequate framework for evaluating psychological change. The distinction of different levels of psychological functioning, namely the symptom, attitude, and trait levels, advanced in previous chapters, may provide one such framework.

Superficial therapies may achieve symptom relief; but therapies directed at more fundamental change should initiate changes in test scores related to the deeper and more enduring aspects of psychological functioning. Some suggestive evidence has already been published. Foulds (1959) found that, in neurotic women, symptom measures changed relatively more than personality measures on re-test following one month's treatment of a conventional kind not involving intensive psychotherapy. The attitude tests related to personality type showed no significant change. Martin & Caine (1963), however, found modification in the same attitude tests, as well as symptom relief, following treatment for an average period of five months in the therapeutic community for neurosis at Claybury Hospital. Modification was continued on discharge, as reflected in follow-up testing one year later. No significant change at the trait level was found.

Although the results of these two studies are not directly comparable – since there were sex and personality differences between the two groups, the testing periods were dissimilar, and Foulds's group was not followed up – the approach seemed worth pursuing with a larger sample. The present study is an extension of that described by Martin & Caine. Psychological test score changes accompanying treatment in a therapeutic community are described, using the classifications and related

[1] I wish to thank Dr K. Hope for carrying out the statistical analysis and for the interpretation of results.

Chronic Neurotics in a Therapeutic Community

psychological tests detailed in earlier chapters. Changes are related to a normal sample, tested and re-tested after a one-year interval, to establish a baseline over roughly the same period as the neurotic test series, and to establish the reliability in normal persons of the various types of test over a fairly long period of time.

THE THERAPEUTIC COMMUNITY

The vexed question of what constitutes psychotherapy is left aside as having been treated fully elsewhere by Edwards & Cronbach (1952), Curran & Partridge (1955), Rogers (1961), and Eysenck (1952, 1954, 1955, 1960), to mention only a few authors. Although there is no disagreement in classifying therapeutic community treatment as psychotherapy, there is considerable divergence of opinion among workers in the field as to which constitute the truly therapeutic practices. A full account of the principles of this method as evolved at Claybury has been given by Martin (1962), and the present research was carried out within this framework.

Zilboorg & Henry (1941) have written of two revolutions in the development of psychiatry. The first was associated with the radical transformation of care for the mentally ill initiated by Pinel. The second was accomplished through the work of Freud and the development of the psychodynamic approach in the treatment of mental disorders. Community therapy is considered by some (Moreno, 1952; Dreikurs, 1955; Rapoport, 1960) to represent a third revolution in psychiatry. Here, group methods, milieu therapy, and administrative psychiatry replace the encapsulated, sacrosanct mysteries of the one doctor/one patient/consulting-room relationship.

A number of factors can be distinguished which have combined to promote this movement in psychiatry: (i) growing dissatisfaction with individual psychotherapy, both in terms of substantiated results and in terms of failure to cope with the sheer mass of the problem; (ii) the emphasis of such neo-Freudian writers as Fromm (1943), Horney (1951), and Sullivan (1953) on interpersonal relations and cultural factors in neurotic breakdown; (iii) the recognition of the deleterious effects on mentally ill patients and on staff of authoritarian institutional régimes (Martin, 1955, 1962; Barton, 1959); (iv) the application of social scientific theory to psychotherapy (Foulkes & Anthony, 1957); (v) the increasing recognition of the importance of social experience in learning

263

and communication processes in psychiatry, education, and other fields (Jaques, 1951; Johnson, 1953; Anthony, 1953; Martin, 1962). Johnson, for example, discusses the role of attitudes in determining the selection and modification of information presented, quoting the work of Cantril *et al.* (1949) and relating their experimental work to the learning process in free group discussion.

Although therapeutic communities must differ in many respects according to their stage of development, the type of patient they serve, and the personalities and capacities of their staffs, there is general agreement as to their aim. This has been described by Jones (1952) and subscribed to by Bloch (1961) and Martin (1962). In essence, the therapeutic community is one in which a conscious effort is made to employ all the staff and patient potential in an overall treatment programme.

Rapoport (1960, p. 22) has outlined six beliefs which he feels underlie all therapeutic community endeavour:

'(*a*) The total social organization in which the patient is involved – and not only the relationship with the doctor – is seen as affecting the therapeutic outcome;

'(*b*) the social organization is not regarded as a routinized background to treatment; but as a vital force, useful for creating a milieu that will maximize therapeutic effects;

'(*c*) the core element in such an institutional context is the provision of opportunities for patients to take an active part in the affairs of the institution . . .;

'(*d*) *all* relationships within the hospital – those of patients among themselves as well as patients with staff – are regarded as potentially therapeutic . . .;

'(*e*) aside from formal characteristics of structuring relationships, the *qualitative* atmosphere of the social environment is itself considered important therapeutically. This general orientation has reference to what is sometimes called the "emotional climate" of the institution . . .;

'(*f*) a high value is placed on communication *per se*. One basis for this value is an administrative one. It is considered valuable for people in one part of the organization to know what people in other parts are doing, thinking, and feeling. Furthermore, the act of communicating is thought to have an important morale and therapeutic effect for staff as well as patients. The content of communication is also considered valuable for treatment by making available, through a variety of channels, data supplementing the limited information that emerges in the doctor-patient relationship.'

Admirable though these principles may seem, they remain suppositions until their beneficial effects upon patients have been demonstrated. The burden of proof is on the therapeutic community builders, if the 'third revolution' is not to be regarded in terms more of staff ideology than of efficient functioning of the patients. Few would deny that, in both psychotherapeutic and physical treatment, good communications and the quality of group and individual relations have a bearing on therapeutic outcome; but the distinction, in the therapeutic community, between the merely stimulating and the essentially psychotherapeutic has yet to be made.

In individual analysis and group therapy the concept of transference is usually regarded as central, although most group therapists would agree that the transference factor is considerably modified by group conditions (Foulkes & Anthony, 1957). The therapeutic community differs from both these treatments in the opportunities provided for establishing relationships between patients and between patients and staff outside a formal, limited treatment setting. Although these relationships are subject to analysis and understanding in the small groups and ward meetings, it is clear that a further modification of the transference phenomena as described and manipulated in individual *and* group analysis must occur. The roles, in treatment, of other factors, such as learning and conditioning, empathy, identification, and social perception are probably augmented. As Rogers (1961) emphasizes for his non-directive therapist, the personality of the community therapist is likely to be of great importance in effective treatment.[1]

Be that as it may, the first step in establishing the therapeutic community as a form of treatment is to show that it is at least as effective as other forms of psychotherapy. The advent of such communities is of so recent an origin that little published work into their effects is to be

[1] The writer (Caine, 1964) has found a distinctive interest pattern on the Kuder Preference Record (Personal Form A) for therapeutic community nurses, and significant differences between them and general nurses. The former show a marked preference for working with ideas and abstract material rather than concrete things, and a marked absence of authoritarian attitudes. Both groups showed a pronounced preference for facing up to, rather than avoiding, interpersonal conflict in comparison with the general norms of the scale.

found. The reports of Greenblatt, York & Brown (1955) and of Stanton & Schwartz (1954), although dealing with milieu therapy, are of a general descriptive character rather than validative, and are concerned with American hospitals for psychotics at very different stages of development from the neurosis units to be described here. Rapoport's (1960) study of the Social Rehabilitation Unit at Belmont Hospital, associated with the work of Maxwell Jones (1952), represents one attempt at an evaluation of community therapy techniques in a setting more similar to that obtaining at the Claybury Neurosis Units. Unfortunately, no objective measures of psychological functioning were included in the study, the follow-up material is suspect – as the authors point out – and no control group was used in the design. The patient sample, too, was atypical for a mental hospital neurosis unit, being mainly composed of personality disorders drawn from a working-class culture.

A number of criteria can be enumerated against which research designs and research findings can be evaluated in psychotherapy. These include the provision of a control 'no treatment' or 'other treatment' group, objective measures, an adequate criterion of improvement, adequate sampling, and follow-up. As yet no studies in this area have met all these criteria. The present investigation tries to meet all except the first of these criteria, since work in a comparative treatment study is in its very early stages. No claims are therefore made for the superiority of community therapy as such. The aim has rather been to try to establish a baseline for comparing the efficacy of different forms of treatment.

SETTING AND PROCEDURE FOR THE INVESTIGATION

Description of the Units
The investigation was carried out on chronic neurotic patients undergoing treatment in two neurosis units, both of which are run as therapeutic communities. These units, Forest House and Orchard House, comprise two modern villas in the grounds of Claybury Hospital. The two units are run on the same fundamental principles, but differ in some of the details of their day-to-day organization.

Forest House, throughout the work under consideration, was run as a mixed unit with a total of thirty informal patients, roughly in the proportion of one man to two women. One of the first steps to try to provide more adequate psychotherapeutic help for more patients was the introduction of group therapy conducted on group-analytic lines. The second important factor was the introduction of community therapy, and with it the focusing of therapeutic endeavour on the personality as a whole rather than predominantly on symptomatic relief. Physical treatment, including even night sedation, has been abandoned, except for an occasional crisis.

The treatment programme extends from Monday morning to Friday afternoon, the majority of patients going home for the weekend. This is encouraged as part of treatment policy in order to maintain from the start a firm link between the somewhat artificial atmosphere of the unit and the reality problems of the patient's family relationships.

Four days a week a community meeting is held, followed by a staff meeting attended by doctors, nurses, occupational therapists, and a psychiatric social worker. Both types of meeting are free and unstructured. Problems arising out of the community meeting are commonly discussed at the staff meeting. Staff tensions and differences of attitude and opinion are worked through, and any material relevant to the patients' treatment is fed back into this common pool, from which deeper understanding of their emotional problems can arise.

The patients are divided into four small groups of from six to eight for more intensive group psychotherapy. Each group meets twice a week with their doctor, and twice a week with the occupational therapist or staff nurse, in the mornings.

The afternoons are devoted to occupational activities, which are designed to try to throw into relief the patients' problems rather than merely provide diversion or occupation.

Evening social activities are planned by the patients under the guidance of the nursing staff. Every month an evening community meeting is held to which patients who have left the hospital, but feel the need for some further support, can come. On average, four or five avail themselves of this opportunity.

Orchard House, from which a minority of the cases in this study came, is a unit of only twenty beds. Instead of a shift system, there is one sister in charge on spread-over duty, with two student nurses on each shift. During the period under consideration there were no registrars taking responsibility on the unit, the groups being conducted by two more senior doctors. There was no occupational therapist or social therapist. Ward meetings were held daily, but were attended by the doctors only one day each week, being otherwise conducted by the sister.

Empirical Studies

The Research Problem

Views differ greatly about the efficacy of any form of psychotherapy, and exceptional difficulties attend any attempt to establish objectively what it does and how it does it. In the units described much time is devoted by many highly trained staff to a relatively small number of patients. Ultimately this approach can be justified only if it can be shown that it achieves something more than symptomatic relief, which can often be achieved more easily and rapidly by physical treatments and simple reassurance. The average stay of the patients is six to nine months and, again, the length of the period can be justified only if some lasting benefit accrues which is likely to reduce suffering and loss of working time in the future.

Selection of Patients

Only neurotics and a very few psychopaths are admitted to the unit. Within these groups there is little selection, the majority of patients referred by general practitioners or by consultants, within or without the hospital, being accepted. It may be that, as the particular approach to treatment used in the unit has become known, doctors have become more selective, referring mainly patients who they consider might benefit from this protracted, intensive form of treatment. There is no information about how this selection is made; but it is certainly based on intuition and experience rather than on any objective criteria.

Since the majority of neurotics are now treated as outpatients, these inpatient units inevitably receive a large proportion of chronic, inadequate patients who have failed to respond to other forms of treatment, and of those whose domestic situation is very seriously disturbed as a result of the illness. It is fair to say, therefore, that on the whole the patients admitted are those who would generally be considered to have a relatively poor prognosis. They are drawn from a wide area geographically, part of which is suburban London and part rural Essex and Hertfordshire.

For purposes of comparison a sample of 30 normal volunteers (15 men and 15 women) was tested and re-tested one year later on the Punitive scales, the HOQ, and the Depression scale of the MMPI.

The subjects were drawn from local organizations, namely Toc H, Conservative Party Association, the Women's Voluntary Service, National Association for Mental Health, Friends of the Hospital and their friends, and from a firm engaged in the standardization of industrial designs. This was predominantly a middle-class sample and not representative of the general population. The patient sample was, on the other hand, predominantly lower-middle class. However, a comparison of the scores on the Extrapunitive and Intropunitive scales of this sample of normals and of that sample described by Foulds, Caine & Creasy (1960), representing various occupational grades of mental hospital employees and their relatives, showed no significant differences. The MMPI scales used were all within normal limits, and HOQ mean scores were very similar to those of 65 normal subjects (33 women and 32 men) tested in Aberdeen.[1] It seems likely, therefore, that the present sample of normals is a reasonable approximation to that of an ideal general sample.

THE INVESTIGATION

During the period of investigation 86 patients were admitted to the neurosis units. No patient scoring below the 10th centile on the Mill Hill Vocabulary scale was accepted for treatment.

	Treatment completed	*Number of patients*
A	Tested and followed up	48
B	Not tested at discharge	2
C	Not tested on follow-up	9
D	Did not complete hospital testing	3
	Treatment not completed	
E	Self-discharge soon after admission	12
F	Transfer to other units after admission testing	10
G	Still in treatment at end of study	2

The admission scores of groups C to G are analysed below in the light of the scores of A and B, who supplied the data for the main analysis. These 50 neurotics completed a battery of tests on four occasions – on admission to hospital, after six weeks, just before discharge (with two exceptions), and one year after discharge.

[1] I am indebted to J. J. Kear-Colwell, Department of Mental Health, University of Aberdeen, for this information.

Empirical Studies

The symptom and personality breakdowns of groups A and B were as follows:

	Women	Men
Dysthymics of obsessoid personality	14	22
Dysthymics of hysteroid personality	5	3
Hysterics of obsessoid personality	3	0
Hysterics of hysteroid personality	3	0

The diagnostic category was that assigned by the consultant psychiatrist concerned. The personality allocation was derived from ratings of personality traits by medical, nursing, and occupational therapy staff after approximately two weeks of observation (see Chapter 3, p. 41 above).

In addition to tests at follow-up, a brief interview was conducted to help to determine the success or failure of the treatment. Patients fell into three fairly distinct categories. The first was a 'completely successful' group of 29 who were working at follow-up, who had had no further treatment, and who did not anticipate needing any in the future.

The second 'successful' group consisted of 8 cases who were working and claimed considerable improvement, but reported that they had a few residual symptoms which they described as 'ghost' symptoms. They felt able to control these and they anticipated that they would disappear in time. This group had received minimal supportive treatment through attendance at an outpatient clinic or through the general practitioner about once a month or so. These two groups are combined as the Success group.

The third Failure group of 13 stated that they had not benefited from treatment at all, that their symptoms were just as bad, and that they had been able to carry on only with considerable effort. They were receiving regular and frequent supportive treatment. Five had been readmitted to hospital; but 7 were able to work outside the home.

Thus 74 per cent of those completing treatment were considerably better one year after leaving hospital than they had been on admission; 88 per cent were back at work.

Symptom Measures
The Personal Illness scale from the SSI
MMPI clinical scales of Hypochondriasis (*Hs*), Depression (*D*), Psychasthenia (*Pt*)
General Punitiveness (E + I)
The Mooney Problem Check List (MPCL)

The *Hs* and *Pt* scales gave results very similar to the *D* scale throughout, though slightly less efficiently. Accordingly, only the *D* scale is reported.

(E + I) was found to correlate 0·62 ($p < $·01) with the PI scale, and negligibly with the HOQ, in a sample of 56 neurotics, thus supporting findings reported in earlier chapters.

Attitude Measure

Again, results described in earlier chapters with regard to the Direction of Punitiveness were supported by Caine & Hawkins (1963). In his principal component analysis of the E and I sub-scales Hope (1963) found that the best expression of the Direction of Punitiveness measure was by the formula (2SC + DG) − (AH + CO + DH). This measure has usually been significantly related to the HOQ, but not to diagnostic measures.

Trait Measure

The Hysteroid : Obsessoid Questionnaire (HOQ)

The Mooney Problem Check List has been included above as a symptom measure although it is not a standardized test. This was used as a rough and superficial measure of problems and fears as seen by the patients, and to explore further the expression of these by various categories of patient (Foulds & Caine, 1959; Langley, 1963).

Exception might be taken to so heavy and unfashionable a dependence upon questionnaires. In the earliest studies psychomotor, intellectual speed, and projective tests were used to establish diagnostic and personality differences. Questionnaires were in no way inferior to the other types of measure in this classifying function with neurotics and they have advantages from the points of view of administration and scoring.

Hypotheses

1. In the normal sample, no significant change was anticipated on any of the measures.

Regardless of the likelihood that neurotics would fluctuate more than normals in the actual function being measured, they were probably liable to fluctuate more in test-taking attitude and other variables which would tend to reduce test : re-test correlations. They were more likely to fluctuate in these ways during than after treatment.

2. It was, therefore, predicted that test : re-test correlations would follow the descending order: normals, neurotics between discharge and follow-up, neurotics between admission and discharge.

The earliest work in this area, described in Chapter 1 (p. 5 above), was carried out in a hospital which relied mainly on situational, supportive, and drug treatments. It was found that, in this setting, symptom measures changed significantly even in six weeks, whereas neither attitude nor trait measures did so. It was hypothesized, however, that:

3. Successful neurotics, in the community therapy setting, would not change significantly in six weeks, since the form of treatment is exploratory and disturbing rather than psychologically placatory. This would apply to symptom measures as well as to attitude measures, both of which would, however:

4. ultimately change in the direction of normality.

5. No change at the trait level was anticipated, as there is no reason to suppose that the personality traits involved are psychopathological in themselves. Destructive attitudes associated with trait constellations might well be modified without involving a change at the trait level itself. Specifically, all measures, except the HOQ, should ultimately move in the direction of normality in the Success group.

6. No changes should occur in the Failure group.

RESULTS

The mean scores of the neurotics and normals are reported in *Table 75*. A 2×2, sex $\times$ occasion, factorial design in the analysis of variance was applied to the scores of the normal subjects on the four variables: Depression, General Punitiveness, Hysteroid : Obsessoid personality, and Direction of Punitiveness. Only two of the twelve variance ratios exceeded the 10 per cent level, and these were the ratios for the difference between the sexes in Depression and in Direction of Punitiveness. As in previous studies, men are somewhat more extrapunitive than women and somewhat less depressed. Because of this sex difference, the scores of men and women on these two variables were analysed separately.

TABLE 75 *Mean scores of neurotics (five tests) and normals (four tests)*

| | NEUROTICS | | | | NORMALS | | |
| | Successes | | Failures | | | | |
	N	Mean	N	Mean		N	Mean
Personal Illness (PI scale)							
A	34	8·1	11	9·9			
S	22	7·0	6	8·8			
D	17	1·7	5	5·8			
F	23	2·5	5	5·4			
Depression (MMPI *D*)							
Males					*Males*		
A	19	81·9	6	90·0	Test	15	46·4
S	16	70·3	5	88·0	Re-test	13	50·4
D	19	58·5	6	80·3			
F	19	60·9	6	90·3			
Females					*Females*		
A	18	80·4	7	86·4	Test	15	53·4
S	16	83·1	6	87·0	Re-test	15	52·0
D	18	65·7	5	67·6			
F	18	58·4	7	75·9			
General Punitiveness (E+I)							
A	37	19·1	13	20·5	Test	30	11·4
S	32	20·2	11	20·4	Re-test	30	10·2
D	37	16·0	11	19·5			
F	37	12·2	13	19·5			
Personality Type (HOQ)							
A	37	21·6	13	19·6	Test	30	23·5
S	32	20·7	11	17·7	Re-test	30	24·5
D	37	23·5	11	20·1			
F	37	24·5	13	20·5			
Direction of Punitiveness (E−I)							
Males					*Males*		
A	19	4·1	6	6·8	Test	15	−1·3
S	16	1·4	5	6·8	Re-test	15	−2·0
D	19	−1·0	6	7·2			
F	19	−0·4	6	7·3			
Females					*Females*		
A	18	6·1	7	10·9	Test	15	+0·5
S	16	9·1	6	10·8	Re-test	15	+0·5
D	18	5·1	5	4·0			
F	18	2·3	7	6·1			

The neurotics were tested on admission to hospital (A), after six weeks of community therapy (S), on discharge from hospital (D), and on follow-up one year after discharge (F). They were allotted to a Success or a Failure group according to their condition on follow-up.

Normal subjects were re-tested one year after the initial testing.

Empirical Studies

Hypothesis 1 was confirmed: on the four available measures, MMPI *D* scale, General Punitiveness, HOQ, and Direction of Punitiveness, there were no significant changes.

Hypothesis 2 was that the descending order for test : re-test correlations would be normals, neurotics between discharge and follow-up, neurotics between admission and discharge. The correlations are shown in *Table 76*; thus 13 of the 14 conform to expectation.

TABLE 76   *Re-test correlations of normals and of neurotics between admission and discharge and between discharge and follow-up*

Scale	Normals	Neurotics Between admission and discharge	Neurotics Between discharge and follow-up
Personal Illness	—	0·30	0·56
Depression	0·62	0·25	0·55
General Punitiveness	0·75	0·29	0·62
Direction of Punitiveness	0·51	0·20	0·65
Hysteroid : Obsessoid	0·85	0·43	0·74

An examination of the slope of the curve of the Success group (*Figures 6–12*) bears out Hypotheses 3, 4, and 5 to some extent. The obtained regressions illustrated in *Figures 6* to *12* and analysed in *Table 77* are predominantly linear, with the occasional addition of a quadratic element. The relatively flat curve between admission and sixth-week testing contributes to the appearance of a significant deviation from linearity in *Figure 9*. In *Figures 8, 10,* and *12* (Successes) the slope for this period of therapy is contrary to the overall tendency, though the deviations from linearity are not significant.

FIGURES 6–12
REGRESSIONS OF FIVE VARIABLES ON TREATMENT

In each diagram the horizontal axis is drawn at a height representing the average score of normals estimated from previous studies. The four observations represent the mean scores of neurotics tested on admission to hospital, after six weeks of community therapy, on discharge from hospital, and one year after discharge. Patients were allotted to a Success or a Failure group according to the outcome of therapy. All the tests except the Personal Illness scale were administered

274

to a sample of normals, and their test and one-year re-test scores are indicated by the ends of a dotted line. Standard deviations are estimated from the weighted average of the error mean squares of the two neurotic groups.

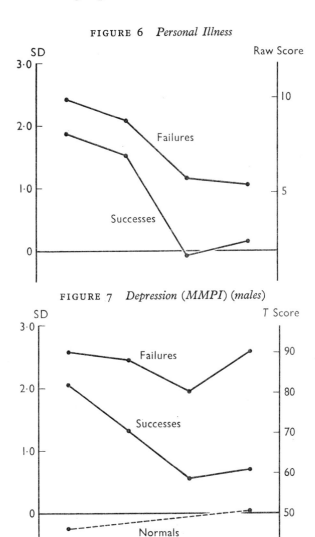

FIGURE 6   *Personal Illness*

FIGURE 7   *Depression (MMPI) (males)*

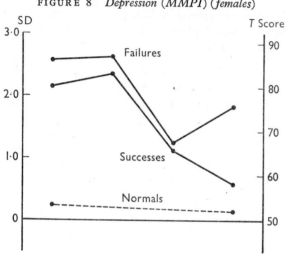

FIGURE 8   *Depression (MMPI) (females)*

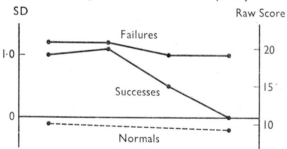

FIGURE 9   *General Punitiveness (E + I)*

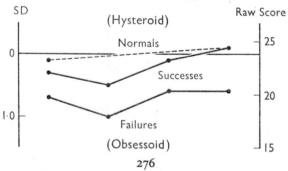

FIGURE 10   *Personality Type (HOQ)*

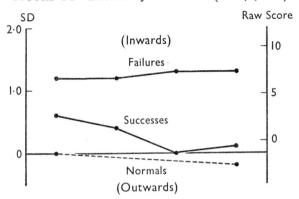

FIGURE 11   *Direction of Punitiveness* $(E-I)$ *(males)*

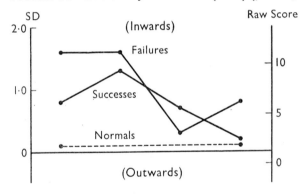

FIGURE 12   *Direction of Punitiveness* $(E-I)$ *(females)*

TABLE 77 *Tests of the regressions of four variables on treatment*

Source	DEPRESSION (MMPI D) Males		DEPRESSION (MMPI D) Females		GENERAL PUNITIVENESS (E+I)		PERSONALITY TYPE (HOQ)		DIRECTION OF PUNITIVENESS (E−I) Males		DIRECTION OF PUNITIVENESS (E−I) Females	
	d.f.	Mean square	d.f.	Mean square	d.f.	Mean square	d.f.	Mean square	d.f.	Mean square	d.f.	Mean square
A. REGRESSIONS OF SUCCESSES												
Linear	1	5082·00	1	6077·04	1	1099·75	1	243·34	1	227·67	1	212·09
Quadratic	1	908·92	1	438·11	1	220·50	1	33·58	1	48·39	1	146·75
Cubic	1	188·61	1	788·56	1	46·62	1	54·95	1	6·41	1	61·37
Error	69	231·08	66	206·20	139	48·76	139	34·39	69	40·12	66	43·35
B. REGRESSIONS OF FAILURES												
Linear	1	12·83	1	816·42	1	10·75	1	15·88	1	1·00	1	137·49
Quadratic	1	207·00	1	92·30	1	0·98	1	16·25	1	0·06	1	7·34
Cubic	1	156·61	1	708·85	1	1·33	1	20·38	1	0·00	1	77·87
Error	19	279·82	21	178·75	44	67·77	44	48·30	19	53·25	21	26·41

Neurotic patients were tested on admission to hospital, after six weeks of community therapy, on discharge, and one year after discharge. They were allotted to a Success or a Failure group according to their condition on follow-up, and the regressions of the two groups are analysed separately. Significant mean squares are italicized.

Figures 6 to *12* are calibrated in units of standard deviation. It can be seen that the Successes show a considerable decline in Personal Illness[1] score which brings them near the normal baseline. This line represents a mean score of 2·0, the approximate average score of normal subjects tested in other studies. The Successes also show a considerable decline in Depression, and a significant drop in General Punitiveness. Thus all three symptom measures decline significantly. On Direction of Punitiveness, both men and women become less intropunitive and approach the normal mean.

According to Hypothesis 6 there should be no significant changes in the Failure group. The only significant changes, in fact, were in Depression and in Direction of Punitiveness, and these changes occurred in women but not in men. It is somewhat puzzling to observe that, while the first four variables show some tendency to change in the normal direction, men become very slightly more intropunitive and women significantly more extrapunitive. *Figure 6* suggests that the Failures show a significant improvement in degree of Personal Illness.

The most obvious improvement among the Successes occurs in the variables of Personal Illness and Depression. It cannot, however, be argued from this that the change in degree of Personal Illness and Depression is greater than the change in, say, General Punitiveness. It is questionable whether a linear relation can be assumed between scores on the PI scale and degree of Personal Illness. Indeed the concept of such a relationship between a numerical scale and a psychological variable is logically difficult to clarify. Even if this difficulty is ignored, differences in reliability and validity must be taken into account (Hope, 1965). The evidence is that the HOQ is the most reliable of the present measures and that it has a fairly high validity. Thus, a tentative conclusion is that the smaller change in HOQ relative to the changes in PI, MMPI *D*, and General Punitiveness is evidence that it is more difficult to modify personality traits than symptoms. This is some confirmation

[1] The usefulness of the Personal Illness scale was not firmly established when this experiment was designed and so it was employed without conviction. Only a few of the normals completed it, and these only on one occasion. These scores have been ignored except in so far as they contribute to the establishment of the normal baseline in *Figure 6*. The number of neurotics who completed the scale varies considerably from one occasion of testing to another. The deviation from orthogonality is such that it did not seem worth while to attempt a statistical test of the regression of this variable on time. The problem of missing values is discussed in the note on non-orthogonality at the end of this chapter (p. 289 below).

of one of the assumptions about the factors distinguishing personality traits from psychopathological signs and symptoms (see Chapter 2).

The Mooney Problem Check List was handled separately from the main analysis. *Table 78* shows changes within and between the Success and Failure groups.

TABLE 78   *Comparison of changes within and between the Success and Failure groups for the Mooney Problem Check List*

	No. increasing score	No. decreasing score	Within-groups significance of change χ^2	$p<$	Between-groups comparison of significance of change χ^2	$p<$
Admission—discharge						
Success	5	32	19·702	·001		
Failure	0	11	9·091	·001	—	—
Admission—follow-up						
Success	2	34	28·444	·001	{ almost	
Failure	4	9	1·231	n.s.	3·589 {	·05
Discharge—follow-up						
Success	10	25	6·428	·02		
Failure	7	4	·364	n.s.	3·040	·10

An examination of the problem areas as indicated by the MPCL was carried out. Too few hysterics had completed the list to make any useful comparison with dysthymics. Obsessoid personalities underlined significantly more items (particularly sex items) and marked more problems as extremely pressing than did hysteroid personalities.

Failures tended to make higher scores than Successes in the social introversion, personality, and sex areas.

Comparisons on First Testing
On admission to hospital there is no significant difference between Successes and Failures on any of the five variables (*Table 79* (A)). *Figures 6–12* show that on every variable the Successes are closer to the normal mean than are the Failures. A multivariate test (analysis of dispersion) of the differences between Successes and Failures on admission yields a non-significant variance ratio ($F_{5, 44} = 1\cdot07$; $p > \cdot25$).

TABLE 79 Comparisons between groups on four variables

Source	PERSONAL ILLNESS (SSI PI)		DEPRESSION (MMPI D)				GENERAL PUNITIVENESS (E+I)		PERSONALITY TYPE (HOQ)		DIRECTION OF PUNITIVENESS (E−I)			
			Males		Females						Males		Females	
	d.f.	Mean square	d.f.	Mean square	d.f.	Mean square	d.f.	Mean square	d.f.	Mean square	d.f.	Mean square	d.f.	Mean square
A. FIRST TESTING														
Neurotics v. Normals	—	—	1	*13141·44*	1	*7711·36*	1	*1212·02*	1	*111·63*	1	*336·00*	1	*455·88*
Successes v. Failures	1	*25·81*	1	*299·58*	1	183·85	1	21·20	1	36·66	1	35·26	1	*113·53*
Error	43	13·93	37	157·77	37	114·04	77	61·67	77	38·20	37	26·29	37	35·63
B. LAST TESTING														
Neurotics v. Normals	—	—	1	(2653·88)	1	(1192·87)	1	(274·56)	1	(19·51)	1	(110·94)	1	(74·91)
Successes v. Failures	1	*34·02*	1	*3937·75*	1	*1537·90*	1	*512·54*	1	*152·00*	1	*274·20*	1	75·29
Error	26	7·19	35	149·75	37	178·95	77	45·79	77	35·22	37	28·89	37	32·25

The groups are:
(a) a sample of neurotics whose therapy was rated successful on follow-up
(b) a sample of neurotics whose therapy was rated failed on follow-up
(c) a sample of normals.

First testing is admission testing for neurotics and first testing for normals. Last testing is follow-up testing for neurotics and one-year re-testing for normals. Significant mean squares are italicized.

Wherever possible a second comparison, orthogonal to that between the two groups of neurotics, has been calculated. This is the comparison of the weighted average of the combined neurotic group with the average of the normal group. For the purposes of this comparison the normals' scores on first testing are compared with the neurotics' scores on admission to hospital, and the normals' scores on second testing are compared with the neurotics' scores on follow-up. *Table 79* (A) shows that the between-groups variance in Depression, General Punitiveness, and Direction of Punitiveness is attributable to the difference between normals and neurotics rather than to the difference between the two groups of neurotics. Although no such comparison is available for Personal Illness because the PI scale was not administered to the normal subjects, *Figure 6* leaves little doubt that the same holds true of this variable. There is no significant difference between normals and neurotics on the variable of personality type (HOQ).

Comparisons on Last Testing
When the follow-up test results are compared with those of normals it can be seen that the situation is the reverse of that obtaining on admission (*Table 79* (B)). The between-groups variance is now attributable to the success-failure comparison rather than to the normal-neurotic comparison. *Figure 6* confirms that this is true of Personal Illness. An apparently aberrant result is the value, for neurotics versus normals, of the mean squares for Depression and for General Punitiveness. This, of course, is not validly estimated in the presence of a significant difference between Successes and Failures. *Figures 7, 8,* and *9* show, however, that the anomaly is an artifact. Depression and General Punitiveness conform to the pattern of the other variables in that the Successes obtain a normal score while the Failures continue to score high. Another aberrant result is the failure to find a significant difference between female Successes and Failures on Direction of Punitiveness. This negative result, together with the (non-significant) deviation from linearity in the regression, may be attributable to the very small size of the sample. Seven is the maximum number of women who completed this test on any one occasion (*Table 75*).

Symptoms, Attitudes, and Traits on First and Last Testing
The symptom and attitude measures all serve to distinguish neurotics from normals when the former are admitted to hospital, but distinguish

Successes from Failures at follow-up. The trait measure does not show these clear-cut movements. Successful neurotics probably do not differ significantly from normals on admission to hospital (*Figure 10*); but they show a significant tendency to move in the hysteroid direction between admission and follow-up. These findings, which are not, at first sight, entirely consistent with one another, may be explained by the observation that the normals move in the hysteroid direction between test and re-test and the Successes overtake them in this movement.

Having exhausted the between-groups degrees of freedom in two orthogonal comparisons it is not possible to test whether the Failures differ significantly from normals on admission. The evidence is that they do in that, although they become slightly less obsessoid, they are significantly different from the Successes on follow-up when the Successes obtain the same score as normals.

Although it may be concluded that the personality of the neurotics is slightly on the obsessoid side of the normal mean, this finding may not be generalizable to neurotics in other hospitals for reasons connected with admission policy. Personality undergoes a slight, but significant, modification during (and perhaps after) successful treatment by community therapy.

Prediction of Outcome

This analysis has so far ignored the correlations between variables which are reported in *Table 80*. The weighted average of the variance-covariance matrices of the admission scores of the Successes and Failures was calculated,[1] and the discriminant function maximizing the distance between the two groups was computed. The calculation of this vector may appear superfluous in the light of the non-significant variance ratio of the analysis of dispersion. This ratio serves to test the significance of the discriminant function in one sense of the word significance (Kendall, 1957, p. 158f). The analysis of dispersion tests the null hypothesis that the samples are drawn from the same population. Although no evidence was found for the alternative hypothesis in the admission scores, the subsequent course of the subjects' psychological processes and illnesses strongly suggests that the null hypothesis should be rejected and an attempt made to differentiate the groups.

[1] The PI scale was not completed by 5 (10 per cent) of the neurotics on admission. The variance and covariances of this test were increased proportionately.

TABLE 80 *Correlations between scores of a sample of 50 neurotics tested on admission to hospital*

	Personal Illness (SSI PI)	Depression (MMPI D)	General Punitiveness (E+I)	Personality (HOQ)	Direction of Punitiveness (E−I)
Personal Illness	(1·000)	·235	·449	·055	·324
Depression	·262	(1·000)	−·164	−·208	·471
General Punitiveness	·477	−·142	(1·000)	·050	−·238
Personality	·007	−·231	·040	(1·000)	−·291
Direction of Punitiveness	·356	·503	−·207	−·314	(1·000)

Lower left: total correlations; upper right: within-group correlations. The sample is split according to the outcome of therapy, and the averages of the within-group variances and covariances (weighted by the numbers in the two groups) are used to calculate the correlations.

The discriminant function gives the following relative weights to the variables, the weight of Personal Illness being taken as unity:

$$PI + 0·54D + 0·86 (E+I) − 0·45 HOQ + 2·10 (I−E)$$

With these values the mean of the Successes is 69·4, that of the Failures is 85·4, and the value half-way between the two is 77·4. *Table 81* shows the effectiveness of the discrimination achieved. The efficiency of the function varies according to the cut-off point. As would be expected with a ratio of three Successes to one Failure, the most efficient cut-off point is on the Failures' side of the half-way value. Indeed, it is to the right of the mean for the Failures. This is in accordance with practical requirements, since it is more important to include Successes than to exclude Failures. With a cut-off score of 93·4, 10 out of the 45 subjects who completed all tests on admission are misclassified. For practical purposes this is not better than the overall efficiency of assuming that all the neurotics belong to the Success group. This assumption would misclassify 11 out of the 45 patients. Nevertheless, the rate of misclassification is low enough to give some confidence in the theoretical implications of the discriminator, bearing in mind the smallness of the sample and the uneven split between the two groups.

TABLE 81 Distribution of neurotics along the discriminant function maximizing the distance between Successes and Failures in the test space

Discriminant function	5·4	13·4	21·4	29·4	37·4	45·4	53·4	61·4	69·4	77·4	85·4	93·4	101·4	109·4	117·4	125·4	Did not complete all tests
Males Successes	1	2			1	4	3	2	2	2	2		1	1			2
Males Failures							2	2	1		1	2		1			0
Females Successes					2	3	2	1	3	4		1	1	1			1
Females Failures									2	1		1	1				2
Not tested on follow-up			1			2	1	3	1	1			1				0
Did not complete hospital testing							1	1	1								1
Discharged themselves soon after admission	1					2	3	1	2		2			1			2
Transferred to other units			1	1				1	1			2		2			1
Still in treatment at end of study													1				1

Empirical Studies

When the discriminant function scores of those who were transferred to other units are compared with the scores of those who discharged themselves soon after admission (*Table 81*), it can be seen that there is a tendency for the latter to be classified as Successes; whereas the former are, to a lesser extent, classified as Failures.

Table 82 shows the value of the maximized distance between the group means and the percentage contribution of the variables to this distance. Over half the discriminatory power is contributed by Direction of Punitiveness. Another 20 per cent is due to the Depression scale.

TABLE 82 *Discriminant function maximizing the distance in the five-dimensional test space between neurotics who are going to recover under community therapy and those who are not*

Variable	Test	Weight (w_i)	Difference between group means (d_i)	$w_i d_i$	$\% D^2$
Personal Illness	SSI PI	·038	1·762	·067	11
Depression	MMPI D	·021	6·915	·143	23
General Punitiveness	E+I	·033	1·484	·049	8
Personality Type	HOQ	−·017	−1·952	·034	6
Direction of Punitiveness	E−I	·080	3·946	·315	52
			D^2	·608	100

The scores are those of patients when admitted to hospital. The mean score of the 13 unrecovered patients is higher than that of the 37 recovered patients on every test except HOQ.

SUMMARY AND CONCLUSIONS

The main conclusions are:

1. There were no significant changes in symptom, attitude, and trait measures among normals after an interval of one year.

2. Neurotics who were classified as Failures in their response to treatment changed very much less than did Successes. On admission, the main difference was between normals and neurotics; whereas, at follow-up, the main difference was between normals and successful neurotics on the one hand and failed neurotics on the other.

3. The period in which most change occurred in the direction of normality was somewhere between six weeks and discharge from hospital, which was, on average, after about six months.

4. The trait measure was probably more resistant to change than the other measures.

5. Patients who were less intropunitive, less depressed, and less nihilistic personally and sexually (MPCL) were more likely to show a favourable response to treatment, or to improve more with the passage of time.

Aside from these test differences between successfully and unsuccessfully treated patients, there were clinical differences. The Failure group had a significantly higher number of patients diagnosed as personality disorders, either on admission or subsequently ($\chi^2 = 5\cdot14; p < \cdot03$). The personality disorder group included such diagnoses as schizoid personality, inadequate personality, or simply personality disorder. Of the patients who were transferred, three were diagnosed as schizophrenic and three as, quaintly, 'genuinely' depressed and, therefore, treatable by ECT. Taking all these cases together in opposition to hysterics and dysthymics, the clinical diagnostic difference between the Failure group (including transfers) and the Success group becomes highly significant ($\chi^2 = 10\cdot58; p < \cdot005$). Thus the Failure group came to be regarded by the medical staff as revealing either deep-seated personality disturbances or psychotic processes. The admission test scores give weight to this view and suggest that this formulation was not simply because these patients had failed to respond to the initial treatment programme. There were no significant differences between the groups in respect of age, chronicity, or length of stay in the community wards. All the Success group were thought to be 'improved' or 'recovered' on discharge; but so were all but two of the Failure group.

Such changes as occurred cannot be attributed unequivocally to community therapy; but there are reasons for doubting the adequacy of a 'spontaneous remission' explanation. Eysenck (1960) states that 90 per cent of neurotics may be expected to recover in five years without psychotherapeutic – or, presumably, conditioning – treatment. The spontaneous remission theory does not seem to be the most plausible or parsimonious explanation of the facts of the present investigation. The average duration of illness of the patients was seven and a half years, a period well beyond that quoted by Eysenck. It seems unlikely that these patients would spontaneously remit within six months or so of entering hospital and remain relatively well for the next year. When such an elaborate treatment and testing programme, specifically designed for initiating and measuring symptom and attitude change, is shown to achieve its aim, to invoke coincidence seems the least probable explanation. Particularly is this so when patients, in retrospect, can relate incidents occurring in the treatment process to their altered view of themselves and of others.

At follow-up interview, those who claimed to have changed were asked to what they attributed the change. The responses may be classified as follows:

Greater understanding of self	14
Greater understanding of personal relationships	13
Relationships with other patients	11
Greater understanding of other persons	9
Relationships with staff members	3
Understanding and acceptance by others	2

Seven patients mentioned that they had a continuing relationship with at least one other patient at the time of follow-up. One couple had married and two other couples were courting. Almost all asked after at least one other patient.

Some support for Foulkes & Anthony's (1957) 'mirror process', and for Asch's (1957) opinion that 'we learn about others through ourselves and conversely', came from two patients who described how they developed insight from seeing their own feelings and attitudes mirrored by another patient talking in the group, while they themselves sat silent. From the above figures it seems likely that this kind of learning was of more frequent occurrence than these spontaneous comments would indicate.

Another explanation for the results is that patients have merely learned what to say. Although this may be true to some extent, the clinical evidence suggests that emotional factors are also involved and that insight has been accompanied by emotional reorganization. The stability of the discharge and follow-up scores appears to represent some real modification in attitude and symptomatology, since it is unlikely that patients would remember just how they had answered some 700 odd questions one year previously.

Finally, this study has sought to provide a baseline for comparative

Chronic Neurotics in a Therapeutic Community

investigation of types of treatment and, in so doing, has underlined the importance of distinguishing between various levels of psychological functioning such as the symptom, attitude, and trait levels.

NOTE ON NON-ORTHOGONALITY

Apart from the effects of the lack of consistency in administering the PI scale (discussed in a footnote on p. 283 above), the number of missing values is small (*Table 75*). Seven patients – five Successes and two Failures – left hospital about six weeks after admission, and their test scores at that time were counted as discharge rather than sixth-week records. Two Failures were not tested on discharge. These slight departures from orthogonality were ignored in the analysis of *D*, General Punitiveness, HOQ, and Direction of Punitivenes in *Table 77* (A), and in the analysis of *D* and Direction of Punitiveness in *Table 77* (B). In these analyses weighting coefficients (Snedecor, 1956, p. 348) were applied to the group means and appropriate corrections were made. In all the other regression analyses strict orthogonality was preserved by modification of the vectors of weights.

The five Successes who were discharged about six weeks after admission tended to obtain, on their discharge testing, scores which were lower than the mean for all Successes on discharge. If separate sixth-week scores had been available for the five patients these would most probably have lowered the mean sixth-week scores for the Success group, thus making the departure from linearity less than is shown in the graphs.

Admission and follow-up samples are complete on all tests except the PI scale. The weighting vectors for the comparisons in *Table 79* were all designed to ensure orthogonality.

REFERENCES

ANTHONY, E. J. (1953). Group psychotherapy. In J. Burton (Ed.), *Group discussion in educational, social and working life.* London: Central Council for Health Education.
ASCH, S. (1957). *Social psychology.* New Jersey: Prentice Hall.
BARTON, R. (1959). *Institutional neurosis.* Bristol: J. Wright.
BLOCH, C. (1961). *Aspects of the psychiatric service in Great Britain.* Report sponsored by WHO. Brussels: Psychiat. Inst. of the Brugmann Univ. Hospital.

CAINE, T. M. (1964). Personality tests for nurses. *Nursing Times*, 24 July.

CAINE, T. M. & HAWKINS, L. G. (1963). Questionnaire measure of the hysteroid-obsessoid component of personality. *J. consult. Psychol.*, 27, 206.

CANTRIL, H., AMES, A., HASTORF, A. H. & ITTELSON, W. H. (1949). Psychology and scientific research. I, The nature of scientific enquiry. *Science*, 110.

CURRAN, D. & PARTRIDGE, M. (1955). *Psychological medicine*. Edinburgh: Livingstone.

DREIKURS, R. (1955). Group psychotherapy and the third revolution in psychiatry. *Int. J. soc. Psychiat.*, I, 23.

EDWARDS, A. L. & CRONBACH, L. J. (1952). Experimental design for research in psychotherapy. *J. clin. Psychol.*, 8, 51.

EYSENCK, H. J. (1952). The effects of psychotherapy: an evaluation. *J. consult. Psychol.*, 16, 319.

EYSENCK, H. J. (1954). A reply to Luborsky's note. *Brit. J. Psychol.*, 45, 132.

EYSENCK, H. J. (1955). The effects of psychotherapy: a reply. *J. abnorm. soc. Psychol.*, 50, 147.

EYSENCK, H. J. (1960). The effects of psychotherapy. In H. J. Eysenck (Ed.), *Handbook of abnormal psychology*. London: Pitman Medical Publishing Co.

FOULDS, G. A. (1959). The relative stability of personality measures compared with diagnostic measures. *J. ment. Sci.*, 105, 783.

FOULDS, G. A. & CAINE, T. M. (1959). Symptom clusters and personality types among psychoneurotic men compared with women. *J. ment. Sci.*, 105, 469.

FOULDS, G. A., CAINE, T. M. & CREASY, M. A. (1960). Aspects of extra- and intro-punitive expression in mental illness. *J. ment. Sci.*, 106, 599.

FOULKES, S. H. & ANTHONY, E. J. (1957). *Group psychotherapy*. Harmondsworth, Middlesex: Penguin Books.

FROMM, E. (1943). *The fear of freedom*. London: Allen & Unwin.

GREENBLATT, M., YORK, R. H. & BROWN, E. L. (1955). *From custodial to therapeutic care in mental hospitals*. New York: Russell Sage Foundation.

HOPE, K. (1963). The structure of hostility among normal and neurotic persons. Unpublished doctoral thesis, University of London.

HOPE, K. (1965). The structure of aggression. (In preparation.)

HORNEY, K. (1951). *Neurosis and human growth*. London: Routledge & Kegan Paul.

JAQUES, E. (1951). *The changing culture of a factory*. London: Tavistock Publications.

Chronic Neurotics in a Therapeutic Community

JOHNSON, M. L. (1953). The ABC of group discussion: theory. In J. Burton (Ed.), *Group discussion in educational, social and working life*. London: Central Council for Health Education.

JONES, M. (1952). *Social psychiatry*. London: Tavistock Publications. Also under the title of *The therapeutic community*. New York: Basic Books, 1953.

KENDALL, M. G. (1957). A course in multivariate analysis. London: Griffin.

LANGLEY, G. E. (1963). Patients' attitudes to neurosis. *Brit. J. Psychiat.*, **109**, 463.

MARTIN, D. V. (1955). Institutionalization. *Lancet*, 1188.

MARTIN, D. V. (1962). *Adventure in psychiatry*. Oxford: Cassirer.

MARTIN, D. V. & CAINE, T. M. (1963). Personality change in the treatment of chronic neurosis in a therapeutic community. *Brit. J. Psychiat.*, **109**, 459.

MORENO, J. L. (1952). Presidential address to the American Society of Group Psychotherapy and Psychodrama, New York.

RAPOPORT, R. N. (1960). *Community as doctor*. London: Tavistock Publications; Springfield, Ill.: C. C. Thomas.

ROGERS, C. R. (1961). *On becoming a person*. London: Constable.

SNEDECOR, G. W. (1956). Statistical methods. (5th edn.) Ames, Iowa: Iowa State College Press.

STANTON, A. H. & SCHWARTZ, M. S. (1954). *The mental hospital*. New York: Basic Books. London: Tavistock Publications.

SULLIVAN, H. S. (1953). *The interpersonal theory of psychiatry*. New York: Norton; London: Tavistock Publications.

ZILBOORG, G. & HENRY, G. A. (1941). *A history of medical psychology*. New York: Norton.

PART IV

Prospect and Retrospect

CHAPTER FOURTEEN

Some Implications

DIAGNOSTIC IMPLICATIONS

Some implications with regard to diagnosis arise, principally from the use of the continuum of increasing degrees of failure to maintain or to establish mutual personal relationships. It would, for example, be of interest to set up a diagnostic reliability study, utilizing this continuum and the necessary and sufficient conditions for each of the categories, to see whether an increase in reliability could be produced. The *ad hoc* scale for degrees of agreement suggested earlier (Foulds, 1955) could now be given some empirical backing. The questions that should be asked in such a study would be:

1. Is X a personality disorder or normal? (If PD, then . . .)
2. Is X personally ill or a psychopath? (If PI, then . . .)
3. Is X psychotic or neurotic? (If P, then . . .)
4. Is X a non-integrated or an integrated psychotic?

Having ascertained the position on this class continuum, one would proceed to the group distinctions within the class. If X were diagnosed, for example, as an integrated psychotic, the next query would be: Is X manic and/or melancholic or paranoid?

Acceptance of this continuum, with its corollary that the greater contains and takes precedence over the lesser, would rule out, for example, a diagnosis of schizo-affective psychosis and other such illicit unions. It also opens up the possibility that patients who are categorized in the same major class, but differ in their minor class, may require different treatment, have a different prognosis, etc. There is some suggestive evidence, for instance, that melancholics whose neurotic class is anxiety state differ from those whose neurotic class is depression in being more extrapunitive, having wider Scatter of Tapping, and more Crossing of Lines and Lifting of the Pencil on the Porteus Mazes. All of this would be consistent with what one might expect from agitated and retarded melancholics.

Prospect and Retrospect

There is one more finding in this same vein, which arose from dissatisfaction with the differentiation within the neurotic class. Because of this dissatisfaction it was decided to look at a scale that contrasted symptoms that were essentially psychological with symptoms that were somatic. The items, which were drawn from the *a priori* Neurotic scales of the SSI, were as follows:

Psychological Symptoms

A	4	Are there times when you feel anxious without knowing the reason?
A	5	Are you afraid of being in a wide-open space or in an enclosed place?
A	6	Are you afraid that you might be going insane?
A	9	Are you afraid of going out alone?
B	2	Have you lost interest in almost everything?
B	5	Are you depressed because of some particular loss or disappointment?
B	7	Does the future seem pointless?
B	10	Do you ever seriously think of doing away with yourself because you are no longer able to cope with your difficulties?
E	1	Are you distressed by silly, pointless thoughts that keep coming into your mind against your will?
E	3	Are you unnecessarily careful in carrying out even simple everyday tasks, like folding up clothes, reading notices, etc.?
E	4	Are you unable to prevent yourself from doing pointless things – like tapping lamp-posts, touching things, counting windows, uttering phrases, etc.?
E	5	Are you afraid you might do something seriously wrong against your will?
E	6	Do distressing thoughts about sex or religion come into your mind against your will?

Somatic Symptoms

A	1	Does your hand often shake when you try to do something?
A	2	Do you sweat very easily even on cool days?
A	3	Do you suffer from palpitations or breathlessness?
A	7	Have you a pain, or feeling of tension, in the back of your neck?
G	1	Do you ever lose the use of an arm or leg or face muscle?
G	2	Do you ever have fits or have difficulty in keeping your balance?
G	3	Do you ever completely lose your voice (except from a cold)?

Some Implications

G 4 Do you ever lose all feeling in any part of your skin, so that you would not be able to feel a pin-prick; or do you ever have burning or tingling sensations under your skin?

G 5 Do you ever have black-outs, dizzy spells, or faints?

G 6 Have you been in poor health during most of the past few years?

G 7 Do you often suffer from blurring of vision or any other difficulty with your sight which no one seems able to put right?

G 8 Are you often bothered with pains over your heart, in your chest, or in your back?

G 10 Are you worried about your physical health?

The procedure was to draw all 'somatic' symptoms from the *a priori* Neurotic scales only and thus to eliminate somatic delusions as far as possible. These items proved to be the thirteen listed above. The next step was to select thirteen 'psychic' items which, when considered over all six groups in the original SSI standardization sample (see Chapter 8, Appendix C), matched as closely as possible with the 'somatic' items for frequency of positive responses.

The sample to which subsequent results relate was that described in Chapter 9 (p. 196).

Scores on the psychological symptoms correlated -0.292 with scores on the somatic symptoms. This correlation was just short of significance at the 5 per cent level.

The somatic symptoms score was subtracted from the psychological symptoms score, so that positive scores indicated a predominance of psychological symptoms. The majority of schizophrenics were classified as 'psychic' (14 out of 20); the minority of hysterics (7 out of 20) and the remaining groups were evenly divided (being 9, 10, or 11).

Scores on this scale were correlated with various other scales. The results are shown in *Table 83*. The Direction of Punitiveness scale differs from that used earlier, the formula being $(2 \ SC+DG)-(AH+CO+DH)$. Thus positive scores indicate a preponderance of intropunitiveness.

Mean scores for the groups on General Punitiveness and on Direction of Punitiveness are shown in *Table 84*.

TABLE 83 *Correlations between the (Psychic-Somatic) Symptoms scale and other variables*

	60 Neurotics		40 Integrated psychotics		30 Non-integrated psychotics	
	r	p<	r	p<	r	p
General Punitiveness	·417	·001	·337	·05	·082	n.s.
Direction of Punitiveness	·377	·01	·500	·001	·289	n.s.
Hysteroid (HOQ)	·178	n.s.	—·296	n.s.	·203	n.s.
Mill Hill Vocabulary	·215	n.s.	—·064	n.s.	·156	n.s.
Age	—·219	n.s.	—·093	n.s.	·301	n.s.

TABLE 84 *Mean scores of 'psychics' and 'somatics' within neurotic and psychotic groups on General Punitiveness and Direction of Punitiveness*

	General Punitiveness	Direction of Punitiveness
SCHIZOPHRENICS		
Psychic	25·35	6·09
Somatic	26·71	1·86
PARANOIACS		
Psychic	17·60	1·60
Somatic	14·50	—2·40
MELANCHOLICS		
Psychic	25·08	12·92
Somatic	20·75	6·50
HYSTERICS		
Psychic	18·14	9·86
Somatic	13·77	3·77
ANXIETY STATES		
Psychic	18·60	7·80
Somatic	13·00	3·20
DEPRESSIVES		
Psychic	22·50	7·00
Somatic	17·70	5·60

Some Implications

Table 85 shows the mean scores for psychoneurotics and for somato-neurotics and for hysterics and dysthymics on the two punitive measures and on age.

TABLE 85   *Mean scores of psychoneurotics, somato-neurotics, hysterics, and dysthymics on two punitive measures and on age*

| | Sample divided into: | | | | |
| | 20 Hysterics | | 40 Dysthymics | | |
	Mean	s.d.	Mean	s.d.	*p*
General Punitiveness	14·90	6·41	17·95	7·56	n.s.
Direction of Punitiveness	5·90		5·90		n.s.
Age	37·30		40·27		n.s.

| | Same sample divided into: | | | | | |
| | 27 Psychics | | 33 Somatics | | | |
	Mean	s.d.	Mean	s.d.	*t*	*p*
General Punitiveness	19·93	5·59	14·73	7·53	2·97	·01
Direction of Punitiveness	8·04	5·10	4·15	5·98	2·72	·01
Age	34·33	12·48	43·33	8·98	3·14	·01

Thus:

1. Psychic and somatic symptoms tend to be negatively correlated.

2. Schizophrenics were predominantly 'psychic', hysterics 'somatic', and the remainder evenly split.

3. On General Punitiveness, in five out of six groups the 'psychics' score higher than the 'somatics'. It may, therefore, be that somatization converts General Punitiveness.

4. On Direction of Punitiveness, in all six groups the psychics score higher (i.e. more intropunitively) than the somatics. It may, therefore, be that somatization converts predominantly intropunitiveness and can thus be regarded as another form of intropunitiveness.

5. Since psychic melancholics differ from somatic melancholics, psychic paranoids from somatic paranoids, and, on one measure at least, psychic schizophrenics from somatic schizophrenics, it would seem that the neurotic symptoms of psychotics are of some significance. This finding adds support to the class continuum: not only are all psychotics neurotic, but it is of importance to know what type of neurotic.

6. In all three neurotic groups, the psychics are younger than the somatics; but this does not hold with the psychotics.

7. Within neurosis, psychics differ significantly from somatics on General Punitiveness, Direction of Punitiveness, and age; but hysterics and dysthymics differ on none of these. It will be worth investigating more fully, therefore, whether the psychic *v.* somatic split in neurosis is a more useful one to make than the hysteric *v.* dysthymic split. The division into hysterics, anxiety states, depressives, and obsessionals may be considered at the next level down. Hysterics appear to be predominantly somato-neurotics and anxiety states and depressives to be rather evenly divided. It would be expected that obsessionals would be predominantly psychoneurotics.

8. In view of the finding of reduced General Punitiveness and, in particular, of reduced intropunitiveness in the somatic cases, it would be of interest to apply these scales to psychosomatic cases, especially in conjunction with more covert measures of hostility.

A further use for the Symptom-Sign Inventory would be in studies designed to assess the degree of constancy or of change in diagnoses of the same individual on successive breakdowns. The implicit assumption that one is dealing with unchanging entities bedevils diagnostic work and begs many questions. If, after an interval of time, a patient is given a different diagnosis by a different psychiatrist, the assumption usually made is that at least one of the psychiatrists (and probably the first) has erred rather than that the patient may have changed. In our present state of ignorance parsimony should not be invoked, because it entails that the hypothesis 'once an X always an X' cannot be disproved. From this argument the main contribution of the past history is as an aid to determining what was wrong with the patient in the past. An instrument such as the SSI, which is more standard from situation to situation than would be two different psychiatrists on two occasions separated by a considerable time, could be useful in determining what sorts of patient changed their diagnostic category, and in what direction and how often. It could then be examined why this should be so.

THERAPEUTIC IMPLICATIONS

If the view were accepted that mental illness is illness of the person and not merely of the organism and that the different types of illness represent varying degrees of failure to maintain or establish mutual personal relationships, and if the archaic epiphenomenalism that pervades much psychiatric thinking were discarded, it would follow that the terminal treatment for personal illness must be some form of psychotherapy, some form of psychological guidance.

Acceptance of this view would entail a drastic revision of psychiatric training. At the present time only psycho-analysts are adequately trained in psychotherapeutic procedures in Great Britain, where it is still considered more important for a psychiatrist to have the Membership of the Royal College of Physicians.

During the past thirty years the physical treatments in psychiatry have run their cyclothymic course – starting in mania and subsiding gradually into depression. By the time these words appear the attitude to tranquillizers and anti-depressants will be somewhat less than euphoric and there will be a greater readiness to appreciate that the role of physical treatments in psychiatry is the very valuable one of serving as adjuvants to psychological treatments, their main function perhaps being to bring back the most severely disturbed patients to the possibility of adequate communication. No physician would rest content with prescribing an analgesic as the sole treatment for a severe and undiagnosed pain.

The clearest fact about treatment in psychiatry is that, in the majority of psychotic depressives, ECT produces a marked change which by any reasonable standards must be regarded as a change for the better. It is almost equally clear that the relapse rate is very high (Karagulla, 1950). If it be the case that psychogenic factors can frequently be revealed when the ability to communicate has improved through physical treatment, then psychotherapeutic treatment at this stage might reduce the relapse rate. The lip-service paid to this principle should be given a more sustained and active trial.

The length of outpatient interviews is in itself strong presumptive evidence that many psychiatrists, willingly or unwillingly, rely almost exclusively on tranquillizers and anti-depressants. Inadequate training in psychotherapy naturally tends to promote acceptance of this position. It is not inconceivable that anxiety can be reduced by the use of tranquillizers or by behaviour therapy to such an extent that the patient and his most intimate associates are presented with a new opportunity to develop more satisfactory personal relationships. That more recently acquired patterns of behaviour should be the first to be broken up by physical treatments is readily understandable. The expectation would then be that the older ones, which presumably had laid the foundations for the final disruption, would be re-established. What is required is that a new pattern of behaviour should be established at this time. The fact that the patient should so often have to face this critical period unaided by expert advice and guidance is certainly nothing less than unfortunate. It would be of great interest to know, for example, whether those cases which relapsed rapidly after behaviour therapy (Cooper, 1963) were those in which the symptoms had not become functionally autonomous. It may be that there is a small number of cases in which the symptoms have perseverated beyond their teleological function and no longer have important ramifications in the personality. It is for such cases that behaviour therapy seems likely to be most effective.

The Road to Recovery

Five points have been posited on the continuum of failure in maintaining or establishing mutual personal relationships:

   (i)   Normal
   (ii) Personality disorder
  (iii) Personal illness
  (iv) Psychosis
   (v) Non-integrated psychosis.

When treatment results in some change in the clinical condition, it is usually thought of in terms of an individual in, say, class (iv) becoming less (iv) or even becoming (i). On the present hypothesis, it would be possible for the (iv) to become a (iii), a (ii), or a (i). If this were so, it would have definite implications for treatment, the most important of which would be that treatment is increasingly tending to stop too soon.

The data given below concerning improved and unimproved psychotics and neurotics are unsatisfactory in that patients were re-tested after four to six weeks and the period between such re-testing and discharge was variable.[1] Usually, however, the interval was very short and it is probable that the figures to be presented would have been reduced by not more than 10, or at most, 20 per cent. They are perhaps worth presenting as an illustration of the argument and to indicate the lines along which a more accurate study might proceed.

[1] This sample of patients is described in Chapter 9 above. Of 120 cases, 88 were re-tested (see p. 196).

Some Implications

Table 86 shows the number of psychotics who were still diagnosed on re-test on the Symptom-Sign Inventory as psychotic or as neurotic, and the number of neurotics who were still diagnosed as neurotic.

TABLE 86   *Diagnosis of improved and unimproved psychotics and neurotics on SSI re-test*

SSI re-test diagnosis	37 Improved First SSI diagnosis:		51 Unimproved First SSI diagnosis:	
	Psychotic 20	Neurotic 17	Psychotic 16	Neurotic 35
Psychotic	7	0	12	0
Neurotic	8	9	1	29
Normal	5	8	3	6

Thus, on re-test, roughly 35 per cent of the improved psychotics would still be classified as psychotic on the SSI; 40 per cent would still be classified as neurotic; and only 25 per cent would be classified as normal. Of the unimproved or slightly improved psychotics, three-quarters remain psychotic.

Of the improved neurotics, about half remain neurotic; of the unimproved or slightly improved neurotics, more than four-fifths remain neurotic.

It would be of interest to institute a long-term follow-up study to try to determine whether those psychotics, for example, who are discharged when still assessed on the SSI as psychotic or as neurotic have a different subsequent history from each other and from those who are discharged as normal. From Caine's report (Chapter 13) it would appear that neurotics are not discharged from Claybury Hospital until they are within normal limits, as assessed at least by his measures. To achieve this kind of result takes longer. We urgently need to know whether this extra time is well spent: it may be that the time is well spent in the case of neurotics, but that a different policy is optimal for psychotics, or for some types of psychotic. All these questions require investigation.

Perhaps one reasonably straightforward study that could be set up would be one in which 50 successive admissions with a diagnosis of psychotic depression were allocated to each of two treatment groups – one receiving ECT and psychotherapy and the other receiving ECT alone. A five-year follow-up would probably be desirable and objective measures should be used throughout.

Prospect and Retrospect

The recent policy change towards treating more of the personally ill in units attached to general hospitals perhaps carries the implication that the future direction of treatment will be the opposite to that advocated here. The movement towards the general hospitals will be satisfactory to the extent that the influence of psychiatric on physical treatment exceeds that of physical on psychiatric treatment.

THEORETICAL IMPLICATIONS FOR SCHIZOPHRENIA

Attempts have been made to account for schizophrenic symptomatology from two quite distinct and opposed theoretical standpoints. Both these standpoints, which may be designated 'the unconscious conflict theory' and 'the defective attention theory', though important, are inadequate and for substantially the same reason. A third possible description is discussed below.

The Unconscious Conflict Theory

Federn (1953) believes that schizophrenic *symptoms* are defensive activities purposefully related to unconscious conflicts over interpersonal difficulties.

Such a theory as Federn's can be a sufficient condition for schizo-phrenic symptoms only in so far as the nature of the unconscious conflict is so specific that it occurs in schizophrenia, but not in other conditions. Owing to errors of measurement and of diagnosis, the last part of the statement is reduced empirically to 'occurs significantly more frequently in schizophrenia than in any other condition'. Unfortunately, in almost all psycho-analytic studies the representativeness of the examples provided is suspect, since no attempt is made to obtain an adequate sample of the group of cases in question or to compare such a sample with adequate samples of other types of case.

The unconscious conflict that Federn suggests might well constitute a necessary condition. As yet the evidence is, of course, exiguous. Leaving this aside, however, his claim that schizophrenic *symptoms* are defensive activities purposefully related to unconscious conflicts over interpersonal difficulties seems improbable as an overall explanation, even if the word teleologically be substituted for purposefully to make it clear that the defensive activities are not conscious and deliberate or intentional.

304

Some Implications

Psycho-analytic theories seem more likely, and perhaps more importantly, to account partially for withdrawal and for behavioural content than for behavioural processes. It is dubious to regard over-inclusive thinking or the knight's move as teleological, let alone intentional. It is dubious because the evidence is ambiguous. Painstaking and sensitive interpreters, such as Laing (1960), provide evidence of the apparently intentional use of thought disorder by schizophrenics to prevent people making communicative contact with them; but this evidence generally seems to be obtained from patients who have at least partially recovered. The ambiguity lies in the fact that they may be rationalizing or following Bartlett's (1932) theory of remembering and reorganizing their past experience in a way more meaningful and familiar to themselves. Again, the apparent gibberish that schizophrenics talk to themselves when not aware of or not concerned about being overheard is difficult to bring within Laing's explanation. Altogether, the impression is given by such writings that schizophrenics are thought to be much more alert to, and indeed in control of, social situations than seems to be the case, except perhaps in the very early stages of an insidious onset or in patients whom many would prefer to call schizoid psychopaths. Many schizophrenics, particularly hebephrenics, complain that there is something wrong with their mind, and give the impression that they are being overwhelmed by a tidal wave rather than that they are steering the ship into untroubled waters. This accords better with the notion of a disorganization outside either their conscious or their unconscious control. It is true, however, that certain catatonics give the impression of saying 'I shall be schizophrenic and nobody will stop me'.

The Defective Attention Theory

McGhie & Chapman (1961) reject Federn's view that schizophrenic symptoms are defensive activities purposefully related to unconscious conflicts over interpersonal difficulties and prefer to argue that 'breakdown in interpersonal difficulties was a reaction to the primary cognitive disturbance'. This primary cognitive disturbance they see as a loss of the ability to direct attention focally. The schizophrenic's attention is 'directed radially in a manner which is determined, not by the individual's volition but by the diffuse pattern of stimuli existing in the total environmental situation'.

Payne, Mattussek & George (1959) speak of a 'defect in some central filter which is responsible for screening out stimuli, both internal and external, which are irrelevant to the task in hand'. With this McGhie & Chapman are in agreement and feel that the reticular system is probably implicated. Presumably none of these authors is envisaging a homunculus within the brain-stem which can decide what is relevant and what is irrelevant. A defective reticular system, along with any other hypothetical abnormal physiological substrate, may be a necessary condition for schizophrenia and for various somato-psychological states, such as dementia paralytica or Korsakow's syndrome. In order for it to be a necessary and sufficient condition the defect would have to be demonstrably specific to schizophrenia (within the limits of experimental and diagnostic error). This would not, of course, entail acceptance of a specific defect in the reticular formation as the sole cause of schizophrenia. There might, in addition, be valid necessary psychological conditions. These sets of conditions might be dependently modifiable or they might be unmodifiable.

They might be dependently modifiable when someone who has sustained brain-cell destruction, which is irreversible, is enabled, by appropriate training methods, to function at an improved level. Such improved functioning would not, however, presumably occur – to express it as generally as possible – without some physical reorganization. Alternatively, the physical condition might be the focus of therapeutic attention. Improvement produced by penicillin in GPIs is accompanied by improved psychological functioning.

On the other hand, the conditions might be unmodifiable. At least beyond a certain stage of Alzheimer's disease, the process and the deteriorating behaviour seem to be substantially irreversible. There is no reason why a psychological dysfunction should not become substantially irreversible, as indeed it may be in some very long-standing cases of hebephrenia or simple schizophrenia, though these cases may be exceptional.

As with the reticular formation, the inability to direct attention focally cannot be a sufficient condition for schizophrenic symptoms unless it can be distinguished from what appears to be a similar inability in, for example, some toxic confusional states and some hypermanics. It may be a necessary condition for schizophrenic symptoms, provided that paranoid states are separated from the schizophrenic category.

The third description may be designated 'withdrawal without the intention of, or motivation for, returning'.

Some Implications

Withdrawal without the Intention of, or Motivation for, Returning

It has been argued that it may be useful to think of a continuum of increasing degrees of failure to maintain or establish mutual personal relationships, from psychopathy, through neurosis and integrated psychosis, to non-integrated psychosis. Though this last group has been regarded as probably synonymous with schizophrenia, this is still uncertain, and it may be that the subsequent remarks should apply to non-integrated psychosis rather than strictly to schizophrenia.

As Murray's (1938) pre-potency theory so clearly points up, we are not interested in food if we have not got enough oxygen. We are not interested in the diction of Jane Austen if we have not got enough food. Somewhere along a hierarchy of needs we require, if we are to live as persons rather than merely as organisms, intellectual and emotional interchange with other persons. We require mutual personal relationships. From this schizophrenics have opted out even more completely than the Beatniks, since they do so alone. They have no reference group.

As Macmurray (1961) argues, the infant is born into a personal relationship. He is endowed with the impulse to communicate. It is from the inevitable withdrawal and return of the mother that he learns to discriminate the other. Without the negative aspect, the withdrawal, he could not learn of his own existence. The infant's rudimentary motives are governed by the intention of the mother. Without the positive intention of an adult, he could not survive. The human infant, unlike most animals, not only learns, but is taught. He has to be taught and to learn that withdrawal is not necessarily withdrawal of love, and later he has to be taught and to learn to formulate his own intentions and to become fully a person, which entails entering into mutual personal relationships, or at least one such relationship.

This withdrawal and return, to use Macmurray's terms, are perhaps of particular relevance to schizophrenia. Loss of awareness of the self as agent, thought-process disorder, and affective incongruity are each separately a sufficient condition, and the presence of at least one is a necessary condition, for making the diagnosis of schizophrenia. It is the present thesis that this characteristic symptomatology may be an epiphenomenon of withdrawal without the intention of, or motivation for, returning to action, particularly to communication with others. Morris (1963), using the Crichton Royal Standard Psychological Interview with 50 schizophrenics, found an important feature of her results to be a disturbance of *intentional* behaviour in general. Though this

307

finding does not lend positive support to the view here expressed, contrary findings would have been damaging to it.

In order to support the present thesis the relationship between intention, motivation, set, and attention must first be considered, followed by some discussion of the relevant aspects of normal withdrawal and return.

Motive or attention or set can be present without intention; but intention cannot be demonstrated without motive, without attention, or without set. This seems to allow of three possibilities: one may be motivated without any intention; or one may have an intention which is accompanied either by a motive which is consonant or by a motive which is dissonant with one's intention.

Motivation without intention: Normal subjects suffering from food deprivation tended to perceive food in ambiguous stimuli more frequently than did subjects not so deprived (Sanford, 1937). These subjects were clearly motivated to develop a presumably unconscious set, that is a preparedness to attend selectively to facets of a situation. They probably did not *intend* to look for food symbols. This finding was not reproducible with schizophrenic subjects (Michaux, 1955). It would appear, therefore, that schizophrenics were not even unconsciously set to attend selectively.

Motivation consonant with intention: A subject may intend to develop a set for perceiving embedded figures. If he is principally motivated to seek the approval of the experimenter, motive and intention will be consonant. Such consonance is not, of course, always found even among normal subjects.

Motivation dissonant with intention: A subject may consciously be irked by the experimenter and intend *not* to develop a set for perceiving an embedded figure. He may, however, unconsciously fear the consequences of offending the experimenter and, as a result, give an erratic performance. Alternatively, the subject may intend to develop a set for perceiving an embedded figure; but, if the experimenter happened to be a woman with a very beautiful figure, he might be unconsciously motivated to imagine the beautiful figure embedded. Again, dissonance between the intention and motivation might lead to an erratic performance.

Even if initially the schizophrenic takes over the experimenter's

Some Implications

intention and makes it his own, his habitual tendency to withdraw from what he regards as frightening personal relationships may prove too strong and he may lose hold of the intention, and with this will go his set and he will fail to see the embedded figures. It may indeed, from time to time, be the distracting autistic thoughts into which he has withdrawn to avoid personal contact that determine his set. He may then – as a consequence of this withdrawal without the intention of, or motivation for, returning – produce some bizarre, some highly idiosyncratic misperception.

Intention must be conscious. Without intention, or without the residue of past intentions, one cannot organize one's experience in such a way as to make it comprehensible to others. There is no question that very many schizophrenics cannot do this; but, if Thurstone (1924) is right in saying that organization may be introduced pre-cognitively into processes that precede articulate thought, and that consequently thoughts may sometimes be very extensively organized before they are accessible to logical control, at what stage does schizophrenic disorganization occur?

Harding's (1963) vivid metaphorical account of the putative processes involved in the organization of experience may help to pinpoint the problem:

'We stand at the harbour of our mind and watch flotillas of ideas far out at sea coming up over the horizon, already in formation of a sort; and though we can re-order them to a great extent on their closer approach, we cannot disregard the organization they had before they came in sight. They are all submarines, partly under water the whole time and capable of submerging entirely at any point and being lost to sight until analytic techniques undo the repression. But it constitutes a fundamental difference whether an idea is out of mind because it has been forced to dive or because it has not yet come up over the horizon. Sometimes repressed ideas may be close in-shore, forming the co-conscious that interested Morton Prince. Others may be both under water and at a great distance; they find expression in some sorts of dreaming, especially the sorts that have most interested the Jungians. And in creative work great numbers of ideas, more or less organized, are simply out of sight beyond the horizon and can be brought into view only through the redispositions we make amongst the in-shore mental shipping that we *can* see and control.'

Prospect and Retrospect

'Flotillas of ideas far out at sea coming up over the horizon, already in formation of a sort' – are the ideas of the schizophrenic 'already in formation of a sort'? The schizophrenic has not always been a schizophrenic, so that Thurstone's pre-cognitive organization will most probably have been going on, though perhaps with diminished efficiency, at some time in the past. How does this pre-cognitive organization come about? Is it, as Macmurray has argued, that consciousness is primarily motive? At the lowest level of consciousness all that the infant can discriminate is comfort and discomfort. Any organization, be it conscious or unconscious, must involve attention, which must involve selection, which must involve evaluation of data in terms of what is relevant or irrelevant to our intention, or, if the aim or end be too ill-defined to be fully conscious, relevant or irrelevant teleologically. One suspects that, at this level, schizophrenic's ideas are in formation of a sort. Just as literary critics may be able to elucidate what a poet did not know that he meant, so psychiatrists or psychologists may be able to elucidate what a schizophrenic did not know that he meant. The schizophrenic who produces a knight's move may not be able to explain the missing link. Thus, 'He has got his head turned. It looks as though his mind is turned.' It can be conjectured that the missing link was something after this fashion: 'The mind is associated with the brain. The brain is within the head. Therefore, if the head is turned, the mind must also be turned.' His statement implies 'formation of a sort', and we can provide at least a feasible reorganization on closer approach. Or again, 'It looks as though it's a blind girl, because it does not show her face.' Here the missing link may be something of this sort: 'I can't see her face . . . can't see . . . blind . . . a blind girl . . . because I can't see her face.' Finally, 'The man is trying to understand the woman by passing his hand across his eyes.' Here the consequent has been taken for the cause. There is a failure to allow for the negative instances, the passing of the hand across the eyes for purposes other than as an aid to understanding. Thus, a condition which is neither necessary nor sufficient is taken to be sufficient or both.

No doubt some of the schizophrenic's ideas have been forced to dive and some have not yet come up over the horizon; but these latter he does not seem able to bring to closer view because he is unable to re-dispose the in-shore mental shipping. It might be conjectured that there is some pre-cognitive organization, but that these thoughts cannot be brought into the kind of intentional organization necessary for

Some Implications

complete comprehensibility to the subject himself and to others with whom he might on occasion wish to communicate. The in-shore mental shipping is too disorganized to permit of assimilation to it of the new fleet emerging over the horizon. In these circumstances the encroaching thoughts may never be given expression, resulting in apparent poverty of ideation; alternatively, expression may be given to pre-cognitively loosely organized ideas at that stage, so that the thoughts may be no more comprehensible to the schizophrenic himself than to his audience. The process is probably not dissimilar to and perhaps very little less successful than that undergone by the present writer in attempting to communicate views which are almost as elusive for him as he fears they may be for the reader.

If, in a sense, the body thinks, is the intentional person miscoding information from the sub-intentional organism? Or is the organism sending out garbled messages? If the latter occurred, it would presumably be regarded as a more complete stage of disintegration than miscoding. This is probably what occurs with secondaries in the brain; but the neologisms, the word-salads, the knight's moves, palaelogical thinking (Napoleon was a great man. I am a great man. Therefore, I am Napoleon), even the passivity phenomenon (the belief that one's thoughts, one's feelings, one's actions are somehow not one's own) – all these seem more like the person miscoding information from the organism.

Our ignorance in this field is manifestly great. What we can be sure of is that very many schizophrenics do withdraw from interpersonal relationships. They may do so without the intention of, or motivation for, returning. They certainly often fail to communicate intelligibly with others, even when sporadically they are apparently trying to do so. There is no intention of implying that they never at any time wish to do so.

If one withdraws from action in order to reflect on possible courses of future action, the reflection will be governed by that intention to return to action. One would thus be disposed to organize one's thoughts in such a way that they will be communicable to others, when others are likely to be involved in the actions. In this sense one's thinking is reality-orientated and it can be confirmed or disconfirmed in future action.

A normal person may intend, or be motivated, to withdraw into daydreaming for a time, with no lofty artistic creation as his goal, with indeed no clear goal at all. He may merely be putting his intellectual

311

feet up. In so far as such activity may be said not to influence future conduct, to that extent it may be said to be autistic. The intention, or motivation, to return ultimately to action – even should he be prevented in fact from so doing – may be what distinguishes him from the schizophrenic.

Cameron (1947) has claimed that 'schizophrenic disorganization and desocialization involve principally the withdrawal or escape techniques'; but it may be only withdrawal without the intention of, or motivation for, returning that is a defensive activity related teleologically, though not intentionally, to certain unconscious conflicts and that the process disorders of thought and affect are a consequence, an epiphenomenon, of this withdrawal without the intention of returning to interpersonal relationships. A very complete impoverishment of interpersonal relationships may be accompanied by and lead to further incongruity and flattening of affect and to thought disorder. If the lack of intention be crucial, fully adequate experimental models for schizophrenia will not be possible. You can lead a man to the bar; but you cannot make him *intend* to drink. It may, however, be that appropriate therapy can induce the schizophrenic to abandon his negative motivation, his fear of others, whether or not this involves working through it. In time he may then develop sufficient confidence to begin to formulate his own intentions.

How might it be that schizophrenics lack the intention or motive to enter into mutual personal relationships? The process of formulating his own intentions can be hindered in the child, as McGhie (1961a, 1961b) has shown with better-designed studies than his predecessors, by a mother who does not want her child to become fully a person, to become independent of her, and who is herself somewhat inchoate and consequently provides a poor model for reality-testing. This has been made familiar by Bateson *et al.* (1956) as the 'double bind'.

Since, then, the mother of the schizophrenic is herself somewhat disorganized and since she likes having babies but not children, any such child will have been exceptionally deprived of favourable opportunities to learn to formulate his own intentions. He will, therefore, tend to remain dependent on the other for his existence. Lacking any intention and motivated by a free-floating anxiety, his only possible retreat is into fantasy; but even here he is not free. He is hounded. His thoughts, his feelings, his actions are not his own. They are being forced upon him – and, of course, he is quite right. They are not his own; they are his mother's. The self is no longer experienced as agent. He is moved, driven by alien forces. The continuum of increasing failure to maintain mutual personal relationships, which begins with the inability to empathize, the inability to act for the sake of the other, ends in this utter loss of the self-schema, when I am no longer experienced as I. It is no longer I who act, therefore I am not. The schizophrenic *is* out of his mind. Alienation of the person from the rest of humanity can go no further. No person is an island and no human island is a person.

If the individual does not intend, or is not motivated, ever to return to action, to communication with others, reflection will be governed by no such intention and may, therefore, tend to become unorganized and its products ultimately more or less incommunicable. Unlike action, thought can in itself determine nothing, can add not a cubit to our stature. Divorced from action, divorced even from communication with others, it can be neither confirmed nor disconfirmed and is, therefore, not reality-orientated.

It could be that very prolonged deprivation of interpersonal communication, with the consequent lack of feedback, is itself sufficient to induce schizophrenia; but this seems unlikely. Those who have been stranded for long periods on rafts, who presumably retained their intention to return to action and who were far from completely sensorily deprived, might be able to provide useful evidence for discriminating between these two hypotheses. That such people invent devices, such as imaginary companions, for, as it were, averting schizophrenia is well known. That imaginary companions cannot provide feedback is self-evident. That such people are ever schizophrenic when rescued has not been reported, as far as the writer is aware.

Hare (1956) found that schizophrenics tended to come from two quite different social areas (high class and low class); but both were characterized by having a high percentage of single-person households. Such studies make a valuable contribution towards determining whether schizophrenics drift into psychologically unsatisfactory environments or whether unsatisfactory environments contribute to schizophrenic breakdown. Adoption of either view still, of course, omits possibly essential aspects of schizophrenic illness. The possibility remains that those who actually become schizophrenics are those who have withdrawn without the intention of, or motivation for, returning.

If the schizophrenic does lack the ability to formulate and sustain his own intentions, particularly in interpersonal situations, and is not motivated to return to personal relationships, he will increasingly lose the ability to organize his own experience, to form sentiments or, indeed, any adequate schemata. There will no longer be any value system, no criteria by means of which to give greater or lesser weight to different characters of experience. It is not so much that he cannot inhibit what is irrelevant as that he has no means of knowing what is irrelevant. In the extreme, which may never in fact be quite reached, the completely unorganized and non-colour-blind schizophrenic should be unable to perceive the figures in the Ishihara test.

Such a hypothesis would then help to explain thought disorder and much perceptual disorder. Withdrawal from interpersonal relationships would also entail that the schizophrenic would pay less attention to all modes of communication, including affective expression. It might be expected, therefore, that the schizophrenic who is flattened in affect would actually make less use of the affective category when differentiating between stimuli which can be distinguished in terms of several categories, the remainder of which involve much less direct, or do not involve, means of communication. This problem is being investigated by Penelope Dixon, who presents pairs of pictures of people and asks the subject to say in what ways they differ. Normal subjects are very consistent in utilizing differences in emotional expression among their responses. Schizophrenics (who had been rated by two judges independently as markedly flattened in affect – agreement $r = 0.58$; $p < .0005$, 1 tail) tend to use the various non-communication categories, such as 'One is dark, the other fair' or 'One is well-dressed, the other not', almost as often as normals; but the difference in emotional expression is seldom remarked upon. The association between ratings of flattening for 32 schizophrenics and number of emotional responses was:

Rater A: Chi-square (1 d.f.) 7.9; $p < .005$, 1 tail.
Rater B: Chi-square (1 d.f.) 5.2; $p < .025$, 1 tail.

All this is not to deny the relevance of body-build or of genetic loading. It is highly probable that the actual schizophrenic breakdown is multiply determined. It is likely to be analogous to the concatenation of circumstances necessary to produce a road accident. This would account for the extraordinary degree of similarity within the condition as well as for the diversity. Some of the potentially contributing factors appear to be genetic loading, asthenic physique, and a psychological environment militating against the development of mutual personal relationships. Prominent in that psychological environment are the social isolation described by Farris & Dunham (1939) and Myers & Roberts (1959); and the mother, described by McGhie and many others, who does not wish her child to become independently viable, who does not realize that there is anything amiss with him, who is herself somewhat inchoate, and consequently provides a poor model for reality-testing. These factors are themselves probably interdependent.

IMPLICATIONS FOR MEASUREMENT

The necessary and sufficient conditions could usefully serve as focal points for measurement. In general, those scoring high on the Non-integrated Psychotic scale should score high on any measures of loss of awareness of the self as agent, of thought-process disorder, and of incongruity of affect (or flattening). Those scoring high on the psychotic scale should manifest more perceptual disorder than those scoring low, and should show thought-content disorder. Those scoring high on the Personal Illness scale should give evidence of affective disproportion. Those scoring high on General Punitiveness, whether or not they score high on Personal Illness, should score high on any measure of egocentricity or lack of empathy.

Such measures would not only serve a diagnostic function; but they could contribute to an understanding of important processes. No attempt is made to cover this area exhaustively; but a few suggestions are offered below.

Loss of Awareness of the Self as Agent
If those who score high on the Non-integrated Psychotic scale show some blurring of boundaries and loss of a clear self-concept, they should be relatively incapable of becoming ego-involved in test situations. There are a number of well-known areas of psychological measurement in which the results vary according to whether the subject is or is not ego-involved. Among such areas are the Zeigarnik Effect, Level of Aspiration, and Need Achievement. It would be predicted that those scoring high on the NIP scale would show no difference between performances under stress and performances under non-stress, or under ego-involved and non-ego-involved, conditions; whereas those scoring low on the NIP scale would show variation as between the two sets of conditions.

315

Results obtained on any task administered individually and in conditions of competition with others should show less between-task differences in non-integrated psychotics than in any other groups.

Thought-process Disorder

Non-integrated paranoid psychotics should, according to Payne, Caird & Laverty (1964), show more evidence of over-inclusion than non-paranoid schizophrenics as well as all other groups. There are two reservations about this: the first is that manic patients would almost certainly over-include; and the second is that Chapman (1961) found that, by varying the instructions, schizophrenics could become under-includers.

Non-paranoid schizophrenics, with the possible exception of simple schizophrenics, should show weakness and inconsistency of conceptual construct systems, together with lack of social agreement concerning them, compared with all other groups (Bannister, 1962). It may be, however, that a table of random numbers would produce all of these disorders.

It is conceivable that we have not as yet demonstrated anything about schizophrenic thought disorder other than that some schizophrenics do it wrong and others cannot do it at all.

Affective Flattening

Non-integrated psychotics should make relatively little use of the affective category when asked to distinguish between pairs of pictures which differ on this and several other categories (Dixon[1]). The ratio of emotional to non-emotional words written down in one minute, using some restricted category, might produce similar results.

Non-integrated psychotics should more often fail to make mutual choices in the typical sociometric studies.

Perceptual Disorder

Three processes can be distinguished: seeing what is not there; not seeing what is there; misperceiving what is there, either by distorting the ground and failing to perceive the figure or by distorting the figure.

1. Seeing what is not there: Hallucinations may involve distortions or projections of private stimuli; but they do not involve public stimuli. They would appear to be unmeasurable; but time-sampling observations by two or more judges could be compared with admission of hallucinations by the subject.

[1] Personal communication, 1964.

316

2. Not seeing what is there: This might be particularly characteristic of non-integrated psychotics. If they lack the ability to sustain attention and intention, they should be unable to determine what is relevant and what is irrelevant. They should, therefore, be relatively incapable of perceptual organization. In extreme cases, they might fail to perceive the figures of the Ishihara test, to effect closures on Mooney's closure test (Mooney & Ferguson, 1951), and to perceive embedded figures.

3. Misperceiving what is there: The initial percept is a hypothesis which has to be checked. Walking home tired at the end of a cold winter's day, the writer once perceived a poster in the peripheral field as 'Whisky Drive'. This poster was no doubt selected from among others because of its position in the visual field and because it was readily distortable to fit the reigning schema, based upon fairly long-established habit patterns of dealing with the English climate. The percept was, however, sufficiently startling to promote checking behaviour. Checking revealed 'Whist Drive'.

The paranoid's need to defend his immaculate self-concept is so desperate that he has to feel so certain of his apperception of the sign that it requires no checking. He cannot allow himself to be shaken in his belief.

The dynamisms of denial and projection, which are productive of persecutory delusions, appear to operate in perceptual tasks. One paranoid patient, who had cracked his psychiatrist's ribs on the day prior to being given the TAT, saw the boy with the violin as a boy with a machine-gun. The boy kneeling with a gun beside him caused great perturbation – initially in the subject and subsequently in the tester. He stuttered and stammered and clenched his not inconsiderable fists. Eventually he blurted out that it was a boy kneeling with a bottle of ink beside him, which had been spilt. After being leucotomized, he said right away that it was a gun. When the aggressive symbol was absent, he projected it; when it was present, he denied it.

Another well-preserved paranoid, who gave nine verbally well-organized and perceptually competent stories, said in the tenth that the boy had shot the old man in the chair. When asked where the old man in the chair was, he traced round the revolver, saying, 'there's his bald head, nose, moustache, back of the chair'. The writer could then easily share his percept; but the perspective was grossly distorted. He had evidently achieved a condensation, since the one object was both gun and old man in chair.

In these examples 'willingness to report' seems to have little explanatory relevance. The first subject would have to be thought of as willing, at one moment, to report a gun, but not a violin; and, at the next moment, as willing to report a bottle of ink, but not a gun.

Psychotic patients (in common, it would sometimes seem, with Gestalt psychologists) go beyond 'as if' perception, the 'willing suspension of unbelief'. A normal person who had taken an overdose of barbiturates might have unusual sensations which led him to say that it felt as though a cloud were passing over his head; a psychotic patient, who had taken such an overdose, said that there was a cloud constantly passing just over the top of his head. From time to time he would put up his hand to try to feel it. The psychotic, in short, mistakes relations of similarity for relations of identity.

Not all misinterpreted stimuli appear to be threatening. When presented with a picture of a child blowing bubbles, a paranoid schizophrenic perceived this as a child holding a mirror. Part of her hair was evidently seen as the handle of the mirror. The percept was inappropriate in another respect, namely that part of the child's face could be seen through the 'mirror'. A child holding a mirror is likely to be of more frequent occurrence than a child blowing bubbles. Having acquired this set, the stimuli are organized to fit and some incongruities are ignored.

Another picture showed a boy (three-quarter length) tilted at a slight angle. A paranoid schizophrenic decided that it was a boy on a bicycle. There was no sign of a bicycle and the interpretation was made presumably solely on the basis of the tilted angle, which might have suggested pressing down on one pedal. The fact that he would have had to ride through dense bushes was ignored. The second example is clearly one of acting on minimal cues, and both illustrate lack of checking.

Clinicians have long remarked that there is something peculiar about the eyes of paranoid patients. They have a fixed stare. It might conceivably be that they do not scan to the normal extent, but fixate on one portion of the field and in consequence see much more peripherally. They would thus, in so doing, unstructure their own stimuli; turn a TAT into a Rorschach, as it were. Such a process could contribute towards some, at least, of their misperceptions. Appropriate experiments to test such a hypothesis could be set up.

318

Some Implications

Thought-content Disorder

In the main, delusions are fairly readily elicited by questioning and are rather inaccessible to other techniques. It may be, however, that Caine's Scrambled Sentences (Caine, 1960) have a contribution to make in this area. He presents four words on a card thus:

Him	Saw
Hit	He

The subject is asked to say the first sentence he sees with three words. Melancholics give an excess of 'Guilt' sentences over neutral, whereas paranoids give an excess of 'Projected Hostility' sentences, but not of Acting-out Hostility. When subjects are instructed to give two sentences, normals show a significant increase in emotional over neutral sentences given first, whereas psychotics change scarcely at all. It would seem that, under the first set of instructions, normals are in touch with the social situation and suppress what they consider to be undesirable; psychotics, driven by the intensity of their needs, have lost touch and are more likely to say what they in fact saw first. Added to this, paranoids appear to be more sensitized to extrapunitive stimuli and melancholics to intropunitive.

Affective Disproportion

It is difficult to know just where to draw the line between some possible work in this category and in the previous category. Some sort of distinction could be made if psychotics obliged by responding to delusional sounding material to which neurotics did not respond.

Those who score high on the Personal Illness scale should show an excess of emotional words if pairs of emotional-neutral words are presented in a Synoptophore, with suitable control for eye-dominance. Reaction times could be established for neutral-neutral, emotional-emotional, and emotional-neutral pairs. By these means it should be possible to distinguish selective perception from willingness to report.

Egocentricity

On Kelly's Role Repertory Construct technique (Kelly, 1955), those scoring high on General Punitiveness should rate most favourably those who are conceived as being most helpful to the subject.

Hysteroid : Obsessoid
Here, too, it would be desirable to attempt to measure objectively various traits such as the field-dependent *v.* the field-independent approach (with intelligence suitably controlled); speed – accuracy preference; dependency – independency; extremes and variability of judgements; affective expressivity and lability, etc.

If the continuum be a continuum of increasing degrees of distortion and of disintegration of basic personality characteristics, it should follow that, as one moves along this continuum, the influence of diagnostic measures will increase. There may, for example, be considerable differences in certain performances between, say, an anxiety state of hysteroid and an anxiety state of obsessoid personality; whereas there would be no such difference between a schizophrenic who had previously been of hysteroid and a schizophrenic who had previously been of obsessoid personality. In remission, differences might reappear.

If the results of researches such as have been suggested pointed to the need for major revisions, this would still provide no adequate ground for abandoning classification. It has become fashionable to decry psychiatric classification and to substitute nothing but worse chaos or to fly prematurely to aetiology. Aetiology must wait upon nosology, and for the problem of psychiatric nosology at the present time the most appropriate generalization would appear to be that the situation is serious, but not hopeless, and not, as the commentator on the French political scene between the wars would have it, that it is hopeless, but not serious.

REFERENCES

BANNISTER, D. (1962). The nature and measurement of schizophrenic thought disorder. *J. ment. Sci.*, **108**, 825.

BARTLETT, F. C. (1932). *Remembering.* London: Cambridge University Press.

BATESON, G., JACKSON, D., HALEY, J. & WEAKLAND, J. (1956). Towards a theory of schizophrenia. *Behavioral Sci.*, **4**, 251.

CAINE, T. M. (1960). The expression of hostility and guilt in melancholic and paranoid women. *J. consult. Psychol.*, **24**, 18.

CAMERON, N. (1947). *The psychology of behavior disorders.* Boston: Houghton Mifflin.

CHAPMAN, L. (1961). A reinterpretation of some pathological disturbances in conceptual breadth. *J. abnorm. soc. Psychol.*, **62**, 514.

Some Implications

COOPER, J. E. (1963). A study of behaviour therapy in thirty psychiatric patients. *Lancet*, No. 7278, 411.

FARRIS, R. E. L. & DUNHAM, H. W. (1939). *Mental disorders in urban areas of Chicago*. Chicago: Chicago University Press.

FEDERN, P. (1953). *Ego psychology and the psychoses*. London: Imago Publishing Co.

FOULDS, G. A. (1955). The reliability of psychiatric and the validity of psychological diagnoses. *J. ment. Sci.*, **101**, 851.

HARDING, D. W. (1963). *Experience into words*. London: Chatto & Windus.

HARE, E. H. (1956). Mental illness and social conditions in Bristol. *J. ment. Sci.*, **102**, 349.

KARAGULLA, S. (1950). Evaluation of electroconvulsive therapy as compared with conservative methods of treatment in depressive states. *J. ment. Sci.*, **96**, 1060.

KELLY, G. A. (1955) *The psychology of personal constructs*. New York: Norton.

LAING, R. D. (1960). *The divided self*. London: Tavistock Publications.

MCGHIE, A. (1961a). A comparative study of the mother-child relationship in schizophrenia, I. *Brit. J. med. Psychol.*, **34**, 195.

MCGHIE, A. (1961b). A comparative study of the mother-child relationship in schizophrenia, II. *Brit. J. med. Psychol.*, **34**, 209.

MCGHIE, A. & CHAPMAN, J. (1961). Disorders of attention and perception in schizophrenia. *Brit. J. med. Psychol.*, **34**, 103.

MACMURRAY, J. (1961). *Persons in relation*. London: Faber, 1961.

MICHAUX, W. (1955). Schizophrenic apperception as a function of hunger. *J. abnorm. soc. Psychol.*, **50**, 53.

MOONEY, C. M. & FERGUSON, G. A. (1951). A new closure test. *Canad. J. Psychol.*, **5**, 129.

MORRIS, JANE. (1963). An analysis of schizophrenics' interviews. *Brit. J. med. Psychol.*, **36**, 283.

MURRAY, H. (1938). *Explorations in personality*. New York: Oxford University Press.

MYERS, J. K. & ROBERTS, B. H. (1959). *Family and class dynamics in mental illness*. New York: Wiley; London: Chapman & Hall.

PAYNE, R. W., CAIRD, W. K. & LAVERTY, S. G. (1964). Over-inclusive thinking and delusions in schizophrenic patients. *J. abnorm. soc. Psychol.*, **68**, 562.

PAYNE, R. W., MATTUSSEK, P. & GEORGE, E. I. (1959). An experimental study of schizophrenic thought disorder. *J. ment. Sci.*, **105**, 627.

SANFORD, R. N. (1937). The effects of abstinence from food upon imaginal processes. *J. Psychol.*, **3**, 145.

THURSTONE, L. L. (1924). *The nature of intelligence*. New York: Harcourt, Brace.

CHAPTER FIFTEEN

Summary

Chapter 1 sets out the main arguments of the book. The functional psychoses and the neuroses are regarded as illnesses of the person and not merely of the organism. A case is argued for the usefulness of considering the major classes of illness as lying along a continuum of increasing degrees of failure to maintain or establish mutual personal relationships. An attempt is made to describe what is meant by mutual personal relationships. This continuum can be schematized as follows:

Personality disorders	Personally ill	Psychotics	Non-integrated psychotics
Psychopaths			
Neurotics	Neurotics		
Integrated psychotics	Integrated psychotics	Integrated psychotics	
Schizophrenics	Schizophrenics	Schizophrenics	Schizophrenics

The idea that certain dimensions can be considered, on the basis of particular experiments, as an absolute means of differentiating between psychosis and neurosis is rejected.

When, in the present scheme, the subject has been allocated to his class, one then looks at the differentiae between groups within that class. It is hoped that, by this means and by adhering more strictly to the distinction between the symptoms and signs of illness on the one hand and the basic personality characteristics on the other, the reliability of psychiatric diagnosis might be increased.

Studies are reviewed which utilize the psychiatric syndrome : personality type distinction. Measures relating to the former tend to change over time more readily than those related to the latter. The intention of moving from dichotomies to scales is stated and brief reference made to the content of succeeding chapters.

Summary

In *Chapter 2* the principal argument is that the personality traits and attitudes emphasize the continuities of behaviour; whereas symptoms and signs of illness emphasize the discontinuities. The criteria for the distinction are that traits and attitudes are universal, ego-syntonic, and relatively enduring; whereas symptoms and signs are non-universal, distressful, and relatively transient.

Traits are regarded as concerned with the 'how' of behaviour, with the process, the manner of doing; whereas attitudes are concerned with the 'what' or the content of behaviour. Within the characteristics of mental, or personal, illness, a distinction has been made between symptoms, and subjective and objective signs in terms of degrees of awareness on the part of the patients.

In the case of a symptom, the individual has some awareness of her experience and is able and willing to communicate it because she wishes to be rid of it. In the case of the subjective signs, the individual is able and willing to communicate her experience, but is unaware of its significance. In the case of the objective signs, the individual is unable or unwilling to communicate an experience of whose significance she may or may not be aware.

Since personality traits and attitudes are considered to be in a different universe of discourse from symptoms and signs of illness, Eysenck's use of hysterics and dysthymics as criterion groups for extraversion and introversion is criticized.

In *Chapter 3* the history of the concepts of hysteroid and obsessoid in the description of personality types is reviewed. Although the problem of the relationship between symptoms and traits remains unsolved, the great majority of authors do distinguish them. There is an increasing tendency to regard the hysteroid and obsessoid traits as falling within the normal range, as having some ego-syntonic value, as pre-dating any illness, and as being altogether more enduring. Despite the emphasis on the possible constitutional aspects of trait development by many authors, including social psychologists, it is difficult to believe that social pressures do not have a profound effect on the expression or inhibition of certain reaction patterns and that these pressures will not vary from culture to culture and from class to class. Developmental and cross-cultural studies in the normal field are, however, notably absent.

A questionnaire (the HOQ) has been devised which places people along a hysteroid : obsessoid personality continuum. It was validated against observer ratings of the traits from which the questionnaire items had been derived. Agreement between ratings and questionnaire, when each was dichotomized, was around 80 per cent. The re-test reliability for neurotics, after six weeks and with treatment intervening, was just below 0·8. There was no relationship with sex or with vocabulary level; but there was a slight relationship with age – the older subjects being somewhat more hysteroid. There was a significant relationship between the HOQ and diagnosis, with dysthymics tending to be more obsessoid; but the relationship with observed personality type was much greater. This supports the need to separate traits from symptoms.

Both the ratings and the HOQ were normally distributed; but neurotics tend to be somewhat more obsessoid than normals. Either obsessoids tend to be at slightly greater risk of a neurotic breakdown or neuroticism results in subjects distorting their self-description in an obsessoid direction.

In *Chapter 4* the nature of classification is considered and the view accepted that classification is essentially a selective process in which we attend to certain resemblances among our data which are relevant to our intention. In so doing we choose to neglect certain other resemblances which are not relevant to our intentions. These neglected resemblances might be relevant to other purposes.

Classification fell into disrepute in psychiatry because the once-for-all and nothing-but notions were thought to be intrinsic to it and because many of the methods of classifying were so illogical that they inevitably led to chaos. To abandon classification because some forms have been proved inadequate rather than because all forms have been proved unsuitable is to throw out the baby with the bath water. The choice lies between intentional and unintentional classification.

Studies dealing with the reliability of psychiatric diagnosis have been critically reviewed. The earlier and more adverse results can be shown to ensue from the illogical nature of the classifications used. The more recent and better-designed studies show a fair measure of agreement with each other, and suggest that the reliability of diagnosis is satisfactory as between psychosis and neurosis and within psychosis. It is, however, unsatisfactory within neurosis. It is, indeed, so unsatisfactory that, unless it can be improved, there is little to be gained in trying to distinguish between types of neurotic breakdown. If the distinction between symptoms and signs of illness and the more basic traits and attitudes of the personality were more carefully adhered to, such an improvement might be achieved.

In *Chapter 5* a classification system has been outlined. It has been suggested that mental illness is essentially illness of the person and that the person is only a person in relation to other persons. The main categories of personal illness can, therefore, be regarded as constituting a continuum of failure to maintain or establish mutual personal relationships. Thus, it is argued that all non-integrated psychotics are psychotic, are personally ill, and are personality disorders; that all psychotics are personally ill and are personality disorders; that all the personally ill are personality disorders. Those who are personality disorders, but not personally ill, psychotic, or non-integrated psychotic, are psychopaths; those who are personally ill, but not psychotic or non-integrated psychotic, are neurotic; those who are psychotic, but not non-integrated psychotic, are integrated psychotic; those who are non-integrated psychotic are non-integrated psychotic (probably schizophrenic).

The necessary and sufficient conditions for distinguishing between the various classes are set out, and scores on a measure of General Punitiveness are shown to distinguish between personality disorders and normals. With one exception the scores, in fact, follow the suggested continuum. The exception is that psychopaths are the highest scorers. It is argued that symptoms may tend to drain off punitiveness and that this might account for the observed order of results.

Criteria for distinguishing between the personally ill and the organically ill and their admixtures are suggested.

The necessary and sufficient conditions for diagnosing the main classes within personality disorders are given as follows:

Non-integrated psychosis: Loss of awareness of the self as agent and/or thought-process disorder and/or incongruity (including flattening) of affect.

Psychosis: Delusions (implying a self-schema) and/or gross perceptual disorder (including hallucinations).

Personal illness: Such disproportionateness of affect as leads to the inference that the response is to some covert stimulus from which the overt stimulus is a displacement.

Personality disorder: Egocentricity, with lack of empathy and persistent treating of people as objects.

Y   325

In each case the necessary and sufficient conditions for the diagnosis of the minor illness in the hierarchy constitute necessary conditions for the illnesses which are at a higher level in the hierarchy.

The pure personality disorders form the bridge between the normal and the personally ill in that their disability may or may not be distressful, is not universal in the degree to which it is present in them, but is much more enduring than is the case with symptoms.

In *Chapter 6* the Symptom-Sign Inventory, with its possible advantages and disadvantages, has been described and applied to a large sample of women.

The Non-integrated Psychotic *v.* Integrated Psychotic, the Psychotic *v.* Neurotic, and the Personal Illness *v.* Normal scales were all virtually unidirectional. There were several items, in other words, on which the first group significantly exceeded the second; but there were scarcely any items on which the second group exceeded the first.

Non-integrated psychotics were high scorers on all three scales, integrated psychotics on the second two scales only, neurotics on the last one only, and normals on none at all. Some support was, therefore, obtained for the view that all non-integrated psychotics are psychotic and personally ill; that all psychotics are personally ill; and that all the personally ill are not psychotic. Furthermore, the empirical scales were rather congruent with the hypothetical formulations about the necessary and sufficient conditions for making the respective diagnoses. Thus, most of the items on the Personal Illness scale could be subsumed under the heading of 'affective disproportion'; most of the items on the Psychotic scale were 'delusional' items; and most of the Non-integrated Psychotic scale items could be subsumed under some such heading as loss of the self-schema, loss of boundaries, etc.

The continuum of non-integrated psychotic – integrated psychotic – neurotic is not reversible. Thus, it is possible to speak of a schizophrenic with psychotic depressive features or with obsessional features; it is possible to speak of a melancholic with hysterical features. It is not, however, possible to speak of an anxiety state with melancholic features, or of a melancholic with schizophrenic features. The major syndrome in the hierarchy takes precedence. This has been described as 'the King Lear principle' of 'Where the greater malady is fixed, the lesser is scarce felt'.

Summary

In *Chapter 7* the groups within integrated psychosis and within neurosis are considered in relation to the SSI. Numbers are as yet insufficient for consideration of the groups within non-integrated psychosis and within personality disorders.

The necessary and sufficient conditions for making the group diagnoses are described. The empirical results were again found to be reasonably congruent with these formulations. The distinctions within integrated psychosis were better than those within neurosis. The general conclusion would appear to be that the level of agreement between the SSI and the clinical diagnosis is about the same as that between any two psychiatrists.

The empirical scales for distinguishing between groups tend not to be unidirectional, suggesting that these groups are on the same level of classification. Thus melancholia, for example, does not take precedence over paranoia, or anxiety over hysteria.

In *Chapter 8* the SSI scales for comparisons between the psychotic and neurotic groups have been considered. These distinctions can, of course, be made with comparative ease. The most difficult, as would be expected, is that between psychotic and neurotic depression; but even this is not too unsatisfactory. Of those tested, 66 per cent were allocated in agreement with the diagnosis of psychiatrists; 19 per cent were uncertain; and 15 per cent were in disagreement.

An overall comparison of the clinical and the SSI diagnoses showed that, out of 250 women, 62 per cent were allocated in agreement; 8 per cent remained uncertain; and 31 per cent were in disagreement.

As would be expected from the relative unreliability of clinical diagnosis within neurosis, SSI diagnosis within neurotics was less successful than SSI diagnosis among psychotics or between neurotics and psychotics. The SSI tended to over-diagnose melancholics and to under-diagnose hysterics; but it was thought that the latter might be a benign error since the diagnosis of hysteria is sometimes made on the basis of florid personality attributes rather than on symptomatology.

Frequency tables in the various groups were used to distinguish between frequency of occurrence of a symptom in a particular group and its differential power as between groups. Utilizing this distinction, a description was given of the characteristics of six groups of women – schizophrenics, paranoids, melancholics, anxiety states, hysterics, and neurotic depressives.

Prospect and Retrospect

In *Chapter 9* various scales from the SSI and the HOQ were used as criterion diagnostic and personality measures respectively. These were almost always unrelated. Correlations were run between each of these in turn and various other measures, notably the Extrapunitive and Intropunitive scales.

The subjects were 120 women, made up of 20 in each of the following psychiatrically diagnosed groups: schizophrenics, paranoids, melancholics, hysterics, anxiety states, and neurotic depressives. Thereafter the psychiatric diagnosis was ignored and the correlations were calculated over the whole group.

The results lent support to the view that there is a continuum from non-integrated psychotics through integrated psychotics to neurotics. The non-integrated psychotics tended to have all the symptoms that were characteristic of psychotics as a group and that were characteristic of the personally ill as a group. In addition, they had their own rather specific symptoms which were of rare occurrence in other groups. The integrated psychotics tended to have all the symptoms that were characteristic of the personally ill as a group, plus those which they shared with non-integrated psychotics. The neurotics had symptoms which were shared with all psychotic groups, and scarcely any of their own.

The correlations showed that certain test scores, for example, Extrapunitiveness, could be accounted for in terms of diagnostic differences; other scores, for example Direction of Punitiveness, could be accounted for largely in terms of personality differences; and yet others, such as Self-criticism, in terms of an interaction between the two.

Measures associated predominantly with diagnosis tended to change significantly after an interval of about five weeks; measures not so associated tended not to change significantly. Some support was thus lent to the hypothesis that personality variables are more enduring than are symptoms and signs of illness.

In *Chapter 10*, again using the SSI and the HOQ as criterion diagnostic and personality measures respectively, the depressive continuum was examined. The SSI (Melancholic) scale and the HOQ were related (r being -0.343). Thus there was a slight tendency for the more psychotic depressives to be more obsessoid in personality.

Although a continuum from psychotic to neurotic depression can be made, the results suggest that a distinction can usefully be made and

that this distinction centres on the presence of delusional ideas. Indeed it is probably better described as a step-function.

Three measures were shown to relate more closely to personality than to diagnosis and these three measures did not change significantly over all patients rated clinically as much improved, though they did change somewhat for all improved psychotics. Improved psychotic depressives tended to become somewhat more hysteroid and more extrapunitive, and to scatter their tapping more. It may be, therefore, that a deep psychotic depression results in a distortion of the 'true' personality which does not occur in a neurotic depressive.

Four measures, which were more closely related to diagnosis than to personality, all changed significantly in the group of patients rated as much improved. Whereas diagnostic classifications disappeared on re-test, the personality measures continued to classify people in the same categories. Personality measures were thus again shown to be more stable than diagnostic measures.

This detailed investigation of psychotic and neurotic depressives went some way towards demonstrating the utility of a double classification system which takes account of both symptom and personality variables.

In *Chapter 11*, using a similar methodology, the paranoid-melancholic continuum was examined. This continuum is of particular interest in that it illustrates the fact that opposites are more alike in psychology than mere differences.

With these two groups the diagnostic measure (*Pa-Me*) from the SSI correlated 0·347 with the HOQ. Thus there was a tendency for the more depressive patients to be more obsessoid in personality. The association was sufficiently low, however, to suggest that the HOQ continues, even among these two psychotic groups, to measure variables which function somewhat independently of diagnosis.

The direction of delusional blame (Delusional Hostility — Delusional Guilt) was strongly related to diagnosis and to personality. Thus hysteroid paranoids had the highest scores and obsessoid melancholics the lowest scores. While the non-psychotic direction of blame (Acting-out Hostility + Criticism of Others) — Self-criticism is, like the psychotic measure, associated with both diagnosis and personality, the correlation with diagnosis is a good deal lower and with personality somewhat higher in the non-psychotic measure. This might suggest that the non-psychotic direction of blame is a measure of rather more habitual

attitudes; whereas the psychotic (DH-DG) reflects a somewhat transient and exaggerated deviation from, or even reaction against, the patient's usual attitudes.

Although some of the specific predictions about particular measures were inaccurate, the re-test results again supported the belief that personality measures are more stable than diagnostic measures.

As predicted, melancholics showed greater changes on re-test than did paranoids.

In *Chapter 12* particular attention was given to the paranoid schizo-phrenia-paraphrenia-paranoia continuum. Some psychiatrists have included the whole continuum within the schizophrenia class; others have taken the whole continuum out of schizophrenia; yet others, notably Kraepelin, have put some cases within and some outside this class.

Each of the psychotic groups was split on the Non-integrated Psychotic *v.* Integrated Psychotic scale of the SSI. Only in the case of the non-integrated *v.* integrated paranoids were the differences on various other measures beyond chance expectation. The paranoid schizophrenics were, in addition, almost identical with the non-paranoid schizophrenics (except on the Paranoid *v.* Schizophrenic scale); whereas the melancholics and the paranoiacs were different from each other and each from the schizophrenics. It was concluded that the data supported the position of Kraepelin and that, in fact, a useful division could be made at a point on the continuum further away from 'pure' paranoia than has been considered acceptable up to the present time.

When the Non-integrated Psychotic *v.* Integrated Psychotic scale and the Psychotic *v.* Neurotic scale were combined to make a Psychosis scale more comparable with that of Trouton & Maxwell, and the present results on this and on the Personal Illness scale were compared with theirs, the results were found to be remarkably similar. Two notable features were that, on Trouton & Maxwell's psychoticism dimension, all the schizophrenic groups exceeded the non-schizophrenic groups, suggesting that their data contained a concealed non-integrated psychotic scale and that, as in the study reported here, paranoiacs were much the lowest scorers of all groups on neuroticism. The re-analysis of their data by Lorr & O'Connor (1957) brings this out more clearly. They considered the first two rotated factors to be second-order factors appearing at the first level, the first being a schizophrenic reaction and the second

Prospect and Retrospect

one year after discharge. Broadly speaking, on admission the main difference was between normals and neurotics; whereas, at follow-up, the main difference was between normals and those neurotics who had been rated as having responded favourably to treatment on the one hand and those neurotics who had been rated as having responded little, if at all, to treatment. The period in which most change in the direction of normality occurred was somewhere between the sixth-week testing and discharge testing. The trait measure proved to be more resistant to change than did the remaining measures. Patients who were less intropunitive and less depressed at the time of admission were more likely to show a favourable response to treatment, or to improve more with the passage of time.

Although the results cannot be attributed unequivocally to the effects of community therapy, reasons are advanced for the belief that spontaneous remission provides a less likely explanation.

It is a striking finding, worthy of more detailed investigation, that patients seem to attribute the favourable changes in their condition more to interaction with other patients than to interaction with the hospital staff. Many of the latter share this view and regard themselves principally as catalysts. If this interpretation is correct, it might well be that more professional endeavour should go into selecting the appropriate people with whom to bring the patient into contact. This should perhaps be done at an early stage even in those cases for whom individual psychotherapy seems appropriate, since it would tend to reduce the danger inherent in the asymmetrical doctor-patient relationship of increasing the patient's already crippling egocentricity.

In *Chapter 14* some diagnostic implications have been considered. It is proposed that the diagnostic process should proceed from the widest to the narrowest classes and that, when the appropriate class has been decided upon, one should then proceed to the differentiae between groups within that class.

It is further proposed that, for example, the neurotic diagnoses of members of any psychotic group may be pertinent to differences within that group. The neurotic group diagnoses are, however, unsatisfactory, and it is suggested that more useful neurotic groups might consist of those who complain of apparently 'somatic' symptoms on the one hand and those who complain of predominantly 'psychic' symptoms on the other. Some tentative evidence is presented.

332

Summary

Additional diagnostic uses for the SSI are mentioned.

Two therapeutic implications are discussed, and it is argued that some form of psychotherapy is required in all cases of neurosis and of psychosis no matter what somatic treatments may be its necessary precursors.

It is shown that, as assessed by the SSI, some psychotics are discharged while still psychotic, some while no longer psychotic but still neurotic, and some when they are within normal limits. Long-term follow-up comparisons seem to be indicated.

An alternative theory to the 'unconscious conflict' and the 'defective attention' theories of schizophrenia is proposed, which is described as 'withdrawal without the intention of, or motivation, for returning' to interaction with others. It is highly probable that an actual schizophrenic breakdown is multiply determined and that the suggestions put forward, if relevant, constitute only part of the explanation.

Finally, the necessary and sufficient conditions for the class diagnoses are taken as focal points for measurement, and a number of possible investigations are outlined.

REFERENCE

LORR, M. & O'CONNOR, J. P. (1957). The relation between neurosis and psychosis: a re-analysis. *J. ment. Sci.*, **103**, 375.